THE MODERN SUBJECT

SUNY Series in Contemporary Continental Philosophy
Dennis J. Schmidt, Editor

The Modern Subject

CONCEPTIONS OF THE SELF IN CLASSICAL GERMAN PHILOSOPHY

Edited by
Karl Ameriks
and
Dieter Sturma

STATE UNIVERSITY OF NEW YORK PRESS

Published by
State University of New York Press, Albany

Printed in the United States of America

For information, address State University of New York Press, State University Plaza, Albany, N.Y. 12246

Production by Diane Ganeles
Marketing by Nancy Farrell

Library of Congress Cataloging-in-Publication Data

The modern subject : conceptions of the self in classical German philosophy / edited by Karl Ameriks and Dieter Sturma.
p. cm. — (SUNY series in contemporary continental philosophy)
Includes bibliographical references (p.) and index.
ISBN 0-7914-2753-6 (hard : alk. paper). — ISBN 0-7914-2754-4 (pbk. : alk. paper)
1. Philosophy, German—18th century. 2. Philosophy, German—19th century. 3. Self (Philosophy) 4. Subjectivity—History—18th. 5. Subjectivity—History—19th. I. Ameriks, Karl, 1947- . II. Sturma, Dieter. III. Series.
B2628.S34M63 1995
126'. 0943'—dc20 95-4244
CIP

10 9 8 7 6 5 4 3 2 1

Contents

Acknowledgments

Work on this project was made possible primarily by a TRANSCOOP grant from the Alexander von Humboldt Foundation of Bonn, Germany. The University of Lüneburg (Germany) has also provided substantial support. Matching funds for a conference on this topic in April 1994, at the University of Notre Dame (Notre Dame, Indiana), were provided from a number of sources at Notre Dame: the Paul M. and Barbara Henkels Visiting Scholars fund of the Institute for Scholarship in the Liberal Arts, the Nanovic Center of European Studies, the departments of Philosophy, History, Theology, English, Romance Languages and Literatures, Government, Classical and Oriental Languages, and the Program of Liberal Studies. Special thanks are in order for Gary Gutting, Robert Wegs, Rev. Thomas O'Meara, Steve Watson, Manfred Kuehn, and Rudolf Makkreel. Help with the translation of the German contributions was provided by Günter Zöller and Eric Watkins. Louis MacKenzie provided help with translating a French contribution. Invaluable assistance with the final stages of the manuscript came from Mitch Clearfield and John Davenport. An essential role in clarifying the issues discussed here was also played by other participants at the Notre Dame conference: Felicitas Munzel, Zbigniew Zwolinski, Jane Kneller, Jeffrey Hoover, and David Carr. In addition to serving as a featured speaker at the Notre Dame conference, Manfred Frank's enthusiastic involvement with this project in the period before and after the conference has been enormously helpful. He also made possible a further very fruitful discussion of the issues with the editors of this volume in Tübingen in October 1994. The editors would also like to thank Mr. William Eastman of SUNY Press for his timely help and encouragement, as well as all the contributors, who committed themselves to working together in a truly cooperative and productive manner.

1

Introduction

Dieter Sturma/Karl Ameriks

The Project of *The Modern Subject: Conceptions of the Self in Classical German Philosophy*

The era of classical German philosophy, from Kant to Hegel, is unique in the history of philosophical theories. Within barely forty years there arose: the main works of Kant, the *Elementarphilosophie* of Reinhold, the *Wissenschaftslehre* of Fichte, the philosophical works of the young Kantians and post-Kantians, including, above all, Hölderlin and Novalis, and idealist systems of philosophers from Schelling to Hegel. Moreover, recent research has uncovered the philosophical significance of a series of previously little known thinkers in the period of the transition from Kant's transcendental philosophy to German idealism.[1]

For a large of variety of issues, current philosophical attention has also become focused on the argumentative value of the philosophical ideas developed in this era. The full potential (which is not a merely quantitative matter) of this period has certainly not yet been adequately appreciated. Each age poses new questions, and a classical period is distinguished by the fact that, in retrospect, it can be presented in ever new intellectual configurations, and in that way it is able to give ever new answers to changing questions. This point emerges especially clearly in the context of the problems of current philosophy concerning the subject and subjectivity. Against the background of the tendencies of current philosophy, which are very critical of, and even antagonistic to, subjectivity,[2] classical German philosophy takes on an overwhelming significance, because from its very beginning, this philosophy has combined perspectives that construct and criticize the standpoint of subjectivity. The great complexity of its arguments concerning the subject makes for a contrast with current philosophy, since these arguments avoid the exaggerations of pronouncing a death of the subject or the inevitability of its unlimited decentralization.

The various theoretical perspectives of classical German philosophy are distinctive in that they take up, in very different ways, justified criticisms of subjectivity and justifiable claims of its decentralization, but without thereby giving up the notion of the self.

Against the background of this historically and theoretically complex constellation of issues in German idealist thought, this volume undertakes the task of presenting new historical evaluations of philosophical movements in the classical German period, as well as a systematic reconsideration of the foundations of classical German theories of the subject. Behind our title, *The Modern Subject: Conceptions of the Self in Classical German Philosophy*, there also lies a transatlantic research project carried out together by American and European scholars of German philosophy. Its founding idea is the conception of a continuing "transatlantic workshop" that will include attitudes and perspectives coming from different traditions and bring them to bear on a common object of research. In this way, the theme of this project is programmatic. Whatever the differences in their theoretical intentions, all the participants agree that systematically sustainable answers to questions about the subject are to be sought not in the controversies going back and forth in our era about the general decentralization of the fundamental concepts of modernity, but rather in an argumentative engagement with the philosophies of subjectivity in the era of classical German philosophy.

The main points of the philosophy of subjectivity in classical German philosophy emerge primarily in the context of the study of the history of philosophy, whereas in the systematic efforts of contemporary philosophy the invocation of classical German philosophy usually proceeds only with hesitation. The only exceptions here are Kant, who now as before is a common point of reference for many divergent philosophical orientations, and in part Hegel, whose influence in contemporary Anglo-American philosophy has remained limited primarily to social philosophy. The other great names of this period, such as Reinhold, Fichte, Hölderlin, and Schelling show up in systematic discussions only occasionally, at best.

Furthermore, the analytic philosophy which has dominated the Anglo-American realm for so long has had difficulty in thematizing the self and self-consciousness. Even when it has not followed primarily reductionist interests, it has hardly tried to get close to the ideas of classical German philosophers. However, there have been some indications that the reception of these philosophers is clearly changing, for the significance of the theory of subjectivity in classical German philosophy has not remained wholly unnoticed in the systematic context of Anglo-American philosophy. For example, in the work of P. F. Strawson, Hector Neri Castañeda, John Rawls, and Charles Taylor there are investigations which put contemporary problems of subjectivity directly into relation with the classical positions. The same can surely also be said of philosophers like Thomas Nagel, Roderick Chisholm, and Robert Nozick, though they are less interested in the reconstruction of particular positions in the history of philosophy.[3]

The growing interest of Anglo-American philosophers in the traditional figures of classical German idealism may come in part from the stimulus of Continental philosophy, but to a significant extent it also comes from a dissatisfaction with the thematic narrowness that analytic philosophy has brought along with it. On the Continental scene, where the most important source for the systematic rehabilitation of idealistic philosophy of subjectivity is to be found in the so-called Heidelberg school (represented mainly by the works of Dieter Henrich and more recently, Manfred Frank), there has also been a growing interest in the methods of analytic philosophy. This school is also primarily responsible for the newfound interest in post-Kantian theories of self-consciousness among Continental thinkers.

Against the background of this theoretical situation, there has developed in Continental philosophy a trend of combining research into classical German philosophy with the methodological insights of contemporary systematic philosophy. All the contributions in this volume are indebted to this methodological advance. This cooperative transatlantic project shows how one can exploit and develop the overlaps in the different theoretical perspectives in a more fruitful way than would be possible if one stayed wholly within the context of the discussions in separate theoretical traditions.

The Contributions

The thematic approaches in the contributions to this volume follow roughly the path of the development of the determinations of the self and self-consciousness in classical German philosophy. As is well known, this path takes its starting point from Kant's epistemological analyses of self-consciousness, then moves to Fichte's speculative theory of self-positing, and culminates in Hegel's broadening of subjectivity into intersubjectivity.[4] Kant's theory of the self, in its systematic as well as historical context, is the central focus of the essays by Henry Allison, Georg Mohr, and Véronique Zanetti.

Henry E. Allison investigates the connection of spontaneity and autonomy in Kant's concept of the self. He thereby brings the relation of theoretical and practical reason within a strict Kantian conception of the self as an explication of the freedom of the person. For Allison, the concept of the self finds its concretization in the "Incorporation Thesis," according to which incentives can determine the will only when a person takes them up in the form of a maxim. Allison uses this thesis to give a new defense of what he has called Kant's "Reciprocity Thesis," that freedom and the moral law reciprocally imply each other. Allison concludes by arguing that objections to this thesis have failed to see that Kant is making a "conceptual," not a "metaphysical" claim, and that he is contending only that the reality of freedom cannot be denied "from a practical point of view."

Georg Mohr puts forward an argument that includes a developmental history that brings together the different fundamental stages of the eighteenth century philosophical accounts of the consciousness of freedom: introspection (in Wolff and the pre-Critical Kant), moral consciousness (in the Critical Kant), and intersubjectivity (in Fichte). These developmental stages find their thematic correlates in new interpretations of the philosophical concept of freedom, which is taken first in a psychological, then a moral, and finally a social sense. In conclusion, Mohr calls for opening up the perspective of Kantian theory in the direction of a Fichtian conception of intersubjectivity and interpersonality—a conception that identifies essential conditions in the formation of subjectivity that should not be neglected by contemporary philosophy.

Véronique Zanetti draws attention to the rarely noticed connection between the concept of the self and the notion of teleology. There is a tension between regulative and constitutive principles of teleology in Kant's later philosophy that finds a tentative solution in the moral positing of a transcendent divine principle. This positing is reinterpreted by Kant's successors, notably Schelling, in a Spinozist manner. According to Zanetti, Schelling deserves credit for having exploited the argumentative potential of the *Critique of Judgment* for the purposes of an idealistic theory of the self and above all for developing the concept of teleology in a new way.

In his study of the philosophical foundations of early romanticism, *Manfred Frank* explores the immediate reactions of the first successors to Kant. Here Frank elucidates two rarely noticed argumentative developments in early post-Kantian idealism in the period between 1789 and 1792. The first development is the influence of Friedrich Jacobi's book on Spinoza, the second (and not first) edition of which was decisive for the early romantic rejection of Reinhold's and Fichte's philosophy of a first principle. The second development is the work of Novalis and Niethammer, who following Jacobi, were responsible for the original form of the early romantic critique of the philosophy of a first principle. Frank also presents Novalis's philosophy of consciousness, which went far beyond Kant, Fichte, and Hegel in its claim that consciousness has its root in being, which transcends consciousness.

Fichte is the central point of reference for the next post-Kantian developments of the idealist theory of the self. His main idea—that the self is essentially to be conceived as unconditioned activity—became a stimulus for new interpretations which ultimately led the German romantics to a decisive critique of Fichte's starting point. In presenting investigations of the internal structure of the early forms of Fichte's *Wissenschaftslehre*, *Günter Zöller* and *Daniel Breazeale* aim to provide a substantive basis for examining the objections raised against Fichte's starting point. Zöller provides a critical reconstruction of Fichte's account of the human subject in terms of its theoretical and practical activities. Zöller traces the radicalization of Kant's transcendental idealism in Fichte's theory of ideal and real thinking and stresses the systematic supposition of some ultimate prediscursive reality underlying all activity of the I in Fichte.

While Zöller provides a critical reconstruction of the real and ideal activities in the notion of the 'I' in the early forms of the *Wissenschaftslehre*, Breazeale analyzes variations in the meaning of Fichte's theory of an *Anstoss* (or "check"). Breazeale's thesis is that, when we understand Fichte's theory of the *Anstoss*, contrary to many prejudices in the history of its reception, it becomes clear that Fichte's theory of the self is neither dogmatic nor inappropriately idealistic. Rather, from its very beginning, Fichte's conception of the self contains an element of finitude.

Hegel's dialectic of negativity is often taken to be the end point of, and the departure from, the idealist theory of subjectivity. Hegel's dialectic is usually interpreted as orienting itself according to the formal structure of reflection but no longer holding on to an independent concept of the self. The contributions of *Ludwig Siep* and *Robert Pippin* show that such interpretations significantly underestimate the subtlety of Hegel's attitude toward subjectivity. Siep determines the conception of individuality in *The Phenomenology of Spirit* in light of its chapter on reason. Accordingly, at the center of Siep's elucidations there are systematic analyses of the concepts of self-relation, self-actualization, and the synthesis of individual conscience with the *Sittlichkeit* (or "ethical life") of law-governed society. Pippin investigates Hegel's development of the problems of practical philosophy. He shows that Hegel's conception of action is much closer to Kant's than to Hume's, contrary to what is held often and incorrectly in contemporary philosophy. Nonetheless, Pippin says that Hegel's critique of Kant's implicit subjectivism is justified. We are to follow Hegel's proposal that reason can satisfy itself only in social and political institutions.

The analyses of Siep and Pippin are "truly Hegelian" in that they go along with Hegel in opening up the philosophy of subjectivity to the realms of the political and the cultural. To that extent they can be understood as direct responses to debates about the pros and cons of the project of modernity, to which Hegel took a critical but in the end affirmative position.

The works of Sturma and Ameriks, as well as the second contribution of Frank, complete the systematic connection drawn between the classical idealist theories of the self and contemporary philosophy of the subject. *Manfred Frank* critically engages some typical attempts at an elimination of subjectivity and self-consciousness. Precisely in view of the present spirit of the age, which is pushed back and forth by a manifold of streams of reductionism, from physicalism to neostructuralism, Frank's presentation of the ineliminability of subjectivity and self-consciousness expresses an original challenge. Frank's fundamental conviction is that the special task of philosophy is to make explicit in as undistorted a form as possible the importance of subjectivity. The ultimate motive for such a thesis lies not incidentally in the fact that it is a vital interest of human existence that rational individuals can understand themselves as subjects.[5]

The final contributions by Sturma and Ameriks are attempts at the systematic rehabilitation and development of Kant's theory of the self. *Karl Ameriks* reconstructs the argumentative path that the idealist theory of the self has taken from Kant to the present. Ameriks essentially accepts the defense of the ineliminability or irreducibility of the idealist concept of the self, as it has been presented by the Heidelberg school, and especially Manfred Frank. But Ameriks also draws attention to the fact that Kant's theory of the self anticipates later philosophers and is to a certain extent compatible with the Heidelberg school theory of subjectivity, which is known to be more oriented toward Fichte. In particular, Ameriks defends Kant against objections that his account of consciousness rests on an absurd "Reflection Theory."

Dieter Sturma makes a plea for a reconsideration of Kantian arguments in the effort to formulate a nonreductionist theory of the self. Sturma develops an argument for irreducibility that has at its center the concept of a subjective perspective which, because of its behavioral implications, can also be employed in the determination of practical rationality. Sturma also argues that Kant, who is often maligned for being stuck helplessly in dualism, provides a basis for making a step from the self to the Other and a corresponding step from theoretical to practical philosophy.

Future Perspectives

A look back at the theories of the self in classical German philosophy is always also a look forward to various methodological options. Behind the transitions from Kant to Fichte, and from Fichte to Hegel, there are hidden deep theoretical and methodological conflicts and fundamental decisions that remain controversial even today. To this day philosophy has still not come to a final judgment as to whether the appropriate model for subjectivity is the epistemological critique of speculative idealism or rather an encompassing concept of social philosophy.

Methodologically, it is crucial to explain and reconstruct the often opaque texts of classical German philosophy, and in particular the speculative systems of German idealism, in such a manner that for systematic purposes, one brackets from the beginning those presuppositions and arguments which are no longer justifiable in light of the criteria and methods of contemporary theories. The important question then becomes whether, in this way, one can get beyond the classifications of the history of philosophy and make a philosophically significant contribution to solving systematic problems.

The analysis of the classical texts of German idealism must also live with the uncomfortable fact that the meaning and significance of its concepts is determined essentially by their justificatory position in a philosophical system. The need for a kind of coherence theory has the immediate consequence that the arguments and positions developed by German idealism cannot be isolated; they must always be investigated against the background of their systematic context.

While Kant has always received great attention, the speculations of German idealism have remained largely unnoticed, at least in systematic contexts. However, this difficulty in gaining recognition is unjustified by the facts. German idealism contains insights that are of great systematic interest and that can be brought profitably into current efforts to develop theories of self-relations in modernity. Of course, from a current perspective one can follow the positions and solutions of German idealism only to a certain degree.

It is still not possible to determine with certainty the position of classical German philosophy and in particular the full relevance of its contribution to the theory of the self and its self-relations. The contributions of this volume make clear in any event the methodological difficulties and the various thematic perspectives that must be mastered in such a project. It is not clear whether the context of philological and historical work will receive adequate attention in contemporary systematic philosophy. It is to be expected that systematic interest will arise primarily from those unsolved problems that have to do with the project of modernity. Classical German philosophy has a contribution to make in this context that has at last received the beginning of an adequate hearing.

But the intention of this volume is not simply to gain a hearing for the theories of subjectivity developed in classical German philosophy; the articles in this volume are also concerned with presenting to contemporary philosophy a more differentiated picture of its own historical presuppositions. Precisely in regard to the question of the modern subject, which our age has placed on the agenda with so much emphasis, it is unavoidable that we take a look at that era of philosophy that was most intensely focused on the issue of the interconnection of subjectivity and reason.

When the pros and cons of the project of modernity are weighed, it is commonly said of the era of classical German philosophy that at no other time was so much entrusted to human subjectivity and reason, theoretically and practically. However, it would be too partial and too distorted a picture if one characterized this era unrestrictedly as the high age of human subjectivity and reason. Such an estimate seems plausible only because this era made subjectivity and reason a topic of reflection and speculation in a way that has in fact remained unparalleled in its extent and intensity. But the result of these efforts is by no means an overly optimistic claim about a far-reaching effectiveness of human subjectivity and reason, as is often maintained; rather, it is a recognition of the deep contextual dependence of human self-relations. In German idealism, speculative reflection leads to an uncovering of the finitude of human self-relations and not at all to the implication that human existence transcends its contexts and conditions. Here above all is where the contribution of classical German philosophy is to be recognized for its efforts to gain a more differentiated view of the project of modernity.

Notes

1. For a systematic and historical analysis of the philosophy of this period of transition, see Dieter Henrich, *Konstellationen: Probleme und Debatten am Ursprung der idealistischen Philosophie (1789–1795)* (Stuttgart: Klett-Cotta, 1991); and, in this volume, M. Frank, "Philosophical Foundations of Early Romanticism."

2. Examples of such tendencies can be found in the works of Nietzsche, Heidegger, Foucault, Derrida, Rorty, and others.

3. It is interesting that the situation is quite different in practical philosophy, especially in regard to Kant. The systematic reconstruction and revision of Kantian moral philosophy is being worked on very intensively, above all in connection with the work of John Rawls. See, e.g., *Grundlegung zur Metaphysik der Sitten: Ein kooperativer Kommentar*, ed. O. Höffe (Frankfurt: Klostermann, 1989).

4. In this context, Schelling's treatise on freedom and his later philosophy take on a special significance that is not covered in this volume.

5. This work of Frank's can be readily understood as the concluding contribution of this volume, but it does not appear at the end simply because the following contribution by Karl Ameriks makes reference to it.

2

Spontaneity and Autonomy in Kant's Conception of the Self

Henry E. Allison

Although Kant never developed what one might call a theory of the self, his virtual identification of selfhood with freedom provided much of the material used by his idealistic successors to develop their own theories. At the same time, however, Kant's actual account of freedom remains among the most perplexing features of his philosophy. One of the major problems is the bewildering variety of ways in which freedom is characterized in different Kantian texts. Thus, Lewis White Beck has distinguished between five different conceptions of freedom in Kant: empirical freedom, moral freedom or autonomy, spontaneity, transcendental freedom, and postulated freedom.[1] Since empirical freedom is nonproblematic, while postulated freedom turns out to characterize the status of the nonempirical freedom that we supposedly possess rather than a distinct kind of freedom, and finally, since transcendental freedom (as applied to humans) is identified with the absolute spontaneity of the will, this list can be shortened somewhat. Nevertheless, this still leaves us with spontaneity and autonomy as distinct species of freedom: the former concerns rational agency in general, that is, the capacity to determine oneself to act on the basis of general principles (whether moral or prudential); the latter concerns moral agency in particular, that is, the capacity of pure reason to be practical (to determine the will independently of inclination or desire).

It is sometimes claimed that the *Wille-Willkür* distinction drawn in the Introduction to the *Metaphysic of Morals* constitutes Kant's attempt to explain the connection between these two conceptions of freedom.[2] And there is certainly some truth to this, although the latter distinction, which amounts to the contrast between the legislative and executive functions of the will, cannot simply be equated with that between autonomy and spontaneity. For one thing, Kant denies that *Wille*, properly speaking, can be regarded as either free or unfree.[3] For another, autonomy applies only to

Wille taken in the broad sense as the whole faculty of volition, not to *Wille* in the narrow sense in which it is contrasted with *Willkür*.[4] Accordingly, the question of the relation between spontaneity and autonomy remains even after this distinction is introduced. Moreover, this question is itself a reflection of a larger issue: namely, whether the foundations of Kant's conception of freedom (and, therefore, selfhood) are to be located in his general views on rational agency or in the specifics of his moral theory.

My concern here is with this larger issue; and although much of what Kant says from 1788 on suggests the latter view, I shall argue for the former. In other words, I shall try to show that it is only in light of the conception of spontaneity that Kant's account of autonomy and the claims that he makes for it become intelligible. The analysis is a development of the account offered in *Kant's Theory of Freedom*. As in the book, I shall be concerned with two theses, the Incorporation Thesis and the Reciprocity Thesis, which I link with spontaneity and autonomy respectively. In contrast to the book, however, I shall here focus directly on the question of the relation between these two theses and their underlying conceptions of freedom. The discussion thus falls naturally into three parts. In the first two I discuss the two theses separately and in the third their connection in the full Kantian conception of freedom.

I

The conception of freedom as spontaneity is clearly expressed in the Incorporation Thesis. Kant's canonical formulation of this thesis is contained in *Religion within the Limits of Reason Alone*, where he writes:

> [F]reedom of the will [*Willkür*] is of a wholly unique nature in that an incentive [*Triebfeder*] can determine the will to an action *only so far as the individual has incorporated it* [*aufgenommen hat*] *into his maxim* (has made it the general rule in accordance with which he will conduct himself); only thus can an incentive, whatever it may be, coexist with the absolute spontaneity of the will [*Willkür*] (i.e., freedom).[5]

There are at least three aspects of this thesis that need to be emphasized. First, although Kant introduces it in connection with the explication of his "rigorism" (the claim that every action and agent must be judged either good or evil—the doctrine of moral bivalence) and suggests that it is of great significance to morality, it actually amounts to a claim about rational agency in general. Kant himself indicates this by stating that it applies to every incentive, "whatever it may be," implying thereby that it covers actions motivated by inclination as well as purely moral considerations.

In fact, the Incorporation Thesis is best seen as a general thesis about how motives function in the case of finite rational agents or about an *arbitrium liberum*, as contrasted with an *arbitrium brutum*. The latter, as Kant indicates in numerous places, is not merely sensuously affected, but also sensuously determined or necessitated. In other words, a subject with an *arbitrium brutum* is causally conditioned to respond to the strongest stimulus or desire, with this strength being determined by physiological factors, independently of any valuation placed upon it by the subject. Such a subject is, therefore, more properly characterized as a patient rather than an agent. By contrast, although a finite rational agent is still sensuously or "pathologically" affected, that is to say, it finds itself with a set of given inclinations and desires, which provide possible motives or reasons to act, it is not causally necessitated to act on the basis of any of them. For such an agent, then, one can no longer speak simply of being moved to act by the strongest desire, as if desires came with pregiven strengths, independently of the significance assigned to them by the rational agent in virtue of its freely chosen projects. Instead, the Incorporation Thesis requires us to regard the agent as acquiescing to the desire, granting it, as it were, honorific status as a sufficient reason to act. As the text indicates, this status is attained by incorporating the desire into one's maxim or principle of action. For example, I may have a strong desire to indulge myself in an ice cream cone, but the mere presence of such a desire or craving does not provide me with a sufficient reason for doing so. It can only become such in light of a rule permitting such indulgence under certain conditions. Consequently, in acting on the desire, I am also committing myself to that rule, and such a commitment must be viewed as an act of spontaneity on my part (of self-determination, if you will), which is not reducible to the mere having of the desire. It is, then, in this commitment and incorporation, which is inseparable from the practical use of reason, that we find the locus of agency.

The second point to be made with respect to the Incorporation Thesis is that it is by no means unique to the *Religion*. On the contrary, as the reference to the necessity of taking up or incorporating an incentive into a maxim indicates, this thesis is nothing more than an explication of what is already implicit in the familiar account of rational agency as based on the "conception of law" or principles in the *Groundwork*.[6] Since maxims are the first-order, subjective principles on which rational agents act, and since maxims are self-imposed (we do not simply have maxims, we *make* something our maxim), maxim-based action involves self-determination and, therefore, an exercise of spontaneity. Moreover, if in the *Groundwork* the

Incorporation Thesis is used without being mentioned, in other texts it is expressly affirmed, albeit not in the precise terms of the *Religion*. A good example of this is *Reflexion* 5611, which belongs to a set of *Reflexionen* that illuminate the discussion of freedom in the *Critique of Pure Reason*.[7] As Kant there puts the matter, actions are to a large part induced [*veranlasst*] but not entirely determined through sensibility, for reason must provide a "complement of sufficiency" [*Complement der Zulänglichkeit*].[8] This idea of a complement of sufficiency clearly corresponds to the incorporation of incentives into a maxim. In both cases the essential point is that reason somehow intervenes even in actions based on sensuous motives. Similarly, in *Metaphysik K3*, dated 1794–95, Kant maintains that, in addition to sensible stimuli, the "concurrence of the understanding" [*concurrenz des Verstandes*] is necessary to determine a rational agent to act.[9] As Karl Ameriks has noted in his discussion of this text, "What Kant has in mind here is . . . a model where the self 'goes along' with what is proposed to it without being compelled by this proposal."[10] Ameriks is perfectly correct in referring to this as a "model," and he is likewise correct in emphasizing that the point of this model is to articulate the key Kantian principle that sensibility of itself, apart from the contribution of the understanding or reason, is insufficient to account for either agency or cognition. To this I would only add that this doctrine of concurrence is nothing new but merely a fresh expression of the view to which Kant had been committed at least since the beginning of the "Critical" period.

The third and for present purposes most important point is that this incorporation is based on what Kant terms the "absolute spontaneity of the will." Although Kant does not discuss the matter in the *Religion*, this is presumably to be contrasted with relative spontaneity, which he sometimes describes as "*spontaneitas secundum quid*." In his pre-Critical metaphysical lectures, Kant compares the latter mode of spontaneity to that of a turnspit because its exercise depends upon a prior determination by an external force and contrasts it with the absolute spontaneity required for genuine agency.[11] Moreover, in a famous passage in the second *Critique* Kant uses precisely the same expression to characterize the "psychological" or "comparative" conception of freedom affirmed by Leibniz, which, in Kant's eyes, effectively reduces the soul to an "automaton *spirituale*."[12] And from this, together with the accounts in the first *Critique*, the *Groundwork*, and the other texts mentioned above, it seems reasonable to conclude that Kant held that the act of incorporation that is supposedly constitutive of rational agency requires more than a merely comparative freedom. More precisely, it requires a capacity to determine oneself to act independently of the "causality of nature," a capacity which can be thought only in light of the transcendental idea of freedom.

As has been frequently pointed out, this account of spontaneity has a parallel in the theoretical sphere, where Kant contrasts the spontaneity of the understanding with the receptivity of sense. Although the issues involved are quite complex, the case for epistemic spontaneity can be expressed fairly succinctly and in a way that helps to highlight the comparison with the practical variety. The main point is that the reception of sensible data is no more capable of accounting for cognition than being sensibly affected is sufficient to account for rational choice. As Kant avers in many places in the first *Critique*, sensibility and the imagination (in its empirical, reproductive function) can present to the mind merely a subjective order of representations (*a–b*), which reflects the contingencies of one's perceptual situation (the fact that one happened to perceive *a* before *b*). But such a subjective order does not of itself possess any cognitive worth; that is, it does not amount to the cognition of an objective connection or order. An objective connection requires that the understanding bring the given representations under an ordering principle or rule (pure concept of the understanding), by means of which the order is determined as objective. Kant characterizes this as an act of spontaneity of the subject, since it is not determined by the sensible data, and it constitutes the epistemic analog to the act of incorporation or concurrence. In both domains, then, we might say that the mind is "underdetermined by the data" and that complete determination requires a contribution on the part of the subject. In the cognitive domain, this contribution (the act of spontaneity) amounts to a determination of the object, whereas in the practical domain it is a genuine self-determination.

Given this parallelism, it is not surprising to find Kant occasionally appealing to a linkage between these two kinds of spontaneity. The best known of these places is in *Groundwork* III, where he appears to move from the epistemic spontaneity of rational beings to their practical spontaneity or freedom, only to draw back from the conclusion that his premises seem to warrant. As Kant there puts it:

> Reason must look upon itself as the author of its own principles independently of alien influences. Therefore as practical reason or as the will of a rational being, it must be regarded by itself as free; that is, the will of a rational being can be a will of his own [*ein eigener Wille sein*] only under the Idea of freedom, and such a will must therefore—from a practical point of view—be attributed to all rational beings.[13]

Since I have dealt with this text and the complex line of argument it involves at length elsewhere,[14] I shall here limit myself to pointing out that Kant's refusal to draw the expected conclusion (that we are warranted in regarding ourselves as free in the practical sense) stems from a significant disanalogy between epistemic and practical spontaneity. This disanalogy does not concern the type of spontaneity (as if cognition requires merely relative and agency absolute spontaneity), but rather the kind of certainty possible with respect to each. Although Kant to my knowledge never expresses himself in this way, it seems reasonable to attribute to him the view that the spontaneity of the understanding (or reason in its theoretical capacity) is self-certifying somewhat in the manner of the Cartesian *cogito*. To doubt one's spontaneity in this sense would be to doubt that one is a thinking being, but this, of course, would itself require an act of thought. The 'I think' must be able to accompany all my representations, even the thought that I am not really thinking. The Critical Kant, however, denies that we are entitled to draw any positive metaphysical conclusions regarding the "I or he or it (the thing) which thinks" from this result.[15] As always, the 'I think' remains "the sole text of rational psychology, and from it the whole idea of its teaching has to be developed."[16]

By contrast, in the practical domain, not even this degree of self-certification is available. Here, then, we must conclude that reflection on the ineliminable moment of spontaneity can yield only the conditional result: if I take myself to be a rational agent, that is, if I take myself to be acting on the basis of reasons and a reflective evaluation of my situation rather than merely responding to stimuli, I must necessarily regard myself as free. In the terms of the *Groundwork*, I can act only under the idea of freedom.[17] Or, as Kant is quoted as claiming in the *Metaphysik Mrongovius*, "Freedom is practically necessary—man must therefore act according to an idea of freedom, otherwise he cannot act [*anders kann er nicht*]. That does not, however, prove freedom in the theoretical sense."[18] As the latter remark indicates, the practical necessity of acting under the idea of freedom leaves in place the epistemic possibility that I am deluded in believing that I am acting or, as Kant sometimes puts it, that my "reason has causality." Here the Cartesian demon is more difficult to dislodge. In fact, it cannot be exorcised by any theoretical means, although it can be safely ignored from the practical point of view.

Finally, in light of these considerations, we are in a better position to appreciate the status of the Incorporation Thesis as the expression of a nonempirical, normative model of agency, which constitutes the Kantian alternative to the familiar Humean, belief-desire model. First, the model is nonempirical because the thought is just that, a thought or idea, rather than an object of possible experience. We cannot, as it were, introspectively catch ourselves incorporating incentives into our maxims any more than we can introspect the act of thinking itself.[19] Accordingly, this act is something "merely intelligible," which cannot be assigned to the self as phenomenon. Second, the model is normative because it is only in light of it that we regard ourselves as acting on the basis of reasons and, therefore, as subject to evaluative norms (whether moral or prudential).

II

Whereas the conception of freedom as spontaneity and the Incorporation Thesis in which it is expressed have pre-Critical roots, the characterization of freedom as autonomy and the associated Reciprocity Thesis are first explicitly formulated in the *Groundwork*. Autonomy is introduced in *Groundwork* II as the culmination of a regressive account of the conditions of the possibility of a categorical imperative. Although Kant confounds matters by referring to a "formula of autonomy," supposedly on a par with the other formulas of the categorical imperative, his major claim is that autonomy is the "supreme principle of morality" in the sense of being the condition of the possibility of action on the basis of this imperative. Autonomy, so construed, is defined as "the property the will has of being a law to itself (independently of every property belonging to objects of volition)."[20] This is contrasted with heteronomy, according to which "the will does not give itself the law, but the object does in virtue of its relation to the will."[21]

If one is to understand fully the significance of this conception, it is necessary to focus on the parenthetical clause. This is because, of itself, the conception of the will as having the property of "being a law to itself" need not take us beyond the Incorporation Thesis. Maxims, after all, are described by Kant as "subjective laws," and they are by their very nature self-imposed or self-legislated. Consequently, it is sometimes argued that the will exercises its autonomy (in the sense of being a "law to itself") in all cases of rational choice, even when it involves immoral behavior.[22] And if this is the case, then we cannot regard autonomy as a new conception of freedom, one explicitly tied to the capacity to act on the basis of the categorical imperative. Even worse, on this reading, heteronomy would not be a contrasting form of agency, but rather a simple lack of agency, a complete subjection of the will to the "causality of nature." Although the latter is precisely how the conception of heteronomy is frequently understood, such a reading makes nonsense of Kant's critique of alternative moral theories as based on the *principle* of heteronomy. As we shall see, this critique turns on the claim that all such theories embody an inadequate account of moral motivation (one which ultimately revolves around the principle of self-love); but this presupposes that the subjects of morality are regarded as agents, who act on the basis of principles rather than merely respond to stimuli.

The parenthetical clause offers the prospect of a way out of these difficulties because it suggests that autonomy involves not simply the capacity of the will to determine itself to act on the basis of self-imposed principles (which would include heteronomous principles), but the capacity to do so in a particular way—namely, "independently of every property belonging to the objects of volition." Accordingly, the task is to determine just what this independence condition involves, and this can best be accomplished by considering a mode of volition that lacks it, that is, one in which "the will does not give itself the law, but the object does so in virtue of its relation to the will."[23]

If the latter is to be understood as a form of agency, it must be one in which all the agent's maxims reflect its needs (directly or indirectly) as a sensuous being, needs which are themselves explicable in terms of the laws of nature. In short, it is not that the agent is causally conditioned to act as a result of these needs (in which case it would not even have an *arbitrium liberum*); it is rather that these needs (including psychological or "ego needs") provide the only available sources of reasons to act. Although this is quite far from the picture of agency presented in Kant's major writings in moral theory, it is arguably the view to which he adhered, at least implicitly, prior to the *Groundwork*.[24] Conversely, an agent with the property of autonomy would not be subject to this limiting condition, and this means that it would have the capacity to recognize sufficient reasons to act that do not stem (even indirectly) from its needs as a sensuous being. Since such reasons can stem only from pure practical reason, the will (as practical reason) would be self-legislative in the fullest sense and pure reason would be practical.

In light of this conception of autonomy, it is easy to see why Kant both regards autonomy as the supreme principle of morality and denies that any view of agency that does not acknowledge autonomy in this sense is capable of accounting for the possibility of morality. The key idea is simply that morality, as Kant analyzes it in *Groundwork* I and II, requires not merely that our actions conform to duty but that they be "from duty," that is, that the duty-motive of itself provide a sufficient reason to act. Expressed in Kantian terms, this means that the recognition of an obligation brings with it an "incentive" [*Triebfeder*] or "interest" in fulfilling it. Such an interest is termed by Kant a "pure" or "moral" interest. Assuming autonomy, this condition can be met, since *ex hypothesi* an agent with this property is capable of being motivated by a non-sensuous incentive. Lacking this property, however, such motivation is impossible, since an interest, stemming from one's needs as a sensuous being, would then be required, in order to have a sufficient reason (incentive) to act. And on that scenario, which is that of heteronomy, moral requirements would be reduced to hypothetical imperatives, since the only incentive for fulfilling them would be their status as necessary means to the satisfaction of some presupposed interest.

So far we have considered Kant's argument to the effect that autonomy is a necessary condition of the possibility of morality. Kant also claims, however, that it is its sufficient condition, and this is where the Reciprocity Thesis comes into play. In order to understand the significance of this thesis, we must recognize that autonomy, as presented above, does not yet involve any necessary connection with morality. The claim that the will has the capacity to legislate to itself, even apart from all sensuous needs and interests, is not equivalent to the claim that the moral law is the law that it legislates. Rather, the introduction of autonomy as a property of the will serves to create the space needed to account for the possibility of moral motivation (the independence condition), but it does not of itself provide anything to fill that space or even to guarantee that it can be filled. For all that we have seen so far, it is conceivable that an autonomous agent might legislate some other law to itself or perhaps determine itself to act on the basis of principles that make no pretense to lawfulness (no claim to universality and necessity). Accordingly, even granting freedom as autonomy, we still need an argument linking it to the moral law. This is the function of the Reciprocity Thesis, which, in the language of the second *Critique*, affirms that "freedom and unconditional practical law reciprocally imply each other."[25]

In the *Groundwork*, Kant introduces this thesis in connection with the distinction between a negative and a positive definition of freedom. After first characterizing the will as "a kind of causality belonging to living beings so far as they are rational," he claims that freedom, negatively construed, is just the capacity of the will "to work independently of *determination* by alien causes." Although incapable of capturing the essence of freedom because of its negative thrust, Kant claims that it leads to a positive definition that does capture this essence. This positive definition is just autonomy, here characterized as the "property which will has of being a law to itself."[26] The argument for this connection turns on the premise that the will, like any "kind of causality," cannot be lawless, that is, it must have a specifiable *modus operandi* or "character." And since, *ex hypothesi*, determination by "alien causes" in conformity with laws of nature is ruled out, nothing remains but to attribute to the will the property of being a law to itself, that is, autonomy as contrasted with a "heteronomy of efficient causes." Finally, Kant continues, the claim that "'Will is in all its actions a law to itself'" is equivalent to the "principle of acting on no maxim other than one which can have for its object itself as at the same time a universal law," which is just the formula for the categorical imperative. And from this he concludes that "a free will and a will under moral laws are one and the same thing."[27]

This argument consists of two moves: one from the negative to the positive conception of freedom or autonomy and the other from autonomy to the categorical imperative. Unfortunately, each of these moves is highly problematic, with the difficulty in both cases stemming from an ambiguity in the central notion of autonomy. To begin with, causal independence (as expressed in the Incorporation Thesis) does not entail autonomy in the full Kantian sense discussed above. As already indicated, the latter involves more than independence from determination by alien causes; it also involves a positive capacity to be motivated by reasons that are totally independent of one's needs as a sensuous being. But this positive capacity simply cannot be teased out of negative freedom, at least insofar as the latter is simply identified with spontaneity.[28] Similarly, with respect to the second move, the claim that the will is a "law to itself" need not mean more than that it is spontaneous, acting on the basis of self-imposed principles, and from this there is no direct route to the categorical imperative.

As I have argued elsewhere, however, the analytic connection between freedom and the categorical imperative that Kant affirms in the Reciprocity Thesis can be established if we thicken our initial conception of negative freedom to include motivational as well as causal independence.[29] In addition to the requisite sense of freedom, this argument, which I can only sketch here in a rough manner, is based on the assumption that the agent in question is rational. This entails that its choices must be subject to a justification requirement. In other words, it must be possible for such an agent to offer reasons for its actions, and since reasons are by their very nature universal, this means that such an agent must be willing to acknowledge that it would be reasonable (justifiable) for any rational being to act in a similar manner in relevantly similar circumstances.

Now, of itself this claim is relatively noncontroversial and yields only a weak sense of universalizability that is far removed from the form required by Kantian morality. The move to the categorical imperative and to the strong sense of universalizability it involves turns on the extension of the justification requirement to the most fundamental maxims of such an agent. This extension is entailed by the nature of the freedom being attributed to the agent. Since such an agent is assumed to have the capacity to determine itself independently of, and even contrary to, its needs as a sensuous being, it cannot simply appeal to a given desire, no matter how strong or "foundational," as if that desire of itself constituted a sufficient reason to adopt a course of action. On the contrary, desire-based action requires a desire-independent warrant. The question thus becomes what could provide such a warrant, and the short Kantian answer is that it can only be provided by an unconditional practical law, that is, one which applies to all rational agents independently of their desires. This is why Kant claims in the second *Critique* that "freedom and unconditional practical law reciprocally imply each other."[30] Consequently, an agent with autonomy must submit its self-legislation to the condition of its conformity to unconditional practical law. And since it can be shown that this is equivalent to recognizing the authority of the categorical imperative, it follows that an agent with autonomy must recognize the authority of this imperative as the supreme condition of its self-legislation.[31]

Finally, before concluding this section, it is important to determine more precisely the thrust of the Reciprocity Thesis. First, of itself, it does not suffice to show that rational agents such as ourselves really are subject to the categorical imperative, since it presupposes rather than establishes the type of freedom (autonomy) that is both a necessary and a sufficient condition of this imperative. Second, it does not entail that autonomous agents necessarily obey this imperative insofar as they act freely. It shows rather that they must recognize its authority and motivational force (as the source of a sufficient reason for action) even when they violate its precepts. As always, for Kant, what is objectively (in the eyes of reason) necessary remains subjectively contingent. Nevertheless, it does establish the inseparability of Kantian morality from a conception of freedom that is distinct from that of spontaneity, even when this is understood in the absolute sense.

III

Up to this point we have examined the two conceptions of freedom and their respective theses separately; our present task is to consider their relationship in the overall Kantian conception of the self. Now, given what we have seen so far, it would seem that Kant's position should be that the two conceptions have different warrants and operate at different levels of reflection. Since we can act only under the idea of freedom, spontaneity, and with it the Incorporation Thesis, must be presupposed in every exercise of rational agency. Correlatively, autonomy is presupposed as a condition of acting from duty. Finally, since acting from duty is a species of acting, autonomy must presuppose spontaneity (and the Reciprocity Thesis the Incorporation Thesis).

Although something like the above seems to be operative in the *Groundwork*, when we turn to the texts from 1788 on, a somewhat different picture emerges. Essential to this later picture is the thesis, first enunciated in the preface to the *Critique of Practical Reason*, that the moral law is the "*ratio cognoscendi* of freedom"; that is to say, apart from our consciousness of standing under the moral law, "we would never have been justified in assuming anything like [*so etwas*] freedom."[32] Far from being an isolated claim, this doctrine of the total dependence of the conception of freedom on the moral law is a constant refrain of Kant's from then on. For example, in *Religion within the Limits of Reason Alone*, the very work in which the Incorporation Thesis is expressly formulated, Kant states of the moral law that "it is the only law which informs us of the independence of our will [*Willkür*] from determination of all other incentives . . . and at the same time of the accountability of all our actions."[33] Similarly, in the *Metaphysics of Morals* he claims that moral laws "first make known to us a property of our choice [*Willkür*], namely, its freedom."[34]

As the citation from the *Religion* makes clear, the claim is not that we are free, or even that we are certain of our freedom, only insofar as we act from duty; it is rather that it is the capacity to act from duty (of which we are aware through our consciousness of standing under the moral law) that makes us aware of our general capacity to determine ourselves to act independently of the "causality of nature." In short, it is through the consciousness of our autonomy that we become aware of our absolute spontaneity and, therefore, of the imputability of our acts. Moreover, this account of the connection between the moral law (itself certified through the "fact of reason") and freedom as spontaneity appears to underlie both the "deduction" of freedom and the doctrine of the unity of reason in the second *Critique*. Thus, Kant there maintains that pure practical reason fills the place left "vacant" by speculative reason by providing practical reality (through the moral law) to the "Idea of freedom as a faculty of absolute spontaneity," which, with respect to its possibility, is an "analytical principle of pure speculation." And, in the same context, he further contends that "Speculative reason does not herewith grow in insight but only in respect to the certitude of its problematic concept of freedom, to which objective, though only practical, reality is now indubitably given."[35]

Since absolute spontaneity (transcendental freedom) is the conception of freedom indigenous to reason in its speculative use, it seems clear that establishing an intimate connection between morality and such freedom is essential to Kant's systematic project of demonstrating the unity of reason. It seems equally clear, however, that this linkage of absolute spontaneity specifically and solely with the capacity to act from duty raises fresh questions about the overall coherence of Kant's position. First, there is the question of consistency, which arises because of the difficulty in reconciling such a view with many of the texts previously considered as well as with the significance attributed to the Incorporation Thesis. Second, the result seems highly counterintuitive; for assuming that Kant is consistent in maintaining that freedom as spontaneity is a condition of rational agency, it would follow that he is committed to the view that it is only through our consciousness of standing under the moral law that we can become aware of our rational agency, that is, of a capacity to set ends, adopt maxims, and the like. But this seems quite implausible; indeed, it is only insofar as we first consider ourselves as agents engaged in a deliberative process that moral claims gain any real hold on us.

One might respond to both the inconsistency and implausibility charges by appealing to texts which suggest that Kant in fact thought that the merely comparative conception of freedom, which can be ascertained through experience, rather than absolute spontaneity, is all that is required to distinguish the *arbitrium liberum* from the *arbitrium brutum* and, therefore, for the attribution of agency in nonmoral contexts.[36] On this basis, then, one might simply deny that Kant held that absolute spontaneity is a condition of rational agency per se. But even leaving aside the difficulty of reconciling any such reading with the Incorporation Thesis, the real problem with it is that it makes it difficult to see how Kant can then deny the possibility of a naturalized account of action from duty as well.[37] Once the adequacy of a thoroughly naturalistic account of rational agency in general is admitted, then it becomes quite difficult to maintain that action from duty constitutes a unique exception. A capacity to act on the basis of reasons that hold independently of one's needs as a sensuous being is one thing, and a capacity to act contracausally, which is clearly what absolute spontaneity involves, quite another. And if Kant does indeed identify the two, then it would seem that he is guilty of conflating a motivational with a causal independence of nature.

Nor can one defend such a conflation on the grounds that motives or incentives for Kant are the psychological causes of action. On this reading, a capacity to act on the basis of a supersensible incentive is just what is meant by a capacity to exercise a supersensible causality; so it would hardly be surprising that Kant identifies the warrant for affirming the latter with the consciousness of the former capacity. Although it must be admitted that Kant does seem to reason this way at times, it cannot be taken as his considered view, since it makes it completely unintelligible how inclination-based actions (which *ex hypothesi* have sensible incentives) can be imputed. As we have already seen, this is conceivable only insofar as we assume that incentives (whatever their nature) are not of themselves sufficient to determine choice but must first be taken up or "incorporated" into a maxim. Such a view, however, clearly requires a sharp distinction between the incentive and the causal determinant of action, with the latter (as the Incorporation Thesis affirms) being attributed to the absolute spontaneity of *Willkür*.[38]

Interestingly enough, these difficulties disappear if we identify the freedom for which the consciousness of the moral law serves as the *ratio cognoscendi* with autonomy rather than spontaneity. Since autonomy (in the specifically Kantian sense) is not a condition of rational agency, we no longer have to attribute to Kant the view that our consciousness of duty first makes us aware of our agency. Nor do we need to accuse him of conflating motives and causes. On the contrary, it would make perfect sense for Kant to claim that our consciousness of duty first makes us aware of our autonomy; particularly since apart from such consciousness we could have no reason to believe that there might be such a thing as a pure or nonsensuous incentive. In short, what the consciousness of standing under the moral law really provides is a determinate content to the otherwise vacuous idea of a motivational independence from our needs as sensuous beings rather than some kind of guarantee of our causal independence from everything in the phenomenal world. This independence is still presupposed as a condition of agency; but this presupposition leaves in place the epistemic possibility that our putative freedom is illusory, that we are automata rather than agents. Although such a view is practically vacuous, since we cannot act on the basis of it, it remains unrefuted theoretically. Indeed, only when the "primacy of practical reason" is taken in a much stronger sense, as it was by Fichte, for example, could such an argument from morality be thought to undermine the very possibility that our freedom might be illusory.[39] But at that point we are no longer on genuinely Kantian ground.

Admittedly, this seems to conflict with much of what Kant says about freedom in the second *Critique*, particularly with the opening claims in the Preface that "With the pure practical faculty of reason, the reality of transcendental freedom is also confirmed."[40] And one paragraph later: "The concept of freedom, insofar as its reality is proved by an apodictic law of practical reason, is the keystone of the whole architecture of the system of pure reason and even of speculative reason."[41] In passages such as these, which suggest that the reality [*Realität*] of transcendental freedom has somehow been established through the moral law as the fact of reason, Kant certainly seems to be denying *tout court* the possibility that our freedom might be illusory. But to interpret such claims in this way is to ignore the explicitly practical context in which they arise. As Kant makes clear at several points, freedom is known only as a condition of the moral law, and this means that, although the law gives practical reality to the notion of an unconditioned, supersensible causality (absolute spontaneity), it does not extend our theoretical insight into such causality—not even to the extent of ruling out the epistemic possibility that theoretical reason leaves open. Once again, then, we find that the most that Kant's argument entails is that the reality of freedom cannot be denied from a practical point of view.

Nevertheless, even this limited result will be rejected by most philosophers, including many who consider themselves Kantians in moral theory. Since the concern of Kantian moral theory is with the question of the nature of moral motivation, why can't we simply abstract from the properly speculative question of transcendental freedom and thus develop a genuinely Kantian moral theory without worrying about this problematic concept? In fact, Kant himself seems to approve of precisely such a procedure when he remarks in the Canon of the first *Critique* that transcendental freedom is a problem, which "does not come within the province of reason in its practical employment."[42]

The response is to insist once again on the centrality of the Incorporation Thesis and to disarm those who might acknowledge this thesis, or something like it, while denying that this need involve any commitment to even the idea of absolute spontaneity or transcendental freedom.[43] In my judgment, this denial is rooted in the mistaken assumption that the appeal to freedom is intended as something like the best explanation for the "phenomenon" of rational agency, understood as our capacity to deliberate, choose, adopt maxims, and the like. Indeed, given this assumption, it is all too easy to dismiss the appeal to absolute spontaneity on the dual grounds that any forthcoming "explanation" would involve an illicit appeal to noumenal capacities and that it neglects sophisticated forms of compatibilism, which are allegedly capable of reconciling everything we view as essential to rational agency with a broadly naturalistic account.

As I have argued elsewhere, however, Kant's insistence on the connection between rational agency and spontaneity is to be understood as a conceptual claim rather than a putative metaphysical explanation.[44] In other words, freedom in the sense of spontaneity is not something that we must add to our conception of ourselves as rational agents in order to make some kind of metaphysical sense out of it; it is rather the defining feature of this very conception. This is the force of the claim that we can act only under the idea of freedom. In Hegelian terms, freedom, so construed, is subject and not a mere predicate. And in this sense Kant provided the inspiration for the later idealistic identification of the self, ego or *Geist* with freedom. Leaving aside the complications introduced by the suprapersonal nature of *Geist*, the essential difference is that for Kant this remained a mere conceptual claim regarding the manner in which we must conceive ourselves insofar as we take ourselves as rational agents, whereas in his idealistic successors it became inflated into an ontological truth. Whether this conception is necessary and, if so, whether its inflation is warranted are, of course, among the big questions posed for us by German idealism.

Notes

1. Lewis White Beck, *A Commentary on Kant's "Critique of Practical Reason"* (Chicago: University of Chicago Press, 1960), pp. 176–81; and "Five Concepts of Freedom in Kant," in *Philosophical Analysis and Reconstruction,* a Festschrift to Stephan Körner, ed. J.T.J. Srzednick (Dordrecht: Martinus Nijhoff, 1987), pp. 35–51.

2. See, for example, Beck, who correlates freedom as autonomy specifically with "*Wille*" and freedom as spontaneity with "*Willkür*," *Commentary,* pp. 199–200.

3. Immanuel Kant, *Metaphysics of Morals,* trans. M. Gregor (New York: Cambridge University Press, 1991), Ak. vol. 6, p. 226. Unless otherwise noted, references to Kant's works will use the pagination of the following edition: *Kants gesammelte Schriften* (hereafter Ak.) (Berlin: Königliche Preussische Akademie der Wissenschaften, 1900 ff.).

4. For my discussion of this issue see *Kant's Theory of Freedom* (Cambridge, New York: Cambridge University Press, 1990), pp. 129–36.

5. Kant, *Religion within the Limits of Reason Alone,* trans. T. Greene and H. Hudson (New York: Harper & Row, 1960), p. 19; Ak. vol. 6, p. 24. References to this work will include the pagination of the translation first.

6. Kant, *Groundwork of the Metaphysic of Morals,* trans. H. J. Paton (New York: Harper & Row, 1964), Ak. vol. 4, p. 412.

7. These are *Reflexionen* 5611–5620 (Kant, Ak. vol. 18, pp. 252–59). For an analysis of these *Reflexionen,* see Heinz Heimsoeth, "Freiheit und Charakter nach den Kant-Reflexionen Nr. 5611 bis 5620," in *Tradition und Kritik,* ed. W. Arnold and H. Zeltner (Stuttgart: Friedrich Frommann, 1967), pp. 123–44.

8. Kant, Ak. vol. 18, p. 252.

9. Kant, Ak. vol. 29, p. 1015.

10. Karl Ameriks, "Kant on Spontaneity: Some New Data," in *Akten des Siebenten Internationalen Kant-Kongresses,* ed. G. Funke (Bonn: Bouvier, 1991), p. 478.

11. Kant, *Metaphysik L1*, Ak. vol. 28, p. 267. See also *Reflexion* 6077, Ak. vol. 18, p. 443.

12. Kant, *Critique of Practical Reason*, trans. L. W. Beck, 3rd ed. (New York: Macmillan, 1993), Ak. vol. 5, p. 97.

13. Kant, *Groundwork*, Ak. vol. 4, p. 448. Another important, frequently discussed text in which Kant argues in a similar manner is the review of Schulz's *Sittenlehre*, Ak. vol. 8, p. 14.

14. See my *Kant's Theory of Freedom*, pp. 214–21.

15. Kant, *Critique of Pure Reason*, trans. N. K. Smith (New York: St. Martin's Press, 1929), A346/B404. (References to this work will use the pagination of the first/second German editions.) Kant does claim, however, that we are able to derive the negative conclusion of the impossibility of a materialistic account of the self (See *Prolegomena to Any Future Metaphysics*, trans. L. W. Beck (New York: Bobbs-Merrill, 1950), Ak. vol. 4, pp. 334, 352, 363; *Critique of Pure Reason*, B420; *On the Progress of Metaphysics*, Ak. vol. 20, p. 308). For my analysis of this, see "Kant's Refutation of Materialism," *Monist* 72 (1989), pp. 190–208.

16. Kant, *Critique of Pure Reason*, A343/B402.

17. Kant, *Groundwork*, Ak. vol. 4, p. 448.

18. Kant, Ak. vol. 29, p. 898.

19. On the latter point see *Reflexion* 5661 (Ak. vol. 18, pp. 318–19), where Kant explicitly denies that we can experience ourselves as thinking.

20. Kant, *Groundwork*, Ak. vol. 4, p. 440.

21. Ibid., p. 441.

22. This is argued by Rüdiger Bittner, "Maximen," in *Akten des Vierten Internationalen Kant-Kongresses*, ed. G. Funke and J. Kopper (Berlin: de Gruyter, 1974), pp. 485–98; and by Gerold Prauss, *Kant über Freiheit als Autonomie* (Frankfurt am Main: Vittorio Klostermann, 1983).

23. Kant, *Groundwork*, Ak. vol. 4, p. 441.

24. This claim is, of course, controversial. I argue for it in "The Concept of Freedom in Kant's 'Semi-Critical' Ethics," *Archiv für Geschichte der Philosophie* 68 (1986), pp. 96–115; and *Kant's Theory of Freedom*, pp. 66–70. For a similar anal-

ysis, see E.G. Schulz, *Rehbergs Opposition gegen Kants Ethik* (Köln: Böhlau Verlag, 1975), pp. 105 n. 35, 162–67.

25. Kant, *Critique of Practical Reason,* Ak. vol. 5, p. 29.

26. Kant, *Groundwork,* Ak. vol. 4, p. 446.

27. Ibid., p. 447.

28. Although he does not draw the contrast between spontaneity and autonomy as two species of freedom, the basic point is also noted by Thomas Hill, who likewise distinguishes between the two kinds of independence and argues that the move from negative to positive freedom requires attributing both kinds to the former. See *Dignity and Practical Reason in Kant's Moral Theory* (Ithaca and London: Cornell University Press), pp. 93–94, 106–10.

29. See my "Morality and Freedom: Kant's Reciprocity Thesis," *Philosophical Review* 95 (1986), pp. 393–425 and *Kant's Theory of Freedom,* chap. 11.

30. Kant, *Critique of Practical Reason,* Ak. vol. 5, p. 29.

31. For the argument linking the notion of an unconditional practical law with the categorical imperative, see my *Kant's Theory of Freedom,* pp. 210–13; and "On a Presumed Gap in the Derivation of the Categorical Imperative," *Philosophical Topics* 19 (1991), pp. 1–15.

32. Kant, *Critique of Practical Reason,* Ak. vol. 5, p. 4 n.

33. Kant, *Religion,* p. 21 n.; Ak. vol. 6, p. 35 n.

34. Kant, *Metaphysics of Morals,* Ak. vol. 6, p. 225.

35. Kant, *Critique of Practical Reason,* Ak. vol. 5, pp. 48–49.

36. See Kant, *Critique of Pure Reason,* A801–03/B829–31; *Metaphysik der Sitten Vigilantius,* Ak. vol. 27, pp. 503–07; and Karl Ameriks, "Kant on Spontaneity: Some New Data," who refers to somewhat similar passages from *Metaphysik K3, Metaphysik Mrongovius,* and *Moral Mrongovius 2.*

37. This is the main thrust of the very influential critique of Kant by August Wilhelm Rehberg, who held that even our consciousness of the moral law ought to be regarded by Kant as an appearance in inner sense and, therefore, as subject to the causality of nature. For a discussion of Rehberg's views, see Schulz, *Rehbergs Opposition gegen Kants Ethik.*

38. Something like the view criticized in this paragraph seems to be proposed by Allen Wood. See his "Kant's Incompatiblism," in *Self and Nature in Kant's Philosophy*, ed. A. Wood (Ithaca and London: Cornell University Press, 1984), pp. 73–101; and "The Emptiness of the Moral Will," *Monist* 73 (1989), pp. 454–83. For my critique of Wood's reading, see *Kant's Theory of Freedom*, pp. 48–52.

39. I take this to have been Fichte's project in the chapter added to the second edition of his published first work, *Attempt at a Critique of all Revelation* (Königsberg: 1792, 1st edition), in which he takes up specifically the question of whether the consciousness of spontaneity might be illusory. See *Johann Gottlieb Fichtes sämmtliche Werke*, vol. 5, ed. I. H. Fichte (Berlin: Veit, 1845–6; reprinted Berlin: Walter de Gruyter & Co., 1971), pp. 16–33.

40. Kant, *Critique of Practical Reason*, Ak. vol. 5, p. 3.

41. Ibid., pp. 3–4.

42. Kant, *Critique of Pure Reason*, A803/B831.

43. For a recent expression of that viewpoint, see Nancy Sherman, "Wise Maxims/Wise Judging," *Monist* 76 (1993), p. 63, n. 25.

44. See my "Kant on Freedom: A Reply to My Critics," *Inquiry* 36 (1993), pp. 458–63.

3

Freedom and the Self: From Introspection to Intersubjectivity: Wolff, Kant, and Fichte

Georg Mohr

Freedom and subjectivity or self are both central issues where many of the interests of the European philosophers of the second half of the eighteenth century intersect. Kant's transcendental idealism and Fichte's *Science of Knowledge* both constitute essentially a theory of the *self* and a philosophy of *freedom*. This double orientation, self-consciousness on the one hand, the primacy of practical reason on the other hand, is a kind of fundamental condition of German Idealism. There are interesting connections between self and freedom which become obvious in the theories of Kant and Fichte. I shall discuss some points made by these philosophers concerning the following question:

> What is the foundation of our consciousness of ourselves as free beings? Could such a foundation be found in a privileged access that we have to our own mind? Or is consciousness of freedom a genuine intersubjective phenomenon concerning practical reason but one that defies any theoretical or epistemological explication?

In discussing this question, I will refer not only to Kant and Fichte but also to Christian Wolff. The philosophical development that I want to follow in this paper starts with Wolff, who constitutes, as it were, a negative background for the arguments presented by Kant and Fichte. More precisely, there can be four basic possible answers to the question concerning our consciousness of freedom.

1. Our consciousness of freedom is based on the privileged access that we have to our own minds or souls *via introspection*.

2. We know our freedom because we are convinced of the validity of the

moral law. Consciousness of freedom is founded in *moral consciousness* as an inexplicable fact of reason.

3. Only in contexts of communication and mutual recognition do we experience ourselves as free. Our consciousness of freedom is based on *intersubjectivity*.

4. The belief in freedom is simply erroneous or illusory.

I shall omit a discussion of position (4) because it holds that there is no positive answer at all to the question of freedom. Nietzsche, for instance, calls the "concept of 'free will'" the "foulest of all theologians' artifices, aimed at making mankind 'responsible' in their sense, that is, *dependent upon them*. . . . Men were considered 'free' so that they might be judged and punished."[1]

I present the positions of Wolff, Kant and Fichte as a development from "introspection" to "intersubjectivity," from (1) to (3). Hence, the division of my paper into three parts. By "introspection" I understand a general notion for all epistemic (theoretical) self-relations, not only inner perception, but also, for example, intellectual intuition. By "development" I mean not a strictly linear, historical succession, but rather the development of arguments that change in their central points during the second half of the eighteenth century.

Introspection

Wolff–In Wolff, the explication of our consciousness of freedom is part of empirical psychology. It is treated in the third chapter of the "Deutsche Metaphysik."[2] The chapter on empirical psychology is entitled "Of the Soul in General, what we perceive of it." It presents the facts which can be obtained by experience. Experience is defined by Wolff as the "knowledge which we obtain when we attend to our sensations and the modifications of the soul."[3] Empirical psychology proceeds by inner perception, self-observation. Following the Cartesian tradition, Wolff starts from self-consciousness in the sense of the *cogito*. First, he demonstrates the existence of the soul and then proceeds to the description of different mental phenomena. In his empirical psychology, Wolff wants to "relate what we perceive from the soul through daily experience" and "to refer only to that which everybody can know by paying attention to himself."[4]

Starting at § 511, Wolff treats freedom as a subject of self-observation. Wolff argues against the idea that freedom consists in arbitrary choice. This would mean acting without any motive when one chooses to act in one way rather the another.[5] Wolff argues that freedom is the human capacity to act according to good reasons.[6] The foundations of voluntary agency are in the soul. Wolff defines "*Willkür*" as the general capacity to be oneself the origin of one's actions.[7] Freedom is "the capacity of the soul to choose according to its own will the one which pleases it more between two equally possible things . . . or, what amounts to the same thing, to determine itself according to that by which it is determined neither by its own nature nor by something external."[8]

It is interesting to see how Wolff *justifies* his claim that the human will is free. According to Wolff, the will cannot be compelled because it follows judgments of reason about what is "good" and what is "bad." These judgments are decisive for the motives according to which the will deliberates. Freedom is not indeterminate arbitrariness but rather the capacity to determine oneself according to knowledge of the best reasons. So, freedom is based at least on the fact that the understanding cannot be compelled to produce representations. In its activity of representing, the understanding is free. But, how can we know that our understanding is free in representing? Wolff's answer is: by experience. "Nobody would think to doubt this because it is confirmed by daily experience"[9]

This "daily experience" of our free will is further supported by the fact that we perceive a correspondence between body and mind. We "perceive the correspondence of our thoughts with certain modifications in our body and then the correspondence of certain movements in the body with certain thoughts of the soul."[10] But this perception of correspondence is not to be confused with a perception of the cause-effect relation. There is no experience of the effect of either the body on the soul or the soul on the body.[11] Experience can establish only the temporal relation of simultaneity but not a causal relation.[12] Nevertheless, from these limitations of our perceptual experience we cannot conclude that there *are* no such causal relations.[13] This question is discussed in the *rational* psychology.[14] But Wolff explicitly claims that there *are* "voluntary movements" that are "determined by a free decision of the soul."[15] This determination by the soul is, according to Wolff, a necessary condition of voluntary movements. The voluntariness of movements consists in the fact that "they would not happen if the soul had not determined them."[16] That is what is meant by saying that the soul "commands" the body.

I come to a first result: according to Wolff, we *experience* that we are free. Consciousness of freedom is empirical. One of Wolff's central arguments says that the understanding is free in producing representations, and that the freedom of the will can be perceived internally by this freedom of the understanding. Wolff is not referring to a perception of the effect of the soul on the body (movements). We cannot experience that a decision of the will causes movements of our body (arms, etc.). By experience, we can establish merely that two things, i.e., thoughts and physical movements, are simultaneous and, hence, that they "correspond" in time, but we cannot perceive that they constitute a relation of cause and effect. According to Wolff, freedom of the will consists in determining one's own actions according to rational principles. The soul is capable of determining voluntary physical movements by a free and rational decision. But how can we *know* that we are free? How can we perceive such a self-determination if causal relations cannot be perceived? It seems that in Wolff, there is an inconsistency between the epistemological claim about the limits of experience, on the one hand, and the empirical-psychological account of our consciousness of freedom, on the other hand. To avoid such an inconsistency, we must suppose that, according to Wolff, consciousness of freedom is *only* and *sufficiently* grounded in an inner perception of the freedom of the understanding in producing representations. This thesis raises three questions: Can the free activity of the understanding really be *perceived as free*? And if so, do we not thereby *presuppose* that the *absence* of external constraint can be *experienced*? And is this an intelligible presupposition? These are three questions that Kant tries to solve when he develops his critical philosophy.

Kant 1–In the so-called *Reflexionen* of the 1760s and 1770s, Kant is searching for an account of our consciousness of freedom. In these *Reflexionen*, in his lectures on metaphysics, and, finally, in the Canon of the *Critique of Pure Reason*,[17] Kant makes a distinction between "practical or psychological freedom" and freedom "in the transcendental sense."[18] This seems to be similar to the distinction that Schopenhauer makes later on between "freedom to act" and "freedom of the will."[19] The first is the capacity to act on one's own decisions without there being any external constraint. The second is the freedom of the will in a more fundamental sense, namely, the capacity to determine one's own will without any compulsion, be it external or internal. There is an experience of the first kind of freedom, the freedom of action, i.e., "practical or psychological freedom," but there is no experience of the second kind of freedom. In *Reflexion* 4338, Kant notes: "Freedom from all external compulsion of our will [*Willkür*] is evident by experience."[20] And according to the *Metaphysik Pölitz,* Kant says: "The practical or psychological freedom was the independence of our will [*Willkür*] from the compulsion by the stimuli. It has been treated in the empirical psychology."[21] In this context, Kant speaks of a "sentiment of freedom": "Man feels a capacity inside himself that he cannot be compelled by anything in the world."[22]

Transcendental freedom, by contrast, cannot be experienced. Concerning transcendental freedom, Kant says: "We cannot demonstrate freedom a posteriori."[23] The reason is that "the lack of perception of determining reasons is no proof that such reasons do not exist."[24] A similar remark is made in the *Metaphysik Mrongovius:* "How do we know that the will is free?— Freedom is not a quality that we know from experience; for we cannot experience something negative."[25]

What matters for Kant is freedom of the will, i.e., transcendental freedom. The experience that we actually have of the freedom to act is not sufficient to justify belief in freedom of the will. Inner experience can perhaps confirm our freedom to act. But even if we would admit a causal effect of the soul on the body (in spite of the objections of Wolff and Hume), we could not verify empirically whether the causally efficient *intention* to act is not caused by something else. Freedom of the will cannot be proved in this way. So, inner experience must definitely be excluded as a medium of the consciousness of freedom. Consequently, inner sense and sensibility in general are excluded. Sensibility can "receive," as Kant puts it, *given* data of the *real* in time. But inner sense is not able to find within itself the capacity to realize the *possible,* to produce spontaneously mental and physical events that are not in the realm of time. There can be no sensible intuition of freedom, either inner or outer.

Nevertheless, from 1769 to around 1775, Kant insists on the notion of intuition. He is looking for some *evidence* of freedom. I must be able to be *aware* of my freedom. But, what does it mean "to be aware"? Kant presupposes, apparently, that such a kind of awareness is possible only by intuition. The character of activity and self-determination that is crucial for what we call free agency cannot be represented by *sensible* intuitions. So, another kind of intuition must be established. "We cannot infer the reality of freedom from experience. But we have a notion of it through our intellectual inner intuition (not inner sense) of our activity, which can be moved by intellectual motives."[26] Thus, Kant refers to *intellectual intuition* in order to explain the consciousness of freedom. Intellectual intuition is conceived of as a non-sensible awareness of spontaneous and free agency. Consciousness of the spontaneity of the understanding is the foundation of consciousness of freedom. The freedom of the will is a consequence of the freedom of the understanding. As shown before, this is essentially Wolff's position, although Kant does not allow *sensible* perception of spontaneity anymore, but only *intellectual* intuition.

The foundation of a consciousness of freedom that is based on a theory of *apperception* can often be found in the *Reflexionen*. In *Reflexion* 4723, Kant notes: "The representation of our free spontaneity is such that we are not affected, hence it is not a phenomenon, but apperception."[27] In *Reflexion* 6860 we read: "The apperception of oneself as an intellectual being which is active is freedom."[28] In referring to intellectual intuition and apperception, Kant is trying to find a way out of the indefensible Wolffian empirical-psychological account of the consciousness of freedom.

Kant himself saw a difficulty that results from this conception. How can we be sure that we are actually aware of our own activity (i.e., of our producing) and not merely of the effects of some production (the products)? In *Reflexion* 4220, Kant formulates this difficulty in the following way: "Freedom is, properly speaking, only the self-activity that one is aware of. When someone has an idea, this is an act of spontaneity; but one is aware not of one's activity, but of its effect."[29] It seems that Kant thinks we can solve this difficulty by his theory of apperception. For this purpose, in the *Metaphysik Pölitz,* Kant analyzes the sense and the conditions of the use of the first person pronoun "I." He seems to presuppose two things: first, that the *use* of "I" entails its *justification* and, second, that the use of "I" entails knowledge of the subject's *ability* to use this pronoun. "If I say: I think, I act, etc. then either the word I is misused or I am free. If I were not free, I could not say: *I* do it . . . But when I say: I do it, that involves a spontaneity in the transcendental sense."[30]

In spite of the suggestive force that this argument might have, one cannot overlook the fact that it depends on a premise that is not established. This *implicit* premise is that semantical implications of the use of the first person pronoun "I" and of intentional verbs such as "to do" or "to act" not only suggest but even prove the truth of certain assumptions about the nature of the subjects using these words. But that is not correct. A theory of freedom has to demonstrate (or refute) that these kinds of assumptions are justified; it may not *presuppose* their truth. A theory of freedom is not justified by the simple fact that people say "I do," "I act," etc.; it has to show that we *are justified* in doing so. Therefore, grounding freedom on an epistemology of the understanding is problematic. Such a foundation is of no use for a justification of the consciousness of freedom. The underlying analogy between epistemic and practical spontaneity does not hold. We are not immediately aware of ourselves as free when we use concepts, even if, perhaps, it makes sense to say that we can *infer* that we are free from the fact of the corrigibility of (our use of) concepts. Moreover, consciousness of the freedom of agency is also not an immediate awareness.

Moral Consciousness

Kant 2–The result of the first part of this paper is that none of our theoretical (epistemic, cognitive) faculties is sufficient to explain consciousness of freedom. Moreover, I have argued that this is also a result of Kant's efforts during the 1770s. Therefore, it is misleading to interpret the Kantian theory of freedom as resting on the basis of spontaneity of the theoretical understanding. By doing so, one would neglect the aforementioned results of Kant's own philosophical development. And, in my view, the argument that consciousness of freedom can be explained on such a basis fails systematically too. Kant himself never returned to it. In his theory of freedom in the *Critique of Practical Reason*, Kant explicitly rejects the idea that our consciousness of the spontaneity of the understanding can prove the reality of freedom and personality. Kant illustrates this by means of a thought experiment. We can imagine an automaton that is able to perform self-conscious intellectual activities but which cannot be said to be free. Self-consciousness may indicate intellectual capacities, but it does not constitute a sufficient proof of freedom. "True, self-consciousness would make the automaton a thinking automaton, but it would be a mere illusion if the consciousness of its spontaneity was taken for freedom."[31]

In the *Critique of Practical Reason*, the thesis becomes crucial that consciousness of freedom is based rather on moral consciousness.[32] Kant explains this relation by using a distinction between *ratio essendi* and *ratio cognoscendi*: "freedom is the *ratio essendi* of the moral law, but the moral law is the *ratio cognoscendi* of freedom." Freedom is the ontological condition for the moral law, but the moral law is the epistemological ground of our consciousness of freedom. The moral law is the "condition . . . under which we can *be conscious* of freedom."[33] In order to have consciousness of freedom, we must first know the moral law. We "discover" freedom by knowing the moral law. Awareness of the moral law is the epistemic condition for the consciousness of freedom. The reality of freedom is the ontological condition for the existence of a moral law and our respect for it.

To this thesis is added another crucial Kantian claim according to which the validity of the moral law is a "fact of reason" that cannot be derived from something else, "because one cannot infer it from preceding data of reason, for instance, from the consciousness of freedom (for the latter is not given prior to it), but it is evident by itself."[34] It is "based on no intuition, either empirical or pure," and an intellectual intuition of the freedom of the will "may not be admitted here."[35] Intellectual intuition is now definitely excluded as a basis for the consciousness of freedom. The Kantian proof of the reality of human freedom is no longer based on a theory of self-consciousness, intellectual intuition, or apperception ("I"). Consciousness of freedom is a kind of "ingredient" of the consciousness of the validity of the moral law as a fact of reason.

Fichte 1–Fichte goes even further than the Kantian thesis that there would be no consciousness of freedom if we were not conscious of the validity of the moral law. Fichte claims that the categorical imperative is a condition of consciousness in general. This argument is clearly stated in § 13 of the *Wissenschaftslehre nova methodo*[36] and in § 3 of the *System der Sittenlehre*. In the latter, the deduction of the "principle of morality" is meant to prove that freedom and the moral law are "one and the same thought."[37] Having formulated this thesis, Fichte cites Kant: "Kant deduces in several passages the conviction of our freedom from the moral law." Nevertheless, according to Fichte, freedom is "no consequence of another thought at all." Freedom is not *inferred* from the moral law; it is no consequence of the latter, but is itself an "immediate fact of consciousness."[38] Freedom can only (philosophically) be *deduced* from the consciousness of the moral law as an immediate fact *entailed* by the latter. The proposition "I am really free" is a "first article of faith,"[39] which cannot be concluded from anything else.

Hence, Fichte agrees with Kant when he establishes a connection between freedom and morality; indeed, he even radicalizes Kant's view by claiming that freedom and morality constitute a unity. Like Kant, Fichte takes freedom to be the *ratio essendi*, the ontological condition of morality and of moral sentiments: if we were not free, we would have no feeling of respect for the moral law. Fichte emphasizes this Kantian thesis. But, in Fichte, the first term of the Kantian distinction between *ratio cognoscendi* and *ratio essendi* is developed further by another important point that has also been prepared by Kant, i.e., intersubjectivity.

Intersubjectivity

Kant 3–In Kant's moral philosophy the idea of humanity as an end-in-itself is central. This quality of being an end-in-itself is not attributed to a human individual as such without regard to anything or anybody else. Kant locates it in the dimension of *intersubjectivity*. It is not the mere fact that a human being is a *rational* animal that makes him an end-in-itself. In the *Critique of Practical Reason*, Kant writes: "The fact that he has reason does not raise him above mere animality."[40] The idea of humanity as end-in-itself rather signifies that acting subjects, when they determine their maxims, consider themselves *mutually as* ends-in-themselves. But it is not only this use of the notion of end-in-itself that shows the importance of the idea of intersubjectivity in the Kantian grounding of moral agency. Freedom is a capacity that is attributed to rational beings as *persons*. The "personality" of such beings, according to Kant, is part of a context of *interpersonality*. Freedom, in Kant, is conceived of as something essentially interpersonal. Intersubjectivity is crucial on all levels of Kant's theory. It is accepted as the initial fact that raises the *problem* of morality, and it is even emphasized by the *solution*, that is, the idea of universality implied in the categorical imperative. Already in the *Groundwork of the Metaphysic of Morals*, in one of the formulations of the categorical imperative, the dimension of intersubjectivity—or interpersonality—is clearly expressed. The famous "formula of the end-in-itself" is as follows: "So act as to use humanity, both in your own person and every other person, always as an end, never simply as a means."[41]

Fichte 2–The two central types of argument to be found in the mature Kant are taken up by Fichte: the argument referring to the feeling of respect for the moral law and the argument referring to the importance of interpersonality. For Fichte, however, it is important that the consciousness of moral obligation presupposes a "discovery." There is a *ratio cognoscendi* for moral consciousness itself that Kant did not render explicit. Moral consciousness is not just "given"; it has to be realized. This "discovery" depends on what Fichte calls a "check" (*Anstoss*) and a "summons" (*Aufforderung*). Only by a summons does a subject get the check of feeling obligation. A summons is an intersubjective act that belongs to a context of communication.

Fichte thus supplements the Kantian argument. According to Kant, freedom is discovered by means of respect for the moral law. According to Fichte, however, this discovery of freedom is possible only through intersubjective communication. A summons as well as intersubjective communication in general implies mutual recognition (*Anerkennung*). Hence, intersubjective communication constitutes the context for mutual recognition. For Fichte, recognition is the "ultimate specific reason for the development of individual self-consciousness and its consciousness of freedom."[42] The theory of intersubjectivity becomes part of the philosophical explication of what our prephilosophical belief in freedom implies.[43] In the *Grundlage des Naturrechts*, Fichte's central thesis is that only intersubjectively can finite rational beings become aware of and attribute to themselves their own freedom. That is what Fichte says in the second principle of the *Grundlage des Naturrechts*: "A finite rational being can ascribe to itself a free causality in the sensible world, only if it ascribes it to others as well. Hence, it must also assume other rational beings besides itself."[44]

It is interesting to take note of a remark by Fichte concerning Kant. According to the *Wissenschaftslehre nova methodo*, Fichte concedes to Kant that his moral principle (the Kantian moral law) actually implies intersubjectivity. In § 13 of the *Wissenschaftslehre nova methodo*, Fichte writes that in Kant the "presupposition of the existence of other rational beings" actually serves as a practical principle. When I accept the Kantian moral principle, "I must already presuppose rational beings other than me, for otherwise, how shall I apply this law to them?" Fichte criticizes Kant, however, for not having given the *epistemic* principle (*ratio cognoscendi*) for the *theoretical* assumption of other minds.[45]

In § 16 of the *Wissenschaftslehre nova methodo,* which contains the deduction of individuality, Fichte argues that the "concept of selfhood of a person is not possible without the concept of other minds." Only if I understand a summons to self-determinate agency do I form the concept of my own freedom and spontaneity.[46] Fichte wants to show that a single individual cannot determine his will: "one individual alone can have no ends" and "one individual alone cannot know himself as free."[47] Consciousness of freedom presupposes a reciprocity of individuals who appeal to (summon) and mutually recognize each other. Fichte even says: "The first representation that I can have is the summons to free willing, to me as an *individual.*"[48] Individuality in the sense of belonging to a context of intersubjective communication is even a condition of self-consciousness: "a rational being cannot posit itself as a being with self-consciousness, without positing itself as *individual,* as one among a number of rational beings, which it assumes just as it assumes itself."[49] Thus, with Fichte the account of the consciousness of freedom is definitely transferred from theoretical to practical philosophy, because even the most fundamental level in Fichte's philosophy, that is, self-consciousness, is connected, as Fichte puts it, to the *practical* "I." That is what Fichte emphasizes in the first Corollary of § 1 of the *Grundlage*: "It is asserted that the practical I is the I of the original self-consciousness, that a rational being perceives itself immediately only when it is willing. It would not perceive itself, nor the world, if it were not a practical being; it would not even be an intelligent being if it were not a practical being."[50]

It is important to consider that according to Fichte's *Grundlage des Naturrechts* and his *Wissenschaftslehre nova methodo,* interpersonality is constitutive not only for the social circumstances of legal communities. That was rather the concern of Fichte's lectures given in 1794, *Some Lectures Concerning the Scholar's Vocation.*[51] From the beginning, the subject of these lectures is interpersonality as a condition of *society*. But that is not a point that could be regarded as remarkable in the history of philosophy at the end of the eighteenth century. After Hobbesian contractualism, at the latest, it was generally admitted that legal rules imply the mutual recognition of the concerned individuals *as legal persons*. This cannot be the point of Fichte's famous introduction of interpersonality into the most fundamental dimension of theoretical *and* practical philosophy.[52] The crucial point is rather that, at the beginning of the *Grundlage des Naturrechts* as well as in the *Wissenschaftslehre nova methodo* and in

The Vocation of Man, the idea of interpersonality is "worked out in a strict transcendental deduction from the principles of subjectivity."[53] Interpersonality is deduced as a condition of subjectivity itself, not only as a condition of society and legal community.

Conclusion

Summarizing the arguments used by Wolff, Kant, and Fichte in order to justify our consciousness of freedom, we can conclude that in eighteenth century German philosophy there is a change of orientation from introspection to intersubjectivity. For Wolff, freedom is a subject of empirical psychology. He focuses on *inner perception* as the foundation of the consciousness of freedom. The earlier, "pre-Critical" Kant in the *Reflexionen* begins by criticizing this empirical account. He defends intellectual intuition and seems to admit the possibility of a "deduction" of practical spontaneity (freedom) from epistemic spontaneity (there are traces of this conception even in the *Groundwork* of 1785). The mature Kant points to *moral* consciousness, which is itself a "fact of reason," as the epistemic reason for consciousness of freedom. Fichte agrees with Kant in this respect and, moreover, develops another crucial aspect of the Kantian foundation of morals: the dimension of intersubjectivity.

It seems to me that the arguments discussed above allow some systematic conclusions. Perhaps the fact that we *are* free has to do with our capacity to have relations to ourselves, relations that must be regarded as a medium and condition of consciousness and rationality. But the *consciousness of* freedom is possible neither by introspection nor by immediate acquaintance (or "familiarity," "*Vertrautheit*"), but only by intersubjective, *mutual imputation* of freedom. Fichte has put it in the influential terms of "summons" and "recognition." In my view, it is convincing to argue, as Fichte does, that we cannot know anything about freedom unless we conceive of freedom as something interpersonal. One does not know by oneself that one is free. Fichte's idea of accounting for intersubjectivity and interpersonality in a theory of the conditions of the formation of subjectivity is still a model for philosophers today. One might hold that "a priori intersubjectivism" is indefensible as an account of subjectivity.[54] But we should not neglect that Fichte has done more than others to clarify that the point of philosophical progress, such as Fichte understood it, is not to invert the hierarchy of principles but to account for the variety and complexity of the conditions that are necessary to ground something so complex as subjectivity and consciousness of freedom.[55]

Notes

1. Friedrich Nietzsche, *Twilight of the Idols*, trans. R. J. Hollingdale (Harmondsworth: Penguin, 1990), "The Four Great Errors," p. 47.

2. Christian Wolff, *Vernünftige Gedanken von Gott, der Welt und der Seele des Menschen, auch allen Dingen überhaupt* ("Deutsche Metaphysik"; hereafter *DM*) (Halle, 1720; 11th edition, Halle and Frankfurt/Oder, 1751), in *Gesammelte Werke*, ed. Jean Ecole et al. (New York: Olms, 1983).

3. Wolff, *DM*, § 325.

4. Ibid., § 191.

5. Ibid., § 511.

6. Ibid., § 522.

7. Ibid., § 518.

8. Ibid., § 519.

9. Ibid., § 522.

10. Ibid., § 527.

11. Ibid., §§ 528–38.

12. Ibid., § 529.

13. Ibid., §§ 530 and 537.

14. In his rational psychology, the question of cause-effect relations between mind and body seems to disappear. Wolff defends the Leibnizian idea of a *harmonie préétablie*. Physical movements are not caused by mental events (by the soul), but they are rather parallel events.

15. Wolff, *DM*, §§ 535 and 539.

16. Ibid., § 539.

17. Immanuel Kant, *Critique of Pure Reason*, trans. N. K. Smith (New York: St. Martin's Press, 1929), A802–03/B830–31 (pagination of the first/second German editions).

18. Cf. Karl Ameriks, "Kant's Deduction of Freedom and Morality," *Journal of the History of Philosophy* 19 (1981), pp. 53–79; Henry E. Allison, *Kant's Theory of Freedom* (Cambridge: Cambridge University Press, 1990), pp. 54–82; Marcus Willaschek, *Praktische Vernunft. Handlungstheorie und Moralbegründung bei Kant* (Stuttgart/Weimar: Metzler, 1992), esp. pp. 48–53.

19. Arthur Schopenhauer, *On the Freedom of the Will*, trans. K. Kolenda (Oxford: Blackwell, 1985).

20. Kant, *Reflexion* 4338, in *Kants gesammelte Schriften* (hereafter Ak.) (Berlin: Königliche Preussische Akademie der Wissenschaften, 1900 ff.), vol. 17, p. 510.

21. Kant, *Metaphysik Pölitz*, Ak. vol. 28/1, p. 267. Cf. *Critique of Pure Reason*, A802/B830 and A803/B831.

22. Kant, *Metaphysik Pölitz*, Ak. vol. 28/1, p. 255.

23. Kant, *Reflexion* 4724, Ak. vol. 17, p. 688.

24. Ibid.

25. Kant, *Metaphysik Mrongovius*, Ak. vol. 29/1,2, pp. 896–97.

26. Kant, *Reflexion* 4336 (1769–1775), Ak. vol. 17, p. 509.

27. Kant, *Reflexion* 4723 (1773–1775), Ak. vol. 17, p. 688.

28. Kant, *Reflexion* 6860 (1776?–1791?), Ak. vol. 19, p. 183.

29. Kant, *Reflexion* 4220 (1764–1770), Ak. vol. 17, p. 462.

30. Kant, *Metaphysik Pölitz*, Ak. vol. 28/1, p. 269. Cf. also *Reflexion* 4220, Ak. vol. 17, pp. 462 f.; and *Reflexion* 4338, Ak. vol. 17, pp. 510 f.

31. Kant, *Critique of Practical Reason*, trans. L. W. Beck, 3rd ed. (New York: Macmillan, 1993), Ak. vol. 5, p. 101.

32. Marcus Willaschek, however, has shown convincingly that Kant's theory of freedom and agency can be accepted independently of the claim that we are free only if we act *according to* the moral law. See his *Praktische Vernunft. Handlungstheorie und Moralbegründung bei Kant* (Stuttgart/Weimar: Metzler, 1992).

33. Kant, *Critique of Practical Reason*, Ak. vol. 5, p. 4.

34. Ibid., p. 31.

35. Ibid., p. 31.

36. Johann Gottlieb Fichte, *Wissenschaftslehre nova methodo: Kollegnachschrift K. Chr. Fr. Krause, 1798/99*, ed. E. Fuchs (Hamburg: Felix Meiner, 1982), p. 143. For a compiled edition of this transcript and the *Hallesche Nachschrift*, see *Fichte: Foundations of Transcendental Philosophy. (Wissenschaftslehre) Nova Methodo*, ed. and trans. D. Breazeale (Ithaca: Cornell University Press, 1992).

37. Fichte, *System der Sittenlehre*, in *Sämmtliche Werke* (hereafter *SW*), vol. 4, ed. I. H. Fichte (Berlin: Veit, 1845–46; reprint, Berlin: de Gruyter, 1971), p. 53.

38. Fichte, *SW*, vol. 4, p. 53.

39. Ibid., p. 54.

40. Kant, *Critique of Practical Reason*, Ak. vol. 5, p. 61. Cf. also *Groundwork of the Metaphysic of Morals*, trans. H. J. Paton (New York: Harper & Row, 1964), Ak. vol. 4, p. 425; and *Religion within the Limits of Reason Alone*, trans. T. Greene and H. Hudson (New York: Harper & Row, 1960), p. 17 n., Ak. vol. 6, p. 26 n.

41. Kant, *Groundwork*, Ak. vol. 4, p. 429. Concerning the implications of interpersonality in Kant, cf. my "Personne, personnalité et liberté dans la 'Critique de la raison pratique,'" *Revue Internationale de Philosophie* 42 (1988), pp. 312 f.; and Dieter Sturma, "Autonomie und Kontingenz. Kants nicht-reduktionistische Theorie des moralischen Selbst," in *Akten des Siebenten Internationalen Kant-Kongresses*, vol. 2/1, ed. G. Funke (Bonn: Bouvier, 1991), p. 581.

42. Edith Düsing, "Das Problem der Individualität in Fichtes früher Ethik und Rechtslehre," *Fichte-Studien* 3 (1991), p. 39.

43. Cf. Peter Baumanns, *Fichtes ursprüngliches System. Sein Standort zwischen Kant und Hegel* (Stuttgart-Bad Cannstatt: Frommann-Holzboog, 1972); and Baumanns, *Fichtes Wissenschaftslehre. Probleme ihres Anfangs. Mit einem Kommentar zu § 1 der "Grundlage der gesamten Wissenschaftslehre"* (Bonn: Bouvier, 1974).

44. Fichte, *Grundlage des Naturrechts* (hereafter *GN)*, § 3, in *SW*, vol. 3, p. 30.

45. Fichte, *nova methodo*, § 13, pp. 150 f.

46. Cf. also Fichte, *GN*, § 3, "Beweis," section III, in *SW*, vol. 3, pp. 32–33.

47. Peter Rohs, *Johann Gottlieb Fichte* (Munich: Beck, 1991), p. 81.

48. Fichte, *nova methodo*, p. 177.

49. Fichte, *GN*, Introduction, *SW*, vol. 3, p. 8.

50. Fichte, *GN*, § 1, Corollarium, *SW*, vol. 3, p. 20.

51. Fichte, *Some Lectures Concerning the Scholar's Vocation*, trans. D. Breazeale, in *Philosophy of German Idealism*, ed. E. Behler (New York: Continuum, 1987), pp. 1–38.

52. Cf. Ludwig Siep, *Anerkennung als Prinzip der praktischen Philosophie. Untersuchungen zu Hegels Jenaer Philosophie des Geistes* (Freiburg/Munich: Alber, 1979), pp. 26–36; and Siep, *Praktische Philosophie im Deutschen Idealismus* (Frankfurt: Suhrkamp, 1992), pp. 19–64.

53. Baumanns, *Fichtes ursprüngliches System*, pp. 175 f.

54. Cf. Manfred Frank, "Die Wiederkehr des Subjekts in der heutigen deutschen Philosophie," in his *Conditio Moderna. Essays, Reden, Programm* (Leipzig: Reclam, 1993), pp. 103–117; and Frank, "Wider den apriorischen Intersubjektivismus. Gegenvorschläge aus Sartrescher Inspiration," in *Gemeinschaft und Gerechtigkeit*, ed. M. Brumlik and H. Brunkhorst (Frankfurt: Fischer, 1993), pp. 273–89.

55. I am grateful to Gabriele Santel, Michael Quante, Ludwig Siep, and Jon Stewart for philosophical assistance and/or help with the language.

4

Teleology and the Freedom of the Self

Véronique Zanetti

Self-consciousness is the first principle of Kant's first two *Critiques*: it serves as the condition of the unification of the categories and therefore of objective judgments in the *Critique of Pure Reason*; it is the essential condition of freedom in the *Critique of Practical Reason*. We are therefore entitled to expect that the third *Critique*,[1] in its function of reconciling the theoretical and practical domains, would also be based on self-consciousness as its first principle. We will see, however, that this is not really the case. The principle of the Critique of Teleological Judgment is a supersensible principle that unifies mechanism with teleology. On the other hand, in being meant to reconcile freedom with the determinism of nature, it is a principle that is structured as a self-relation which is, in and of itself, the cause and the effect of its products. In this way, as Schelling will show later, it takes on the structure of self-consciousness.

The complexity of the Critique of Teleological Judgment derives in large measure from the multiplicity of its tasks. Indeed, if we are required to define its objective in a global way, we might say that this text is as much a matter of *(a)* defining the conditions for the possibility of knowing empirical nature; as *(b)* explaining how organisms can be thought to be natural products; and, finally, *(c)* looking for a link between theoretical and practical philosophy, i.e., between the theses of natural determinism and freedom. Kant brings together these three objectives, which he attempts to reconcile under one and the same principle, the finality of nature. We are, therefore, justified in seeing in the teleological principle the first principle of the third *Critique*. This principle has a double applicability, theoretical and practical. The application is *theoretical* when it serves to establish the necessity of empirical laws of nature or to explain the internal structure of organisms. From this perspective, the teleological principle serves as a sort of transition (*Übergang*) between specific empirical nature and nature in general, as it is constituted by synthetic a priori principles of understanding. The applicability of the teleological principle is *practical* when it serves as a condition for the possibility of the creation of free and moral beings and for the realization of the highest good on earth. In the latter case, the finality of nature serves as the transition (*Übergang*) between the realm of the supersensible (of freedom) and that of the sensible (the final goal attained).

Nonetheless, Kant assures us that, despite this double realm of application, the teleological principle possesses the same status in the two cases, that is, as a regulative principle of the faculty of judgment. But is this really true? On the other hand, what is one looking for when one searches for a point of juncture between nature and freedom? Is one looking for a principle that might allow for "the passage from the *manner of thinking* according to the principles of one to the manner of thinking according to the principles of the other?"[2] Or is one looking, rather, for a principle that might make possible *the passage* from nature to freedom? I will show that the theoretical point of view favors the first version, whereas the practical point of view leans towards the second. In the first case (where it is a question of a passage from one manner of thinking to another), the teleological principle serves as a heuristic principle, and it has the same regulative status as the mechanical principle with which it is juxtaposed. We are dealing, then, with a theoretical philosophy with a double epistemological perspective. In the second case, however, the mechanical principle is subordinated to the teleological principle with a view towards the realization of moral actions. This would have the consequence that the unification of nature and freedom cannot take place except within a principle of supersensible unification. That would result, on the one hand, in running the risk of losing the regulative status of the teleological principle, and, on the other hand, in a reinstituting of the dualism between practical and theoretical philosophy that we have been trying to avoid.

By way of conclusion, I will outline the monist solution to the problem that Schelling will propose: the only possible candidate for bridging the realms of nature and freedom is a principle of identity, situated beyond the two realms. This principle is neither nature nor freedom yet at the same time is both, as Schelling says with regard to the absolute: " . . . the Absolute is in itself the absolute unity of the finite and the infinite, without being the one or the other . . ."[3] The absolute also possesses the structure of a relation to itself, that is to say, it is of itself the cause and the effect of what it produces.

Thus, whether its application is theoretical or practical, the principle of finality represents a point of juncture, the analog of a schema linking the realm of the supersensible to the sensible. However, contrary to what we might believe, the teleological principle is not the ultimate principle of the *Critique of Judgment*. This is because, as Kant says, even while ascribing this principle to itself, the faculty of judging also gives itself another principle that can in fact be incompatible with it, namely, the mechanical principle. Kant claims that the teleological principle itself must find its basis in a superior principle, a supersensible principle of a unification of mechanism and teleology: "the common principle of mechanical deduction on the one hand and of teleological deduction on the other is the supersensible, which we must posit at the very foundation of nature as a phenomenon."[4]

The *raison d'être* for such a point of agreement between the two principles is not self-evident. It implies that the mechanical and teleological principles cannot cohabit as methodological principles and that the only way of making them compatible is to unify them in a supersensible principle of which nothing can really be said. And the adoption of such a postulation seems even less constraining since Kant gives the impression of resolving the friction between the mechanical and teleological perspectives by introducing a double epistemological principle bearing on the real: if we seek to furnish a scientific explanation of natural phenomena, we will have to restrict ourselves to physical and chemical laws and thus to the mechanical view; however, if we want to give meaning to the coherence we see in empirical laws or among phenomena, we will have to adopt the idea of an intentional first cause of the world.[5] The two perspectives present themselves, then, as both being equally indispensable, depending on the different perspectives one takes on things, but in each case, the adoption of the perspective issues from an epistemological *choice*. This reading resembles the one L. W. Beck proposes for the third antinomy of the *Critique of Pure Reason*:

> Always (in science) search for mechanical causes and allow no non-natural causes to enter into the explanation of natural phenomenon,

and

> Always in ethics act as if the maxim of the will were a sufficient determining ground of the conduct to be executed or judged.[6]

In this way, to quote Kant, "we would judge nature according to two principles, without the mechanical mode of explanation being excluded by the teleological mode, as if they were contradictory."[7]

But if we hold to such a reading, it is no longer necessary to turn to a supersensible principle as the center of reconciliation between the two principles: the two points of view as such are perfectly able to coexist.[8] Why then is this solution not held by Kant (or more precisely, why is it not the only one to be held by Kant)?

When it is a question of explaining the mode of production of one and the same thing in nature, Kant says, the mechanical and the teleological principles cannot be linked; they are in point of fact treated as constitutive principles since they determine the makeup of the real and no longer merely the way in which the real is judged:

> If for example I admit that it is necessary to consider a maggot as a product of the simple mechanism of matter . . . I cannot derive this product from this matter as from a final causality. Conversely, if I recognize this product as a natural end, I cannot count on a mechanical mode of production of this product and admit this mode of production as a constitutive principle for judging the possibility of this product, by unifying the two principles in such a way. In point of fact, one mode of explanation excludes the other. . . .[9]

But is this really true? In fact, final causality does not exclude mechanical causality, if by the latter we understand efficient causality: what distinguishes them is that in the final causality there is the presence of a goal acting as a motive; independently of that, the action takes place in conformity with efficient causality. What is more, Kant admits this himself (and in the very paragraph where he lays claim to the incompatibility of the principles) when he says:

> in a teleological judgment, even if the form that the matter receives is judged to be possible only by virtue of an intention, this matter can by its very nature, in conformity with mechanical laws, also be subordinated as a means to a represented goal.[10]

Likewise, in *Critique of Judgment*, § 82, we find in parentheses that in itself the mechanism of production in no way contradicts an origin according to ends.[11] Therefore, if Kant insists on the incompatibility of the two principles, it is because he interprets mechanism as something other than a "simple" efficient causality. In my article "Die Antinomie der teleologischen Urteilskraft,"[12] I examined the two other possible meanings of the term "mechanism." Without going into too much detail, I will explain again how the two are in fact used by Kant:

1. The opposition between mechanism and teleology is not an opposition between efficient causality and final causality, but between a *blind determinism* of nature and *intentional causality*. It is in this sense, moreover, that we can read the "preparation" to the resolution of the antinomy in *Critique of Judgment*, § 71, where Kant says that we cannot exclude the

possibility that there is in the depths of living beings "a form of originary causality completely different" from mechanism, namely one emanating from the will of an architectonic understanding. Now, from at least two perspectives we have a fundamental incompatibility between the two hypotheses of blind determinism and finality: when it is a question of explaining the production of an organism, one cannot affirm that "there is nothing in this product that is useless, without end, or susceptible to being attributed to a natural, *blind* organism,"[13] and simultaneously that it results from evolutionary chance. Secondly, on the scale of nature in its entirety, it would be every bit as contradictory to claim that the regularity with which certain events are produced, as well as the coherence of the empirical rules between them, are purely contingent, while also affirming that they result from a superior understanding which is for the systematicity of the empirical rules what our understanding is for synthetic a priori principles.[14] If one had to admit the existence of accidental causes in the production of natural objects, the rationality of the first organizing cause could not be said to be perfect, and the plan that follows this reason in organizing natural things in a purposive way could at any time be counteracted by chance natural events. These are the conclusions that Kant draws by affirming that "the unity of the supersensible principle must be considered as valid not only for certain species of nature, but also as uniformly valid for the totality of nature as a system."[15] We will come back to this argument when considering the practical aspects of the problem.

2. The term *mechanism* can also be used in reference to the definition at *Critique of Judgment*, § 77, where it is a question of the "mechanical mode of production."[16] In this understanding of mechanism, the whole is the product of the parts, but the parts are not in turn determined by the whole. "Mechanism" in this sense is a "causality completely different" from final causality, as is clear if one recalls that Kant refers to final causality when it is a question of explaining an *organism*, i.e., a structure in which the whole determines and is contained in the parts.

The three definitions of the concept of mechanism give us the following situation in the form of a schema:

	final causality exemplified by an organism	final causality extended to all nature
M_1: efficient causality	compatible	compatible
M_2: blind efficient causality	incompatible	incompatible
M_3: the whole is the product of the parts	incompatible	compatible

If we enlarge the table and take into account the solution to the antinomy that Kant appears to give just after its presentation, we can sum up the branches of the alternative in the following way:

(a) When the mechanism of nature as well as finality are seen as perspectives or points of view bearing on the universe (which is what the solution to the antinomy that treats mechanism and finality as regulative principles of the faculty of judgment suggests), one can reconcile these two approaches, that is, as long as the mechanical principle is understood as the application of efficient causality and not in the sense of a blind causality or of an analyzable totality. However, this sort of interpretation results in making the Second Analogy of the *Critique of Pure Reason* also a regulative maxim.

(b) When mechanism and teleology are considered as constitutive of nature, the two principles are not mutually exclusive if mechanism is defined as efficient causality, necessary but not sufficient for explaining living things.

(c) Since Kant insists on the incompatibility of the two principles and maintains that only the adoption of the supersensible principle allows for its solution, it is clear that by mechanism he understands M_2 or M_3, which is to say blind determinism or an analytical relationship of the parts and the whole.

I will also venture a supplementary hypothesis: if Kant holds to the "strong" version of the antinomy and is not satisfied with a relativity of points of view, it is above all because the practical aspect of the *Critique of Judgment* is at stake. Here is a brief summary of the dilemma involving practical reason:

•The *Critique of Judgment* sets out to explain how the merely mechanistic causality of the laws of nature manages to account for the production of reasonable, free, and moral beings. If there is not to be an inexplicable evolutionary leap, it is necessary to conceptualize nature as containing in itself a productive force aimed at the creation of such beings.

•If nature had physically produced perfectly determined creatures, but ones whose reason required them to act in accordance with a will determining what ought to be and not what is, and if, moreover, the demands of the will could not be met on account of the determinism of natural laws, nature would have produced beings whose freedom and morality could not be translated into action. The categorical imperative would then have directed them to act morally in a world in which morality does not have a place.

It could happen, for example, as Kant suggests in *Idea for a Universal History with a Cosmopolitan Intent*, that the laws of nature might determine human beings to seek out discord, when in fact the categorical imperative requires harmony. In this case, each time that human reason would motivate a noumenal subject to act in conformity with moral laws, the phenomenal subject would necessarily act contrary to these laws; we would then be dealing with a dichotomy within the subject itself. It is in order to avoid this dichotomy that the *Critique of Judgment* insists on the necessity of envisaging a point of connection between the sensible and the supersensible. In fact, Kant concedes this: "an ultimate end imposed as a duty . . . and a nature with no final end . . . but a nature in which this end must take place, are self-contradictory."[17] And we know that the moral law obliges us to tend towards the highest good that can be attained freely in the world (cf. *Critique of Judgment*, § 87). This problem is perfectly summarized in the following quote from *On the Use of Teleological Principles in Philosophy*:

> because a pure practical teleology, in other words a morality, is designed to realize its ends in the world, it cannot ignore the *possibility* of these ends in the world, no more in that which concerns *final causes* given there than in that which concerns the very aptitude of the *supreme cause of the world* to agree with a totality of all ends in terms of its effects; it will therefore be no more able to ignore *natural teleology* than the possibility of a nature in general, that is to say transcendental philosophy, in order to guarantee for the pure practical teleology of ends an objective reality, with regard to the possibility of the realization of the object, that is to say with regard to the possibility of the end it stipulates as realizable in the world.[18]

In other words, it is necessary that nature show itself to be *cooperative* in order to ensure the realization of moral laws, "for without the help of nature to fulfill a condition beyond our abilities, the realization of this goal would not be possible."[19]

> Therefore, *the objective theoretical reality of the concept of the final goal* appropriate to reasonable beings in the world *requires* not only that we possess a final goal which is proposed to us *a priori*, but also *that creation, which is to say, the world itself, possess in terms of its own existence a final goal.*[20]

One will note that these reflections have brought us back to a problem already treated in the *Critique of Practical Reason*, where it served as the object of an antinomy. We therefore see that, in taking up once again the question of the compatibility between natural determinism and freedom, on the one hand, and of determinism and the categorical imperative, on the other, the *Critique of Judgment* finds itself at the intersection of the first and the second *Critiques*. The theses that come into conflict in the *Critique of Practical Reason* are as follows.[21]

> *Thesis:* According to natural laws, "no necessary and sufficient connection for the highest good between happiness and virtue can be expected in this world, from the strict observation of moral laws."
> *Antithesis:* "The realization of the highest good, which contains this connection in its concept (the connection between happiness and virtue) is a necessary object of our will and is inseparably linked to moral law."

The tension issues from the fact that the realization of the highest good is necessary for the will, in spite of the contingency of the facts; it may be that, in fact, the virtuous life is at the same time a happy one, but there is no necessary relationship between the two; even more nettlesome, nothing excludes a case such as Job's where a virtuous life is punished by the gravest misery and physical suffering.

If one remembers that an antinomy is defined as a conflict between two true but contradictory theses, we cannot then maintain that we are dealing here with a real antinomy. The thesis and the antithesis are not logically contradictory, since natural laws do not make the realization of the highest good impossible; they make it only improbable. Nonetheless, if the moral law necessarily demands the pursuit of the highest good, the contingency of its feasibility constitutes a genuine problem for practical reason, given the fact that its moral ends run the risk of being stripped of value if they are not feasible.

Kant first proposes to resolve this difficulty by appealing to the immortality of the soul. But more important for us is the solution that looks to the postulation of the existence of God to take care of reconciling virtue and happiness:

> The highest good is therefore possible in the world only insofar as one admits a supreme cause of nature that has a causality in conformity with moral intention. . . . Therefore the supreme cause, insofar as it must be supposed by the highest good, is a being which, by *understanding* and *will*, is the cause, consequently the author of nature, in other words God.[22]

The demonstration of the necessity of this postulate can be summarized in the following logical relation:

1. The moral law is a fact of reason that is necessarily valid.
2. The moral law determines a priori a final goal that is the pursuit of the highest good on earth.

3. The highest good is attainable on earth only if God exists.

Given the law by virtue of which the logical consequence of a necessary premise is itself necessary, one can affirm that if the moral law is necessary, it is equally necessary that God exist. The move from (2) to (3) is necessitated by the fact that *(a)* as one already knows from the presentation of the antinomy, neither moral will nor natural law ensures a necessary connection between obedience to moral law (virtue) and happiness; *(b)* such a connection is presupposed in the definition of the highest good; *(c)* it is therefore necessary to postulate a transcendent cause containing the principle of connection.

In its theoretical application, the adoption of the teleological principle could cohabit with the mechanistic interpretation of the universe without recourse to a supersensible principle of unification, as long as one does not understand mechanism to mean the blind determinism of the laws of nature. The practical application of the teleological principle, however, demands the intervention of a transcendent principle of connection. But this is not the only difference. By conferring a practical objective on the concept of freedom and morality, the practical interest thereby confers not only greater plausibility but also practical necessity on the concept of teleology. That which had been simply *regulative* for theoretical reason becomes *determining* for practical reason. Thus, while the finality of the organism and of nature in its entirety was placed under the rubric of the "what if" in the theoretical perspective, it becomes a necessity for practical reason in regard to the realization of the categorical imperative on earth. Thus, we witness the appearance, in a constitutive form, of the two pillars on which the faculty of teleological judgment rests. The first is that of a superior reason, the unifying principle of empirical nature, which becomes a principle of wisdom with regard to a final goal;[23] the second is that of an ultimate end towards which all nature tends.

The difficulties discussed above put before us the following alternative:

1. Kant abandons the idea that the realization of the highest good on earth is a moral imperative like the categorical imperative and considers it only as a regulative idea operating as a motivation for our actions and even as a consolation in the face of the evil that exists on earth. Since one is not *obliged* to pursue the realization of the highest good on earth, it is then false to claim that the highest good is a necessary object of pure will. In this case, the hypotheses of God and of natural finality also reclaim their status as regulative ideas. Moreover, in this case, as I have already indicated, taking the two maxims as heuristic rules for the consideration of

nature according to efficient causality or according to final causality would be compatible without it being necessary to turn to a supersensible principle of reconciliation.

But if God and natural finality are merely regulative, the aforementioned danger of the moral requirement not being realizable or the danger of seeing schizophrenia as threatening the integrity of the subject are not avoided in any definitive way. Moreover, Kant seems to take these dangers seriously since he considers that the moral relationship according to which there is a cause of the world acting with intention and directed towards an end "must be a condition of possibility of creation every bit as necessary as the relationship according to physical laws."[24]

2. Kant maintains, on the contrary, that we are obliged to seek to realize the highest good on earth. We would then have to conclude that, for practical reasons, the existence of God as well as the finality of nature are necessary postulates.[25] Then, however, the antinomy becomes unsolvable, nature being unable to conform simultaneously to divine intention and to blind determinism.

Let us summarize the elements we have at our disposal. At first, we could believe that the teleological principle, by serving as the equivalent of a schema, would ensure the possibility of a link between nature in general and particular empirical nature, from a theoretical viewpoint, and between freedom and the blind mechanism of nature, from a practical viewpoint. The teleological principle could then have played the role of the first principle of the faculty of judgment. However, this is not the way it goes, given the fact that the mechanical principle presents itself to the faculty of judgment with a necessity every bit as great as the teleological principle. The two principles are then reconciled within a supersensible principle of unity. I have shown why the need for such a recourse did not impose itself from a theoretical point of view. It remains to be seen if matters are otherwise from the practical point of view. There, it was established that the guarantee of the possible realization on earth of the categorical imperative by the intervention of divine wisdom necessitates recourse to a point of agreement between natural determinism and the pursuit of a final goal. This recourse is necessary only if one assumes that it is an imperative that practical reason look to realize a final end on earth. Without this assumption, we can very well admit the cohabitation of teleological and mechanical maxims, insofar as both have value as regulative principles. Once again, then, why did Kant want to see in the principle of supersensible unity the necessary meeting point of mechanical and teleological principles?

Let us return to the objective pursued in the third *Critique*. At the risk of repeating myself, it is necessary to underline the fact that the faculty of judgment is supposed to make possible the move from the domain of the concept of nature to the domain of freedom. Contrary to what Kant affirms in the *Critique of Practical Reason*, then, freedom in and of itself cannot be "the keystone of the entire edifice of a system of pure or speculative reason."[26] If it were, it would no longer be a question of a *link* between nature and freedom, since nature would then have to be subordinate to freedom.

What then must be the nature of the juncture between nature and freedom? One possible interpretation, supported by Kant's own proposals, is to see in the point of juncture a principle that allows for "the passage from the *manner of thinking* according to the principles of the one to the manner of thinking according to the principles of the other."[27] Since "two principles as heterogeneous as nature and freedom can offer but two ways of showing their difference,"[28] we will agree to adopt two different points of view on the world, according to whether we seek to provide a scientific explanation or an ethical justification of the world. Such was the first reading I had given of the antinomy. But we have also seen that, if Kant clearly leans towards such a solution, he is at the same time putting extra demands on the teleological principle, namely, the possibility of a *passage* from nature to freedom. If this first version did not require a necessary recourse to a supersensible principle of unification, however, the second does indeed require it. But if the supersensible principle is a practical principle, it cannot serve as a link between theoretical and practical philosophy. Only a principle that is neither theoretical nor practical, neither nature nor freedom, can truly serve as a link. Moreover, this is what § 2 of the Introduction clearly states:

> It is therefore necessary that there exist a foundation for the *unity* of the supersensible, which underlies nature, with what the concept of freedom contains in a practical sense, of which the concept, even though it succeeds neither theoretically nor practically in providing knowledge of it, and so does not possess any particular domain, still makes possible the passage from the manner of thinking according to the principles of the one to the manner of thinking according to the principles of the other.[29]

It is in this line of thought that we have to situate the monist solution proposed by Schelling to get around the nature-freedom (or *Natur und Geist*) duality. By way of conclusion, I will briefly present this solution.

In his *System of Transcendental Idealism*, Schelling adopts Kant's theses in the following way:

> Nature in its purposive forms speaks figuratively to us, says Kant; the interpretation of its cipher yields us the appearance of freedom in our-

> selves. In a natural product we still find side by side what in free action has been separated for purposes of appearance. Every plant is entirely what it should be; what is free therein is necessary, and what is necessary is free. . . . Therefore organic nature alone gives me the complete appearance of freedom *and* necessity unified in the external world. . . .[30]

The antinomy between mechanism and teleology is resolved by the fact that, all the while being a blind mechanism, nature is essentially final.[31]

Two essential theses of this monist solution should be kept in mind: first, the fact of an identity between freedom and necessity, and second, the fact that the organism objectifies this identity.

1. Schelling's theory of the identity between the mind (freedom) and nature (necessity) seeks to avoid all materialist or idealist reductionism. In the fragments from the *Weltalter,*[32] the identity is described as a veritable relation between two different elements, $A = B$, which constitute a relation of indifference (*Gleich-Gültigkeit* or *Indifferenz*). This latter signifies a pure virtuality of real difference. The identity does not affirm that A and B are one and same object, but that there is an x, and that, from a certain point of view, the essential quality of this x is A and, from another point of view, it is B. If A represents the predicate 'nature' and B the predicate 'mind,' there exists a substance x such that this x is essentially A, and that it is essentially B. Schelling expresses this in the following way: we cannot say that the soul is a body or that the body is a soul.

> But that which in one respect is body, is in another respect soul. We could say in general: the connection in judgment is never a mere part of it, even, as is assumed, the best part, but is rather its whole essence, and the judgment is only this unfolded connection itself. The true sense of each judgment, e.g. the simplest, A is B, is actually this: that which is A is also what is B, which shows that the connection underlies the subject as well as the predicate. There is no simple unity here, but rather one repeated with itself, or an identity of an identity.[33]

Put another way, the identity $A = B$ contains the following three identities: $A = x$, $B = x$ and $A = B$. This can be formalized in the following way:

> Given two variables x and y and two predicates A and B, one can say that:
>
> $$(x)\ [Ax \rightarrow (\exists y)\ (By\ \&\ x = y)]$$
>
> (for all x: if nature is x, there exists a y such that the mind is y and x is identical to y).[34]

This identity is expressed in the *System der gesammten Philosophie und der Naturphilosophie insbesondere* (1804) in a particularly modern fashion:

> Between the real and the ideal, being and thinking, no causal relation is possible; thinking can never be a cause of a determination in being; nor being a cause of a determination in thinking.—For the real and the ideal are only different views of one and the same substance; thus they can no more effect something in one another than one substance can effect something in itself.[35]

2. The second point to emphasize is the objectification of identity throughout an organism. In an organism, matter (first power) and dynamic process (second power) are linked together in a self-regulating and reflexive structure in that the organism—and here Schelling turns again to Kantian terminology—is the cause and effect *of itself.* In mechanical causality, the cause is not only distinguished from the effect, but the effect is produced by an external cause. Now, that which has its cause outside of itself is non-Absolute: "The non-absolute in general is that which is determined in its existence by another whose affirmation lies outside of it. Each particular in general is not the cause of itself but has its cause in another."[36] Consequently, the absolute is, on the contrary, "that which is from and through itself." The reflexive and self-regulating structure of the absolute is therefore found in the organism in which the relationship of cause to effect is not a relationship of something to a thing that is outside of it but a relationship of self to self. "Accordingly, an organized being is neither the cause nor the effect of a being outside it, thus not something that interferes with the mechanistic connections. Each organized product carries the ground of its existence with itself, for it is cause and effect of itself."[37]

If we summarize the two theses—(1) identity (between mind and nature) and (2) absoluteness (of organism)—we can say: the absolute is by itself cause and product of itself (a formula which, if we recall, can be found in the Kantian characterization of the organism), which means that it is not only both "the affirming and the affirmed," but that it constitutes this identity out of itself. Applied to the Kantian dichotomy of nature and freedom, that means that, insofar as it affirms itself as nature, the absolute also affirms itself as freedom and vice versa; it is neither one nor the other taken alone but rather the inseparable identity of the two:

> God (or the absolute) as the self-affirming is necessarily also the self-affirmed, i.e., it is not merely *A*, but as *A* it is already *B*, or more specifically, it is neither *A* nor *B*, but rather the inseparable identity of both. Likewise, God, as the self-affirmed, is necessarily also the affirming, i.e., it is not merely *B*, but as such immediately *A* too, i.e., it is neither *A* nor *B* in itself, but rather as *A* and *B* the whole undivided absoluteness; and

since *A* and *B* are one and the same, it is as *A* and as *B* one and the same, $A=A$.[38]

In what essential way does Schelling's recourse to the absolute differ from the use Kant makes of it for unifying mechanism and finality? The differences come from the premises on which the philosophical system is built. For Kant, the absolute is an inevitable result of an inadmissible dualism that must be resolved in the unity of the system. But since, by definition, it escapes from the instruments of knowledge, the absolute remains "a mere Idea," or a practical postulate that remains powerless when it is a question of resolving the problems presented. Such a postulate or such an idea would probably not have been necessary if Kant had not sought to resolve the antinomy by turning to a supersensible principle, if he had instead been satisfied with the dialectic of reflective judgment and had described the antinomy as an essential property of reflection. Then it was natural for Schelling to attempt to overcome such a dualism: taking as his point of departure the inadequacy of an epistemology based on the subject-object dichotomy, Schelling from the beginning situates knowledge in a monism. But this comes at the price of the "*als ob*" ("as if") that is so dear to Kant.

Notes

1. References to Kant's *Critique of Practical Reason* will use the pagination of the 1st edition (Riga, 1788) and references to the *Critique of Judgment* will be to the second edition (Berlin: F. T. Lagarde, 1793). References to Kant's other works follow the pagination of the following edition: *Kants gesammelte Schriften* (hereafter Ak.) (Berlin: Königliche Preussische Akademie der Wissenschaften, 1900 ff.).

2. Kant, *Critique of Judgment*, Introduction, § 2; my emphasis.

3. F. W. Schelling, *Fernere Darstellungen aus dem System der Philosophie* (1802), in *Sämmtliche Werke* (hereafter *SW*), ed. K.F.A. Schelling (Stuttgart, 1856–64), vol. 1/4, p. 346; cf. also p. 376.

4. Kant, *Critique of Judgment*, § 78, p. 358.

5. It is in this sense that we can read *Critique of Judgment* § 78, where it is a question of unifying the two principles: "it is infinitely important to reason not to ignore the mechanism of nature in its productions and not to leave it aside in explaining these productions, because without this mechanism we can understand nothing about the nature of things. . . . On the other hand, it is an equally neces-

sary maxim of reason not to ignore the principle of ends in the products of nature. . . ." (pp. 354–55).

6. Lewis White Beck, *A Commentary on Kant's "Critique of Practical Reason"* (Chicago: University of Chicago Press, 1960), p. 193. Cf. also Beck, "Five Concepts of Freedom in Kant," in *Philosophical Analysis and Reconstruction,* A Festschrift for Stephan Körner, ed. J.T.J. Srzednicki (Dordrecht: Kluwer, 1987), pp. 33–39.

7. Kant, *Critique of Judgment,* § 77, p. 352.

8. Here I do not take into consideration the way in which Kant presents the two theses in the antinomy: in their formulation, they are indeed incompatible. See my "Die Antinomie der teleologischen Urteilskraft," *Kant-Studien* 83 (1992), pp. 341–55.

9. Kant, *Critique of Judgment,* § 78, p. 357.

10. Ibid., p. 361.

11. Ibid., § 82, p. 387.

12. See my "Die Antinomie der teleologischen Urteilskraft."

13. Kant, *Critique of Judgment,* § 66, p. 296; my emphasis.

14. Cf. ibid., Introduction, § 4.

15. Ibid., § 67, p. 304.

16. Ibid., § 77, p. 351.

17. Ibid., § 88, p. 458.

18. Kant, *Über den Gebrauch teleologischer Principien in der Philosophie,* Ak. vol. 8, p. 183.

19. Kant, *Critique of Judgment,* § 88, p. 432.

20. Ibid., p. 430; my emphasis.

21. My reading diverges from Lewis White Beck's in his *Commentary* and from M. Albrecht's in *Kants Antinomie der praktischen Vernunft* (New York: G. Olms, 1978). These two authors interpret the antinomy as consisting of the alternative that Kant poses between the two following possibilities:

Thesis: the desire for happiness is a necessary and sufficient condition for virtue.

Antithesis: the maxim of virtue is a necessary and sufficient condition for happiness.

Now the thesis is "absolutely impossible," personal happiness being incapable of founding virtue. The antithesis is equally false in that virtue is not a sufficient condition for a happy life in the sensible world. Given that the two affirmations are false, we are not dealing with an antinomy between the two. Beck can therefore affirm that "the whole antinomy is contrived and artificial" (*Commentary*, p. 227). And if there is no antinomy, there is then no reason for there to be "a critical solution to the antinomy."

22. Kant, *Critique of Practical Reason*, pp. 225–26. Cf. also *Reflexion* 6958, Ak. vol. 19, p. 214.

23. Kant, *Critique of Judgment*, § 85, p. 408.

24. Ibid., § 86, p. 415.

25. "Consequently the postulate of the possiblity of the *highest derived good* (the best world) is at the same time the postulate of the reality of a *primitive highest good*, namely the existence of God. Now, *it was our duty to realize the highest good*, consequently not only a right, but also *a necessity linked as if by a need to the obligation to suppose the possibility of the highest good*, which, since it is possible only if God exists, inseparably links the supposition of this existence with the obligation, that is to say that it is morally necessary to admit the existence of God" (Kant, *Critique of Practical Reason*, p. 226; my emphasis).

26. Ibid., pp. 3–4.

27. Kant, *Critique of Judgment*, Introduction, § 2; my emphasis.

28. Ibid., § 91, p. 474.

29. Ibid., Introduction, § 2.

30. Schelling, *SW*, vol. 1/3, p. 608; *System of Transcendental Freedom*, trans. P. Heath (Charlottesville, Va.: University Press of Virginia, 1993), p. 216.

31. "For what is distinctive of nature is that it is purposive in its mechanism, even if this is nothing other than blind mechanism" (Schelling, *SW*, vol. 1/3, p. 608).

Similarly, in the *System der gesammten Philosophie* of 1804 we can read: "Absolutely regarded, nature is thoroughly organic. . . . Matter and each part of matter is a world in itself, actually infinite. This is matter that appears inorganic, and indeed in every part, there lies the type of the whole, so that it needs its development to appear organic. So-called inorganic nature is this potent, all organic in each part: it is of a sleeping plant and animal world, with which one look of absolute identity would awaken into life" (*SW*, vol. 1/6, p. 380).

32. Schelling, *Die Weltalter, Fragmente*, ed. M. Schrötor, in the original version of 1811 and 1813 (Munich, 1946), vol. 1, pp. 26–29.

33. Schelling, *Weltalter*, vol. I, p. 30; see also *SW*, vol. 1/4, p. 121; vol. 1/6, pp. 165, 173, 187.

34. One can also formalize in the following way:
$\iota x\,(Ax) = \iota x\,(Bx)$, where '$\iota x$' signifies 'an object x such as' (that which is A is also that which is B).

35. Schelling, *SW*, vol. 1/6, pp. 500–01; see vol. I/4, p. 135 n.

36. Schelling, *System der gesammten Philosophie*, *SW*, vol. 1/6, p. 148.

37. Schelling, *SW*, vol. 1/2, p. 40.

38. Schelling, *System der gesammten Philosophie*, *SW*, vol. 1/6, p. 165.

5

Philosophical Foundations of Early Romanticism

Manfred Frank

When it comes to early German romanticism, everyone—at least in the area of so-called intellectual history—deems himself or herself competent. Either one sees in it a high point of European culture whose force and productivity in the most varied areas can be compared only with classical Athens,[1] or one sees in it the essence of the "German special way" in the course of modernity and may even date from it a fatal history that reaches "from Schelling to Hitler."

In truth, however, early romanticism, at least philosophical early romanticism, is the great unknown in the archives of intellectual history, and not only in its "official" archives. Professional philosophers choose to avoid it, because they feel an insurmountable suspicion against philosophers who think in fragments and who, moreover, are able to obtain their laurels in the literary genre as well. To them the capacity to present complex thoughts in a language that is also aesthetically appealing seems a sign of argumentative invalidity—and accordingly, their own style is quite repugnant. Scholars of German literature, on the other hand, are habitually afraid of poets who also can think—especially if they think as complexly as, for example, Hölderlin and his circle or the Jena group around Friedrich Schlegel. Moreover, scholars of German literature have only rarely been able to acquire the knowledge that is necessary in order to judge Hölderlin's and Hardenberg's philosophical writings in addition to their poetry. Yet if one does not comprehend both wings of the early romantic production, then one cannot comprehend the period as a whole.

This peculiar situation, though, does not reflect the self-understanding of Hölderlin and Novalis. Recall the letter of October 13, 1796, in which Hölderlin advises, or rather implores, his brother: study philosophy "even if you have no more money than is necessary to buy a lamp and oil and no more time than from midnight to the crack of dawn."[2] One also seldom realizes that Hölderlin thought himself capable of assuming a lecturing post at the University of Jena, which was then rich in great philosophical talent, and of holding his own philosophical lectures next to Fichte and Schelling. As late as 1801, Hölderlin had not yet given up this plan. As regards Novalis, he writes that his profession has the same name as his bride: Sophie (letter to Friedrich Schlegel of July 8, 1796): "Philosophy is the soul of my life and the key to my inner-most self, and since my acquaintance [with Sophie], I am also entirely fused to these studies."[3] Furthermore, comprehensive research recently undertaken on the intellectual situation at the University of Jena during the decisive years from 1789 to 1795 has thrown so much new light on the "constellation" out of which Hölderlin's thought-sketch "Judgment and Being" emerged that one must say that research in this area has been placed on an entirely new foundation.[4] What now remains to be done above all is to uncover the hidden channels through which the earliest philosophical works of Novalis and Schlegel connected with this constellation. In that regard, the year 1796 provides the *terminus ad quem*, for with Schlegel's notes from the fall of 1796 the turn away from philosophizing based on a supreme first principle is finally accomplished. What followed was a deepened methodical working out and patient elaboration of this turn.

The main piece of information on the intellectual constellation between 1789 and 1792 consists in the fact that Kant's philosophy, in whose tradition everything followed, was received by Hölderlin and Novalis through two hitherto unnoticed textual filters, which have not been reprinted for more than two hundred years. The first of these is the second edition of Jacobi's *Spinoza* of 1789. The second one is Reinhold's philosophical turn during the summer of 1792.[5]

I

Jacobi's contribution to the modification in understanding Kant consisted mainly in two ideas—and both of these can be found in clear form only in the second edition of his Spinoza booklet, which means that the interpretation of Jacobi, which has so far rested exclusively on the first edition, has known nothing of them.[6]

The first of Jacobi's ideas brings together Spinoza's monistic substance, which was understood as the sum total of reality, with the notion of being as reconceived by Kant. Being, just like substance, is something singular, and thus not something that would be new and different in each single being. Rather, every being is characterized by a unitary meaning of 'being'. Thus one can say that each thought about a determined existence always already presupposes an understanding of the priority of unitary being. (In the preface to the penultimate version of his novel *Hyperion*, Hölderlin speaks of "being, in the singular meaning of this word.") However, and here the contrast with substance comes in, being is nothing that can be grasped through concepts (no "real predicate"); it is rather the object of some experience—in this case of a higher, non-sensible experience. (After all, Jacobi's "God or being" is a supernatural being.) Being is simply the same as "position" (*Setzung*), and in that regard, Kant had already thought that one has to distinguish between an absolute and a relative position. A concept is said to be "posited absolutely" if its object exists, as in the sentence *I am*, period. The 'am' does not express a new content that would be added to the concept 'I,' such that the two would be synthesized; rather, it says only that something like an 'I' exists and is not, e.g., a product of the imagination. Something is posited "relatively" if the positing occurs, as in the predicative judgment, through the "relational particle 'is.'" In this case something is not posited absolutely, but a subject expression is posited relative to a predicate expression. Kant had called such relations "judgments." They have the structure of "something as something": the first "something" stands for the object and the second stands for the concept under which the first is being interpreted. Apparently Kant, who in this regard was by no means less decisive than Hölderlin and Novalis, had already thought that the copulative "is" somehow represents a derivative mode of the existential "is." And Jacobi, who again would be followed by Hölderlin and Novalis, added to that the thought of the unity of being: existence and identity are somehow the same, and the synthetic force of the binding particle "is" in the predicative judgment flows somehow from the seamless identity of being. I should mention also that already for Kant existential "being"—the "absolute position" as it is still called in Fichte—is only revealed through perception.[7] Kant also speaks of actuality as the "position of things in relation . . . to perception."[8] This "relation" is naturally different from that other "relative position" that is present in predicative judgment, for through the relation to perception the perceived is, as it were, "absolutely posited." Perceptions belong to the class of intuitions.[9] Since the thought of "being, in the unique sense of the word," has nothing sensible as its object, an "intellectual intuition" corresponds to it. (This is Hölderlin's and Hardenberg's parlance; Jacobi had spoken of "feeling," an expression that is also taken from the semantic field of the sensible. That, too, is taken over by Novalis but not Hölderlin.) Under the term *being* a thought is grasped that concerns us even more closely than "*cogito*."[10] This is why for Fichte and Schelling '*sum*', and not '*cogito*', is the supreme principle.

There is a second idea of Jacobi (to be found in the seventh supplement to the second edition of the Spinoza book) that exercised a strong influence on the intellectual formation of the early romantics. In the seventh supplement, Jacobi shows that the definition of "knowledge" as "grounded opinion" leads to an infinite regress. The demonstration is as follows. What is known are states of affairs, and these are expressed by propositions (thus Kantian "judgments"). If a state of affairs is a fact (thus something known), then it must by definition be grounded. Thus, the proposition expressing it must be grounded in another proposition, for which in turn the same would hold: it, too, has its ground in another proposition, which in turn has it in another one, and so on *ad infinitum*. Now, if it were the case that all of our opining were conditioned by other instances of opining, then we would never arrive at an instance of knowledge. Thus, if we are to retain the strong definition of "knowledge," there must be at least *one* proposition that holds not conditionally but unconditionally. "Unconditionally" means valid precisely *because* its validity is not derived from the condition that another proposition grounds it.[11] Jacobi calls the knowledge that is expressed in an unconditional proposition "feeling" (or "faith"). "Faith" means intuiting a fact as certain per se, without further justification.

Finally, Jacobi brought together the idea of the "being" that is always already thought in every determined "existence"[12] with the idea of the unconditioned beginning, by saying of the latter that it is already presupposed in each "representation of the conditioned"—and this in such a way that we "have of its existence the same and even a higher certainty than regarding our own *conditioned* existence."[13] Jacobi thereby asserts outright that the experience of the conditioned is given only in the context of the representation of the unconditioned. And we can easily understand this after what has just been said, for if the conditioned is to contain an instance of *knowledge*, then a certainty is needed as its credential, and this can be derived only from an unconditioned consciousness. This is the most original component of all consciousness. Even more: it first makes possible the consciousness that we have of ourselves (of our own existence). As Novalis notes, "the ground of thinking—*SUM*."[14]

II

Reinhold's "Elementary Philosophy" took over the thought of an unconditioned beginning in the following way. He called a proposition that is unconditionally valid (valid without reference to another proposition as its condition) a "first principle." From this principle he sought to deduce whatever else can claim validity, through a derivation procedure modeled on Descartes, namely, from the fundamental validity of the first principle or basic proposition and a logical derivation from it. In the early summer of 1792, Reinhold was overcome with doubt concerning this procedure of deduction from an unconditionally valid first principle (a procedure that was to receive its fullest unfolding in Fichte's *Science of Knowledge*). These doubts seem to go back to the Tübingen repetitor Carl Immanuel Diez. But Diez was only one among several highly talented students of Reinhold, who all sought to prove to their master that in his derivation program certain of his premises actually received their full justification only from their consequences, or in other words, that Reinhold had to resort to premises that he could not justify initially but only afterward. Thus, the justification does not proceed from an initially advanced first principle, but from a principle that one would rather have to characterize as the final idea and not the basic proposition of the philosophical system. The principle is an Idea in the original Kantian sense of a relational category that is expanded toward the unconditioned for the purposes of systematizing our knowledge. Now, Ideas hold only hypothetically: they regulate our thinking about the world, but they do not constitute any objects. Thus if ultimate justification proceeds only by way of Ideas, then, to put the matter paradoxically, it never proceeds ultimately. And thus the program of a deduction from a first principle changes into the infinite approximation of a principle that can never be brought to ultimate certainty, i.e., an Idea.

In the case of Reinhold, we are dealing more precisely with the Idea of an "absolute subject," which is the only active element in all the relations addressed by the "principle of consciousness" and which enters into a self-relation in all of the constellations that are predelineated in the "principle of consciousness." Since Reinhold understood all consciousness as representation of a represented object, he could also characterize the consciousness that we have of ourselves only as such an object-relation.[15] Thus, for him grounding subjectivity became an Idea unreachable for representation, which he—like Kant—had to describe as merely regulative. But to turn self-consciousness into a regulative Idea means to renounce the project of ascribing to it being and Cartesian evidence. And thus the "absolute I" is no longer a ground of deduction but is—as Novalis calls it—a "principle of approximation."[16]

During the time when such thoughts were forming slowly among Reinhold's students, Novalis was Reinhold's student and was well acquainted with Niethammer, Benjamin Erhard and Baron von Herbert. (After his departure from Jena, Novalis kept up a correspondence with all of them. That correspondence is known only in parts.) Hölderlin, by contrast, encountered the departure from the philosophy of the first principle only in the version that Niethammer gave it in December 1794 (in the "Announcement" of the *Philosophisches Journal*), where this was done even more decisively than in the programmatic introductory essay of his *Philosophisches Journal* of May 1795. Hölderlin called Niethammer his "teacher" and "mentor," and there is no reason to take this as merely a gesture of modesty.[17]

III

It seems that Niethammer was indeed the first to formulate the basic outline of an alternative to the program of Fichte's philosophy of a first principle—a philosophy in which the smart Jena students saw only a relapse (at the highest level) into the long-since-refuted conception of Reinhold's "fundamental philosophy." In a letter to von Herbert from June 2, 1794, which has only recently been found and published, Niethammer expresses his "conviction regarding the dispensability of a highest and unique principle of philosophy."[18] As already noted, this conviction represented the consensus among Reinhold's students after 1791–92, including Niethammer himself, as well as Novalis-Hardenberg and his friends Benjamin Erhard and von Herbert. On May 19, 1794, Erhard wrote to Niethammer:

> In one respect, Herbert is quite right concerning the one principle. A philosophy which departs from one principle and which presumes to derive everything from it, always remains a piece of sophistry. But a philosophy that ascends up to the highest principle and presents everything else as standing in perfect harmony with it, not deriving it from it, is the true philosophy.[19]

Here for the first time in the history of idealism there is mention of that infinitely ascending procedure that Reinhold had first sketched in his introductory essay to volume 2 of his *Beyträge* and that was to find its most surprising resonance in Schlegel's conception of philosophy in 1800–01, delivered at Jena before an audience that is said to have included Hegel.

The basic argument of Niethammer's introductory essay, titled "Von den Ansprüchen des gemeinen Verstandes an die Philosophie" ("On the Demands of Common Sense to Philosophy"), states that the intuitive convictions of common sense cannot be regarded as fundamental as long as philosophical reason is able either definitely to prove them or to refute them. But precisely because of the lack of a secure foundation, philosophy is unable to do this. For that foundation would either have to be given intuitively—in which case it in turn would need justification—or it would be proven through a justification—in which case this justification, which itself would require grounding, would be caught up in an infinite regress, as shown by Jacobi. Thus, the unrefuted intuitions of common sense must be considered correct (that is, warranted)[20] provisionally or for pragmatic reasons. In particular, Niethammer contests the possibility of a transcendental proof for the fact of experience—in that, he follows the skepticism about philosophy in the *Aenesidemus*.[21] The only way for philosophical reason to discredit the opinions of common sense that are based on intuition would be to point to a foundational principle that surpasses this intuition. In the classical version of the transcendental deduction, this is achieved through the demonstration of a priori laws of our mind from which our assumed convictions can be conclusively derived as consequences. Niethammer seeks to uncover the following circle in this derivation procedure: first, experiences are demonstrated in consciousness; then, there is an inference from these principles to their antecedents; third, those antecedents are taken to confirm the experiences. Now, not only is there no certain inference from consequence to antecedent, there is, in particular, no necessary connection between propositions that are empirical and contingent and others that are a priori and apodictically valid. Thus, Niethammer denies nothing less than transcendental argument.[22]

We have to imagine that among the former students of Reinhold there was a general consensus on this skeptical conviction regarding philosophy, a consensus that was strongly expressed toward outsiders, especially toward Fichte. Only such a consensus could explain what has so far remained totally unexplained in all research on early romanticism, namely, the agreement and above all the immediacy of the critique with which all of them—Sinclair, Zwilling, Hölderlin, Weisshuhn, Herbert, Feuerbach, Novalis, and Schlegel—reacted to Fichte's *Science of Knowledge* (and with it the type of a philosophy of ultimate justification represented by it) between the spring of 1795 and the fall of 1796. The situation in Jena after Reinhold's departure and Fichte's call to be his successor was something like this: The students of Reinhold expected to learn new arguments from Reinhold's successor against the possibility of a philosophy from a first principle. Instead, Fichte appeared in Jena with the consciousness of a mission, namely, that of having to show the Reinholdians how to do philosophy from a first principle. Thus, in spite of all the respect for Fichte's significant, superior intellectual power, his appearance was perceived in Jena as an anachronism in comparison to the state of the basic conviction about metaphilosophy.

I will not examine here why Hölderlin and his circle took up the skepticism regarding philosophy from a first principle and developed it into a speculative metaphilosophy—for this chapter of early idealism is by now well documented and thoroughly researched. By contrast, the train of thought of Friedrich von Hardenberg, called Novalis, is still almost entirely *un*disclosed. And yet his early philosophical notes, the so-called *Fichte-Studien* (erroneously so-called), have been available in a critical edition since 1960. It has been established that Novalis began writing down his notes on Fichte at the latest in September 1795, that is, a little later than Hölderlin.[23] And what was said for the latter ought to hold as well for Novalis: since his manuscript already presents its solution on the very first pages and does not attain it only at the end of complex attempts at understanding himself and Fichte, the intellectual labor on which it is based must fall into the preceding months.

So far the few attempts to elucidate these difficult notes have failed entirely due to ignorance regarding the context of discussion, the outlines of which I have just sketched. In this respect Novalis merits special attention. For in their perspicuity and argumentative agility, his notes are clearly superior to those of Hölderlin and Sinclair. Novalis was well acquainted with the second edition of Jacobi's Spinoza booklet.[24] He had studied with Reinhold during the latter's growing crisis regarding the philosophy of a first principle and was a close friend of his. The same holds for his relation to Niethammer, who invited him from Jena in 1795 to collaborate on the *Philosophisches Journal*.[25] Novalis's former tutor, Carl Christian Erhard Schmid, who remained in friendly relations with his student for the rest of his life, was himself a cofounder of the *Journal* and an opponent of Fichte's philosophy of a first principle.[26] Finally, Novalis was already very familiar with Fichte and his writings due to the fact that his father had taken over from von Miltitz the payment of the stipend that had enabled Fichte to start his career in the first place.

IV

I will organize my interpretation of the earliest independent philosophical notes of Novalis into three theses: first, Novalis solves the problem of how something that is by definition unconscious ("ultimate being" [*Ursein*]) can be mediated with consciousness; second, he aims to show how the conception of a transreflexive unity of being can be reconciled with the conception of an internal articulation of the Absolute (into feeling and reflection, matter and form, synthetic and analytic I, opposition and object, state and object, essence and property, or in whatever form Novalis structures the opposition); and thirdly, Novalis establishes a well-explicated connection between the conception that being is beyond consciousness and the conception of philosophy as an infinite, never-ending approximation. On the one hand, the latter conception integrates the most important result of the critical turn against the philosophy of a first principle from the years around 1792 in the Reinhold circle. On the other hand, it prepares the aesthetic solution of the problem: that which philosophy can grasp only in an infinite amount of time, and thus can never reach, aesthetic imagination is able to grasp in an instant—to be sure, only as something irresolvable. "If the character of a given problem is insolvability, then we solve it by demonstrating its insolvability [as such]. We know enough of *a*, when we understand that its predicate is *a*."[27] This is accomplished by art as the "presentation of the unpresentable."[28]

V

My three theses concerning the basic arguments of Novalis's *Fichte-Studien* are in need of some kind of overture. Reflection on the relation between being and consciousness precedes the question of how the unrepresentable being could nevertheless be represented by consciousness.

Just as in the cases of Hölderlin and Sinclair, Novalis's first independent intellectual attempts take their departure from reflections on the form or essence of judgment. He is concerned with the relation between the copulative "is" and the meaning of "being" as identity or existence. It had already been the conviction of Rousseau's Savoyard vicar and also of Kant (and in general of the logic of the time) that the copulative "is" is some kind of indirect indication of identity: an expression of one semantic class (ordinarily an expression for a subject representation) is identified with an expression of another semantic class (ordinarily standing for a predicate representation), even if only partially or relatively. Thus, the meaning of "being" is essentially "being identical." However, in order to express this identity in the form of a judgment, we must, Novalis thinks, step outside of it: "We leave behind the *identical* in order to represent it."[29] This representation produces a "*pseudo-proposition*." Instead of representing identity, it represents to us a synthetic relation between two expressions. But synthesis is not the same as identity, although it presupposes it.[30] The concession that the seamless identity of original being has to make to linguistic expression (Novalis says to "the sign"[31]) is thus its dis-figuration (*Ent-stellung*) into a relation between two different things.

This corresponds to Hardenberg's double identification of "knowledge" (or "consciousness"), on the one hand, with that which is known through a true judgment, and on the other hand, with the intentional relation to a "something." (Novalis thinks that the German term *knowledge* [*Wissen*] stems from "what" [*was*].)[32] The first of these two identifications is in agreement with Kant's position. With the second identification, he contradicts Fichte, who had declared that some consciousness, viz., self-consciousness, is non-objective—a move with far-reaching consequences. Objective consciousness is also called "positing," because it posits opposite itself the object (or the thought) *of* which it is consciousness, rather than identifying itself with it.[33] This explains a formula that occurs repeatedly in Novalis: "Consciousness is a being in being outside of being."[34] This being "outside of being" is "no real being."[35] Thus consciousness has, so to speak, less being than its object, being. This means that for its quasi-being, consciousness is in need of an intentional relation to being. But the reverse does not hold. Being would still be there if there were no consciousness, no knowledge, no judgment of it (or about it).[36] Consciousness, however, exists only as essentially being-related-to-being. Every relation differentiates, and the determinateness of what is being differentiated is grounded in this differentiation.[37] This, however, prevents consciousness from gaining direct access to the undivided unity of being. The latter could show itself only, according to the linguistic convention introduced by Kant, through some sensation.[38] Following Rousseau and Jacobi, Novalis speaks of "feeling."[39] This would be a mode of consciousness closed off to conceptual knowledge, a state of "not-knowledge."[40] Any thematization through reflection would destroy it.[41]

VI

Thus we have reached the point where my first thesis can be justified. For if it is the case that the highest "being" exceeds the possibilities of our cognitive faculties, then the question immediately arises how there can be any consciousness regarding it. That is the question to which Novalis, who always remained faithful to the basic critical inspiration of Kant and Fichte, has dedicated a series of reflections that one has to call ingenious both because they are without precedent and because of their effect on subsequent intellectual history. These reflections open up nothing less than an independent course of idealist speculation. At its end there does not stand an absolute idealism in the manner of Hegel. Rather, ontological idealism is overcome in favor of an epistemologically enlightened realism. One could also speak of a return to Kant even before absolute idealism has spread its wings. Here I can sketch only the basic thought of Novalis.

At the beginning of Novalis's thought experiment stands a consideration of the etymology of the word *reflection*.[42] Apparently, Novalis was moved to such a consideration because, as we just saw, he thinks of consciousness as related in principle related to an object (or "positing"). From this he does not exempt reflection, i.e., the consciousness through which we are acquainted with ourselves. In that he distinguishes himself radically from Fichte and the adherents of an "intellectual intuition" following Fichte. Even the alleged intellectual intuition which (as in Hölderlin) directly grasps being in its undividedness is, upon closer inspection, characterized by an opposition: that of intuition and intellect (Novalis says of "feeling" and "reflection"). We have to accept this. Now what would it mean, so Novalis's thought goes, if the knowledge we do indeed possess of ourselves could not be made intelligible *from* the thought of reflection? And what if this were the case for the same reasons that prevent us from representing being in a simple predicative proposition ("judgment")? We can only grasp something objective *as ourselves*, if we are already acquainted with ourselves prior to all objectification. For that a special consciousness would be needed, one which Novalis calls "feeling." It would be distinguished by the fact that it would not posit itself opposite that which is felt, as is the case with reflection. And yet Novalis does not really resort to this nonobjective mode of consciousness for his argumentation. "Feeling" is rather the name for an ideal limiting case of consciousness on which we cannot count in an epistemic respect. That is, feeling is originally not a case of "knowledge." Following Jacobi's language, Novalis ascribes to it the epistemic mode of "faith."[43] Thus we have acknowledged a presupposition that cannot be questioned, that cannot be resolved into knowledge, and without which philosophy cannot advance a single step.

We are thus referred back to reflection. Out of it we are not able to explicate our actual *self*-consciousness. But *without* it, we have no *consciousness* of our self. Now a consideration of the meaning of "reflection" shows that the expression refers to a mirroring. All mirroring makes what is being mirrored appear reversed. If I hold an object in front of a mirroring glass, then right and left will be reflected as left and right.[44] Furthermore, the ray of light that runs toward the glass appears to run away from it in the opposite direction. Novalis calls this order, which is characteristic for the finite world of consciousness altogether, "*ordo inversus*."[45] According to it, consciousness is "not what it represents, and does not represent what it is."[46]

Now Novalis asks whether things should be different with the reflection due to which we cognize our self. Could it be the case that it is the fault of reflection that we disfigure being into judgment (thus into the oppositional play of two synthesized expressions)? And that we similarly misrecognize our identity as the interplay of two reflections, an I-subject and an I-object? In that case, the advice of Parsifal would be the only remedy: "The wound can be healed only by the very spear that opened it." In reflecting upon itself, reflection discovers in its own structure the means for mirroring the reversed relations back again into the right order. This is done through self-application or doubling: a reflection that is again reflected upon turns the reversal of relations back around and thus reestablishes the order that obtained prior to the first mirroring. That which first had the appearance of tending "from the limited toward the unlimited"[47] thus reveals itself in the light of doubled reflection as an "apparent passing from the unlimited to the limited."[48]

Novalis takes himself to have established two things: first, the origin of the idealist appearance according to which consciousness comprehends all objects and their sum total, "being," only in the perspective of consciousness, since it starts from itself as that which is first (for itself); and second, the truth of realism according to which being "fundamentally"—i.e., in the ontological order—precedes all consciousness and exists independent of it.

The object of the first reflection is by no means the Absolute itself (that would be a nonsensical, transcendent speculation) but rather its lack. That is why Novalis calls that which assumes the place of the failed object of this first reflection a "what"[49] and later also "matter."[50] Now, reflection indeed has an object but not that which it originally intended: the Absolute. The position of nonobjective being has been taken over by that of the objective appearance. As soon as feeling—the organ of this experience of deprivation—is in turn "observed" (thus reflectively objectified), its "spirit" necessarily disappears: "It [the feeling] can be observed only in reflection. The spirit of the feeling [that which reveals itself in it properly] is then gone. From the product [the intellectual intuition] one can infer the producer, according to the schema of reflection."[51]

Novalis's attempt at a solution is unusual even in the context of the reflection on self-consciousness at the time. Like Kant and Fichte, he does concede to self-consciousness an eminent position and thus distinguishes himself, e.g., from "post-modern" detractors of subjectivity. But he no longer takes self-consciousness to be a principle. It is rather something "dependent" on being.[52] "I *am*," Novalis notes, "*not* insofar as I posit myself but insofar as I suspend myself."[53] Thus a negation of reflection opens the path to being—the dream of the sovereign self-origination of the subject is ended. However, being, which has now assumed the fundamental position, does not exercise the abandoned function of grounding, which the tradition from Descartes to Fichte had assigned to the subject. Being is an ontic, not a logical, matter. Nothing follows from it in the logical sense of the word, except that the self is no longer the master in its own house.

VII

I can touch upon the two other theses only briefly, given the limitations of space. The second thesis states that Novalis—who differs here from the author of "Judgment and Being"—does not simply juxtapose the thought of "original being" and that of the internal articulation of consciousness. For Novalis, this internal differentiation of consciousness follows from its unavoidable reflexivity. Therefore we have to distinguish a reflected and a reflecting. In order not to betray the position of philosophical monism, the differentiation of being in reflection has to be made intelligible by recourse to the very structure of the Absolute. Otherwise the difference would fall outside of the sphere of the Absolute. That, however, would mean that the Absolute was not the sum total of all reality but existed along with something else (independent of it). And that would be an internal contradiction for the being that carries in its very name the specification "*quod est omnibus relationibus absolutum.*"

The determination of this internal differentiation is spelled out by recourse to the opposition of feeling and reflection. Terminological successors to this pair are (in that order) "matter and form," "synthetic and analytic I," "opposition and object" (alternatively, "state and object"), and "essence and property." It is thus always the case that the expression that stands in the position of the subject in the model loses its identity with the application of the predicate and becomes the correlate of a relation. Thus at a higher level, Novalis regains his initial definition of consciousness as "being in being outside of being," viz., through a consideration of the "significant etymology" of "*existence*."[54] We "ek-sist" by standing outside of our own being, thus transforming it into an appearance and relating to it as something lost. Consciousness "is not what it represents, and does not represent what it is."[55] From here it is not far to Hegel's determination of time as a being which is, insofar as it is not, and is not, insofar as it is.[56] Lost being is thus represented under the schema of the past, not(-yet)-Being under that of the future. Split between the two, the self loses its strict identity and is transformed into the continuity of a life history.

VIII

But, you will say: If I can capture pure being always in only one of its predicates and thus fail to reach it properly, how can I be sure being is at all a meaningful concept? To this Novalis responds with desirable clarity that there is no such thing as the pure (as such):[57] "[Pure would be] what is neither related nor relatable. . . . The concept *pure* is thus an empty concept—. . . everything pure is thus an illusion of the imagination—*a necessary* fiction."[58] This fiction is "necessary" because without it we could not understand the connection among the members of the judgment, expressed through the little "relational word 'is.'" It is a "fiction" because we never represent nonrelational being except through the "is" of predication. Thus, it remains the unknown "sum total of the properties known by us,"[59] an ideal, a thought-entity that our knowledge can only approximate infinitely but the content of which it can never exhaust.[60]

And with this thought we enter into the realm of my third thesis. It states that Novalis, unlike Hölderlin, establishes an explicit connection between the thought that being is beyond knowledge and the characterization of philosophy as an infinite, never-ending task.[61] To be sure, Hardenberg's reasoning is inspired by the doctrines of drives and striving with which he had familiarized himself in the meantime by reading the third part of the *Science of Knowledge* (of 1795).[62] These thoughts, which are more radical in their point of departure than those of Fichte, fall totally outside the frame of the philosophy that had trusted self-consciousness with the function of the ultimate foundation of the system of knowledge. For Novalis, the formula of philosophy as "nostalgia for the infinite"[63] thus becomes the indication of philosophy's inconcludability.

This happens in the context of a characterization of philosophy as the search for an absolute ground. This search for a ground, so the argument goes, is necessarily infinite, since an absolute ground cannot be given to consciousness. Now, if "this . . . were not given, if this concept contained an impossibility—then the drive to philosophizing would be an infinite activity—and therefore without end, since there would be an eternal need for an absolute ground which could be satisfied only relatively—and therefore would never cease."[64]

Once one has convinced oneself of the impossibility of completing the search (or rather of the impossibility of realizing what is sought), so Novalis continues, one will "freely renounce the Absolute."[65] "That way, there originates in us an infinite free activity—the only possible Absolute which can be given to us and which we find only through our inability to reach the Absolute and know it. This Absolute given to us can be known only negatively, by acting and finding that what we are looking for cannot be reached through any acting."[66]

> 'I' signifies that absolute which is to be known [only] negatively—which remains left over after all abstraction—That which can be known only through acting and which realizes itself through its eternal lack. / Thus eternity is realized through time, although time contradicts eternity. /[67]

Novalis also calls this impossible "searching for one principle" an "absolute postulate"—like a "squaring of the circle," the "*perpetuum mobile,*" or the "stone of the wise."[68] And from the impossibility of ultimately justifying the truth of our conviction he draws the conclusion that truth is to be replaced with probability. Probable is what "is maximally well connected," i.e., what has been made as coherent as possible without there being an ultimate justification to support the harmony of our fallible assumptions regarding the world. The coherence of our convictions must replace the lack of an evident Archimedean point of departure. If someone wanted more than that, wanted to bring before consciousness the unknowable ground as such, which can only be postulated, that person would land "in the space of nonsense."[69] The fact that the fiction of an absolute justification is called "necessary"[70] does not by itself make it something actual: "we are thus searching for a non-thing."[71]

IX

It has been my intention to document, staying quite close to the text, the conclusion drawn by Hardenberg that philosophy does *not* reach its ideal—and this for the reason that research so far has simply counted Hardenberg among the idealist absolutists. Yet he followed his old tutor Carl Christian Erhard Schmid on the way toward a re-Kantianization of philosophy against the arrogation of absolute knowledge on the part of Fichte and Schelling. The position of these latter was sometimes called "transcendentalism" by Schmid and Niethammer, because it boldly oversteps the limits of knowability. Of course, the fact that the ideal is unreachable by any intellectual effort implies that the propositions obtained by philosophy may never be called ultimately justified. Something that is justified by (Kantian) Ideas is justified only hypothetically. And thus the early work of Novalis fits organically into the constellation surrounding the *Philosophisches Journal,* with its feeling against philosophizing from a first principle.

Early romanticism was much more skeptical and modern than its reputation. However, that reputation is based on ignorance of the texts, and this so much so that it does not survive their examination. What we have learned from our course through the "constellation" of the early romantic philosophy that follows Jacobi and the second stage of Reinhold's work are two insights that the materialist and positivist philosophy of the nineteenth century has repressed rather than forgotten and that could be regained only with difficulty toward the end of our century. The first of these is that self-consciousness has to be described in terms totally unlike those for consciousness of objects and that it therefore cannot be reduced to objective consciousness (not even an objective consciousness that is developed and practiced in intersubjective encounters). The second insight is one of modesty: if self-consciousness is indeed a position that cannot be given up in the economy of philosophy—because otherwise the talk of a distinctive dignity of human beings could not be justified at all—it is still not a principle, especially not one from which eternal truths could be derived. Rather, our self has the double experience that it cannot be made intelligible through a reflective turning upon itself *and* that it depends on some "being prior to all thinking," which it is not itself. At one point, Kant had considered whether the intelligible substrate of "thinking nature" could be thought of as "matter,"[72] or at least as founded in a principle that would equally be the cause of "matter" and of the "subject of thoughts."[73] For Novalis it is established that our mind is not self-sufficient and that it rather has its root in some being (outside of consciousness) that resists its might. The fact that he did not draw any reductionist conclusions from this treatment of self-consciousness is what makes his position so incredibly contemporary.[74]

Notes

1. Thus Dieter Henrich in his report on the "research program on the origin of classical German philosophy after Kant in Jena 1789–1795," which he directed: *Konstellationen: Probleme und Debatten am Ursprung der idealistischen Philosophie (1789–1795)* (Stuttgart: Klett-Cotta, 1991), pp. 217 f.

2. Friedrich Hölderlin, *Sämtliche Werke* (Grosse Stuttgarter Ausgabe), ed. F. Beissner (Stuttgart: Kohlhammer, 1943–1985), vol. 6, *Briefe*, ed. A. Beck, pp. 234–36. Because of the structural and developmental similarities, I also count the philosophical work of Hölderlin and his circle as part of early romanticism.

3. *Novalis Schriften; die Werke Friedrich von Hardenbergs* (hereafter *NS*), ed. P. Kluckhohn and R. Samuel (Stuttgart: W. Kohlhammer Verlag, 1960/75), vol. 4, p. 188.

4. Dieter Henrich, *Der Grund im Bewusstsein: Untersuchungen zu Hölderlins Denken (1794–1795)* (Stuttgart: Klett-Cotta, 1992).

5. Cf., in addition to correspondence, Reinhold's essay "Über den Unterschied zwischen dem gesunden Verstande und der philosophierenden Vernunft in Rücksicht auf die Fundamente des durch beyde möglichen Wissens" ("On the Difference Between Common Sense and Philosophical Reason with Respect to the Foun-

dations of the Knowledge Possible in Each Case"), in *Beyträge zur Berichtigung bisheriger Missverständnisse der Philosophen* (Jena, 1794), vol. 1, pp. 3–45. In the preface, Reinhold himself dates the origin of this text to "at least one and a half years before the origin of the instructive review of *Aenesidemus*" (p. 5) by Fichte, which appeared in the *Allgemeinen Literatur-Zeitung* (Jena, 1794).

6. That is all the more comical since the page numbers of the quotations from Jacobi in Schelling, Novalis, and Friedrich Schlegel all refer to the second edition.

7. Immanuel Kant, *Critique of Pure Reason*, trans. N. K. Smith (New York: St. Martin's Press, 1929), A225/B272 ff. (pagination of the first/second German editions). That is why Kant calls the *cogito* an "empirical proposition" (B422), just as Leibniz before him (apperception is an immediate but nevertheless a posteriori experience: *New Essays Concerning Human Understanding*, bk. 4, chap. 9). Jacobi distinguishes between Spinoza's divine substance as a merely logical ground and God's causal efficacy, due to which God actually begins something in the world. We are unable to think this divine efficacy but must actually experience it: *Über die Lehre des Spinoza in Briefen an den Herrn Moses Mendelssohn* (hereafter *Spinoza2*), new, enlarged edition (Breslau: Lowe, 1789), pp. 415 ff. Jacobi says: "Even of our own existence we have only a feeling, not a concept" (p. 420 n.).

8. Kant, *Critique of Pure Reason*, A235/B287 n.

9. Which Kant defines as conscious sensations (*Critique of Pure Reason*, A225/B272).

10. Jacobi, *Spinoza2*, p. xv: "[I] believe that one must never put the *sum* after the *cogito*."

11. "This brings us to the concept of an immediate certainty which is not only not in need of a grounding but altogether excludes all grounds." (Jacobi, *Spinoza2*, p. 215; cf. esp. pp. 423 ff.).

12. Jacobi, *Spinoza2*, pp. 61, 398 ("of the *being* in all existence").

13. Ibid., pp. 423 ff.

14. Novalis, *NS*, vol. 2, p. 268.

15. This is seen very clearly by Gottlob Ernst Schulze in his *Aenesidemus, Über die Fundamente der von dem Hern. Reinhold in Jena gelieferten Elementar-Philosophie. Nebst einer Vertheidigung des Skepticismus gegen die Anmassungen der Vernunftkritik*, ed. A. Liebert (Berlin: Kant-Gesellschaft, 1991), pp. 86 ff., n. 90, 186–222 and 350 (pagination of the original edition of 1792).

16. Novalis, *NS*, vol. 2, pp. 37 ff.

17. Cf. Henrich, *Grund*, pp. 39 ff. and 113 ff.

18. Reprinted in ibid., p. 832.

19. Quoted in ibid., pp. 11 ff.

20. "Success" decides, says Niethammer ("Von den Ansprüchen des gemeinen Verstandes an die Philosophie," *Philosophisches Journal* 1 [1795], p. 45).

21. Ibid., pp. 22 ff.

22. Ordinarily, transcendental arguments protect themselves against skeptical attacks by recourse to Cartesian evidence in the premises in which what is known a priori is given. Of course, Niethammer knows this strategy—and this all the more since during the decisive years he was Reinhold's student and could experience from up close how his teacher came to doubt this argument, which he himself had been using constantly. Subsequently, Niethammer casts aside the recourse to unquestionable, improvable certainties that do not require any proof in Jacobi's language of "un-conditioned" certainties. He asks: how could there be anything different and better for the feeling of certainty in the case of self-consciousness than in the case of the feelings of certainty with which common sense defends its convictions? This skepticism regarding starting from a Cartesian conception of the subject fits in nicely with the formulation in the text of the "Announcement" (to the *Philosophisches Journal*) "that one has to start with the critique of the subject" (pp. 45 ff.). If I do not succeed in founding the alleged a priori laws of the human subject in anything other than a feeling, then they cannot be considered ultimately justified (p. 32). From this one can already anticipate Niethammer's conclusion "that the claims of common sense have to be regarded as the supreme criterion of all truth in our knowledge" (pp. 32 ff.).

23. Novalis, *NS*, vol. 2, pp. 37 ff.

24. An entry in Niethammer's *Stammbuch* quotes from the preface of the treatise on freedom (Novalis, *NS*, vol. 4, p. 85).

25. Cf. the report by J. L. Döderlein in ibid., vol. 2, p. 32.

26. Fichte punished him for that by brutally "annihilating" him: "Vergleichung des vom Herrn Prof. Schmid aufgestellten Systems mit der Wissenschaftslehre," first published in *Philosophisches Journal* (1795), 12th issue, pp. 267–320; reprinted in I. H. Fichte's edition of the *Sämmtliche Werke* (hereafter *SW*) of his father (Berlin: 1845–6; photomechanical reprint 1971), vol. 2, pp. 421–59, esp. 455 ff. Fichte refers to Schmid's "Bruchstücke aus einer Schrift über die Philoso-

phie und ihre Principien. Zur vorläufigen Prüfung vorgelegt," in *Philosophisches Journal*, 2nd issue of vol. 3 (altogether issue 10), pp. 95–132. Incidentally, in his review of the *Philosophisches Journal* Friedrich Schlegel supports this act of annihilation in a forthright manner (*Kritische Ausgabe* [hereafter *KA*], ed. E. Behler et al. [Munich, Paderborn, and Vienna, 1959 ff.], vol. 8, p. 25). And the correspondence with Caroline (in *KA*, vol. 23) demonstrates that Fichte's annihilation of Schmid satisfied the diabolic exuberance of the Jena circle in general. In spite of the fact that Friedrich Schlegel strongly opposes Fichte's program of a first principle, he calls "the negation of the ordinary objection that philosophy may not go beyond the immediate facts of consciousness, in itself . . . stringent" (*KA*, vol. 8, p. 29).

27. Novalis, *NS*, vol. 3, p. 376.

28. Ibid., p. 685.

29. Ibid., vol. 2, p. 104.

30. Novalis speaks of relative or partial identities. Throughout he defends the thesis that error arises by holding the part for the whole. (Cf. above all *NS*, vol. 2, pp. 176 ff., esp. p. 180: "for appearance is everywhere the half—only the half of a whole is the appearance. . . . Thus appearance originates . . . from elevating the part to the whole . . ."

31. Novalis, *NS*, vol. 2, p. 180.

32. Ibid., p. 105.

33. Ibid., p. 241.

34. Ibid., p. 106. To this corresponds the definition of the I as ek-stasis: "It finds *itself outside* itself" (p. 150). Novalis interprets this ecstatic finding of oneself as sensation (and the latter again, following Fichte), as "sympathetic feeling [*Ein-Innenfindung*] in reality."

35. Ibid., p. 106.

36. Cf. ibid., p. 106.

37. Ibid., p. 171.

38. Kant, *Critique of Pure Reason*, B272 ff.

39. Cf. Rousseau's Savoyard vicar: "*exister, pour nous, est sentir*" (translated in *Émile*, trans. B. Foxley [New York: Dutton, 1977], p. 232).

40. Novalis, *NS*, vol. 2, p. 105; cf. p. 125.

41. Ibid., pp. 114, 115; cf. p. 273.

42. There is a late and surprising echo of this thought in Schelling's so-called Erlangen Inaugural Lecture from January 1821: *Über die Natur der Philosophie als Wissenschaft*, Fichte, *SW*, vol. I/9, pp. 209–246; above all p. 234: "my knowledge does not transform itself but is *being* transformed; *its* respective shape is only the reflex (the *inverse*, hence reflection!) of the shape it has in eternal freedom." Novalis said this already a quarter of a century earlier.

43. Novalis, *NS*, vol. 2, pp. 105, 107.

44. "Image and being change. The image is always the inverse of being. What is right on the person, is left in the image" (ibid., p. 142; cf. p. 153: "/ It is the right side in the observation of the image/—the image is on the left—and the original on the right—/").

45. Ibid., p. 127. Cf. furthermore pp. 128, 131, 133, 136: "sophistry of the I"; vol. 3, p. 65.

46. Ibid., p. 226.

47. Ibid., pp. 114, 115, 117.

48. Ibid., p. 226.

49. Ibid., p. 116.

50. Ibid., pp. 172, 174.

51. Ibid., p. 114.

52. Cf. Novalis, *NS*, vol. 2, pp. 259, 528 ff.

53. Novalis, *NS*, vol. 2, p. 196.

54. Ibid., p. 199.

55. Ibid., p. 226.

56. G.W.F. Hegel, *Enzyklopädie der Philosophischen Wissenschaften im Grundrisse* (1830), ed. F. Nicolin and O. Pöggeler (Hamburg: F. Meiner, 1959), § 256.

57. Novalis, *NS*, vol. 2, p. 177.

58. Ibid., p. 179; cf. p. 247.

59. Ibid., pp. 247 ff.

60. Ibid., pp. 248 ff.

61. The decisive passages can be found in ibid., pp. 250 ff. But they are prepared by the doctrine of drives and striving, which first emerges in No. 32 ("On the Empirical I," pp. 126f.), from where on it runs like a leitmotiv through the developments of the oppositional pairs. Surely these reflections presuppose a reading of part 3 of the *Science of Knowledge*. But they radicalize Fichte's talk of "striving" in a manner that can no longer be reconciled with the notion of an ultimate justification from an evident principle.

62. Cf. Novalis, *NS*, vol. 2, p. 269: "Noteworthy Passages and Remarks on Reading the *Science of Knowledge*."

63. Thus Friedrich Schlegel, e.g., *KA*, vol. 12, p. 7; vol. 18, p. 418; cf. p. 420.

64. Novalis, *NS*, vol. 2, p. 269. Cf. pp. 268f.: "Golden Ages may appear—but they do not bring the end of things—the end of the human being is not the golden age—it is destined to exist forever, and be and remain a beautifully ordered individual."

65. Ibid., pp. 269 ff.

66. Ibid., p. 270.

67. Ibid.

68. Ibid.

69. Ibid., p. 252; cf. p. 254.

70. Ibid., p. 179.

71. Ibid., p. 255.

72. Kant, *Critique of Pure Reason*, B417 n.

73. Ibid., A358.

74. The English version of this essay is based on a translation by Günter Zöller.

6

Check or Checkmate? On the Finitude of the Fichtean Self

Daniel Breazeale

In commemoration of the bicentennial of the publication of the *Grundlage der gesamten Wissenschaftslehre* (1794/95).

"*Das Ich setzt sich selbst schlechthin*"—"The I posits itself absolutely." This is the proposition that stands at the head of Fichte's best-known and most influential work, the *Foundations of the Entire Wissenschaftslehre*, and for two hundred years readers have taken this to be not only the first but also the last word concerning the Fichtean theory of selfhood. Accordingly, this theory has been widely interpreted as a sort of grotesque narcissism: a theory that maintains that nothing is ultimately real but the absolute self, and that everything beyond the self is merely a reflection or creation of the latter, which, on the most charitable interpretation, constitutes for itself an external world as a sort of moral gymnasium—a sphere in which it can dutifully "work out" and where it can have something to "struggle against."

Readers who proceed beyond the first page of this same text often find themselves hard pressed to reconcile the preceding preconception with what they encounter later in this same work and are often perplexed by what appear to be appeals on Fichte's part to the necessary influence upon the I of something wholly alien and "Not-I." This is the doctrine of the *Anstoss*, a word customary rendered into English by translators of Fichte as "check." What is one to make of this appeal to an external "check" upon the striving of the I? Two options are particularly popular with interpreters. One is to explain the "check" in question as nothing more than a roundabout way in which the I surreptitiously "affects" itself (so that it can then go on to posit an external realm for its own moral endeavors).[1] The other popular option is to criticize the doctrine of the *Anstoss* as a pre-Critical or "dogmatic" remnant and thus as incompatible, strictly speaking, with Fichte's declared commitment to transcendental idealism and what is taken to be its "speculative spirit."[2]

In the remarks that follow I wish to explore a third option. I will begin by re-examining what Fichte actually says about the *Anstoss*, particularly in the *Grundlage der gesamten Wissenschaftslehre* (which is where most of the technical occurrences of this term are to be found), but also in other works of the Jena period, in order to determine the precise meaning and function of this doctrine within his early system. I will then employ the results of this reexamination as a basis for a revised interpretation of Fichte's overall theory of subjectivity. The picture of the self that will emerge from this reexamination bears little in common with the prevailing caricatures. The true "Fichtean self," I will argue, is always involved with finitude. It is not the sole author of its own being (though it nevertheless strives to be such), but is always an embodied and temporally conditioned, finite, individual knower and agent.

The Doctrine of the *Anstoss* in the 1794/95 *Wissenschaftslehre*

Let us begin with a question that is perhaps less simple than it at first seems: viz., what does the word "*Anstoss*" actually mean in German, or rather, what did it mean in late-eighteenth century German? A glance at Grimms' *Deutsches Wörterbuch* reveals that this is a term with quite a number of overlapping meanings, plus a number of eccentric and figurative senses as well. Nevertheless, two definitions are most important for our purposes: on the one hand, an *Anstoss* is an "obstacle" or "hindrance" (*Hindernis* or *Hemmung*); on the other, it is an "impulse," "impetus," or even "stimulus" (*Anlass, Impuls, Antrieb*, or *Anregung*). Grimm notes that this latter use was becoming more prevalent during the eighteenth century, and Pierre-Philippe Druet, in his pioneering study of the term, notes that it was a frequently used technical term in the rational mechanics of the period, where it often carried the sense of the "original impulse" that sets a physical system in motion.[3] If Fichte's use of the term *combines* both of these meanings, as is indeed the case, then future English translators of Fichte will have to find a better term for *Anstoss* than "check"—a word that captures but half of the meaning.

Let us now turn to the *Grundlage*, which is the first systematic presentation of the rudiments of Fichte's system, and see how the term that concerns us is employed there.[4] We first encounter the term *Anstoss* near the end of the second, "theoretical" part of the work, just before the famous "Deduction of Representation" with which part 2 concludes. The context is a discussion of whether an explanation of representation should be grounded in the pure activity of the I or in that of the Not-I (which is posited in the first principle of the Theoretical Part as "determining the limited I"). The conclusion of the truly tortuous deconstruction of various strategies for explaining representation, which occupies most of part 2, is that representation can be explained only as a product of the reciprocal "interchange" (*Wechsel*) between the I and the Not-I and only as grounded in a specific, determinate being (*Bestimmtsein*), which can be equally ascribed to either the I or the Not-I. Such a determinate interchange of activity and passivity simply has to be presupposed for the purposes of such an explanation and cannot be further explained by purely theoretical means. If one insists on asking where this particular determinacy comes from, Fichte can only refer him to part 3 of this same work, that is, to the "practical" portion of the *Grundlage*.[5] For the moment, however, let us tarry with Fichte in the theoretical part and concede that the presence for the I of some such determinate mixture of passivity and activity simply has to be presupposed if a transcendental account of theoretical experience (intuiting, conceptualizing, representing, cognizing, etc.) is to be possible at all.

Another way to describe the result of part 2 is to say that it succeeds in establishing the "mediacy of positing," i.e., the principle or law that the I can posit itself only in relationship to what is posited in opposition to the I, that is, only in relationship to a Not-I; and that the I can posit the Not-I only in relationship to an I.[6] Hence, if the I is to posit itself at all—which, according to the chief principle of the entire system, must be the case if the I is to be an I at all—then it can posit itself only as limited and standing in a relationship with something foreign to itself. The theoretical portion of the *Grundlage* establishes the important result that the I can posit itself only as a finite I and hence can *exist* (for itself) only as a finite self, but we still have not discovered the particular *Bestimmtsein* by virtue of which alone it is able to posit itself or anything else. All we can safely say at this point is that, if representational consciousness is to be possible at all, then it must contain an "objective" as well as a "subjective" element or moment, a moment of sheer determinacy or givenness: "Hence something or other [*etwas überhaupt*] must be present, something within which the active I traces a boundary delimiting what is subjective and consigns what remains to what is objective."[7]

Enter the *Anstoss*, which makes its appearance as the most abstract way of designating this "realistic" or "objective" moment of consciousness: the original presence to consciousness of *etwas überhaupt*. In order to provide the latter, it is not necessary to presuppose the *actual presence* within consciousness of this objective element itself; instead, writes Fichte:

> All that is needed, if I may so express myself, is the presence of an *Anstoss* for the I. That is to say, the subjective element [*das subjektive*] must, for

> some reason that simply lies outside of the activity of the I, be unable to extend any further. Such an impossibility of further extension would then constitute the indicated mere interplay or meshing; such an *Anstoss* would not limit the I as active, but would give it the task of limiting itself. All limitation, however, occurs through opposition, and thus, simply in order to be able to satisfy this task, the I would have to oppose something objective to the subjective element that is to be limited and would then have to unite both synthetically, in the manner just indicated. And thus the entire representation could be derived in this way. This manner of explanation is, as is immediately obvious, realistic, yet it is based upon a much more abstract form of realism than any of the other, previously discussed varieties of realism. What it assumes is not a Not-I that is present outside of the I, and not even a determination that is present within the I, but rather, the mere task, on the part of the I itself, of undertaking a determination within itself [*bloss die Aufgabe für eine durch dasselbe selbst in sich vorzunehmende Bestimmung*]—that is, *the mere determinability* of the I.[8]

Brief as it is, this passage is filled with information concerning the specific sense of the term *Anstoss* in the early *Wissenschaftslehre*, and it clearly anticipates several themes explored in more detail in part 3. Five points in particular are worthy of mention.

1. Note that Fichte himself, with the phrase "if I may so express myself," calls attention to the peculiar, indeed, *metaphorical* character of his use in this context of the term *Anstoss*. This should alert us to the fact that the best way to determine what the term means for Fichte is carefully to consider his actual use of it.

2. It is also clear that, whatever else it might be, the Fichtean *Anstoss* is indeed an *obstacle* or *hindrance*—a "check," if I may so express myself—to what is described here only as "the activity of the I," an activity that will be analyzed in considerable detail in part 3. Nevertheless, to the extent that it signifies "an impossibility of further extension," the *Anstoss* is *at least* a "check" on the I.

3. Though the *Anstoss* is admittedly a check upon the I, it does not follow from this that it is necessarily an *external* obstacle to the same. More explicitly, the *Anstoss* is not to be identified with any external object, nor—*pace* the claims of some incautious readers[9]—with the Not-I. All that we can say at present about this abstract remnant of objectivity is that it *functions* within the *Grundlage* as the ultimate real ground upon which all subsequent acts of positing the Not-I (and indeed, as we shall soon see, all subsequent acts of positing the I itself) are based.

Nor is the *Anstoss* to be identified with any particular determination actually present within the knowing I itself (the I qua intellect); instead, as

Fichte puts it, the *Anstoss* does not limit the intellect so much as it "gives it the task of limiting itself." As such, it presupposes and indeed "incites" the I's own capacity for self-determination—which Fichte (in the passage cited) refers to as "the determinability of the I." As we shall soon see, however, there is another sense in which the *Anstoss can* be described as a "determination" of the I—not of the knowing I, or intellect, but of the practically striving I.[10] For the mere intellect, the *Anstoss* is no more than an occasion for further positing.

Thus, even here, in its first technical occurrence, the term does not mean simply "obstacle" or "check" but also has the sense of something that provokes or impels the I to further actions of self-determination, that is, self-limitation. (In passing, it should be noted that the "self-determination" in question here need not be thought of as a *voluntary* action; on the contrary, as the "deduction of representation" quickly makes clear, what Fichte has in mind are those *spontaneous*, albeit rule-governed, acts through which the productive imagination reflects upon and reposits this original *Anstoss*, until finally it obtains to determinate consciousness as a fullyfledged sensible *Vorstellung*. The sense in which an *Anstoss* may indeed be an incentive for truly voluntary self-limitation will be touched upon later.)

4. Even this greatly attenuated "realism" would remain unacceptable on critical grounds were it not immediately synthesized with the fundamental ontological insight of idealism: namely, that all being is being for the I, and hence, that *Sein* = *Gesetztsein*. Accordingly, the *Anstoss* can serve neither as an obstacle nor as a stimulus for the intellect unless it is explicitly posited as such by the latter. Or, as Fichte puts it in a passage that occurs only a few lines after the one just cited: if the *Anstoss* is to assign the I a task, it must exist *for the I*, and thus it cannot be as independent of the I's activity as might at first have appeared. To suppose that the *Anstoss* could be present for the I without any contribution on the part of the I would open this account to all of the well-known objections plaguing any dogmatic attempt to leap from the "real" to the "ideal" series, from the realm of allegedly independent realities to that of consciousness thereof. Hence, if the *Anstoss* is to be a limit or a stimulus for the I, then there must be some sense in which it can be said to "occur as a result of the I's own self-positing." And indeed, this is the case: if the I did not constantly strive to extend itself it could not be *angestossen* in the relevant, Fichtean sense. If there were no outwardly striving activity of the I to be "reflected back into the I," then it is clear that no *Anstoss* could occur to the I, nor could there be any subsequent self-limitation of the I. In this sense, therefore—though only in this sense—the *Anstoss* does depend upon the I, since, as Fichte puts it:

> the *Anstoss* (which is not posited by the positing I) occurs to the I insofar as it is active, and is thus an *Anstoss* only insofar as the I is active. Its possibility is conditioned by the activity of the I: no activity of the I, no *Anstoss*. And *vice versa*: the I's activity of determining itself would, in turn, be conditioned by the *Anstoss*: no *Anstoss*, no self-determination. Moreover, no self-determination, nothing objective, etc.[11]

5. Finally, let us recall that even if the *Anstoss* represents a sort of "limit" or "check" upon the activity of the I, there is a clear sense in which the I must transcend this "limit" even as it encounters and responds to it. The fact that the *Anstoss* must be such *for* the I implies more than that the I must be active in order for its activity to encounter resistance;[12] it also implies that the I must contain another sort of (purely intellectual) activity, thanks to which it can posit for itself its own limitation. Indeed, this is precisely what distinguishes the self-conscious and self-posited limits of a finite self from the determinate, natural limits of a mindless object, and it is why an *Anstoss* can occur only to the former.

Upon the occurrence of the *Anstoss*, the I is supposed to posit the boundary between itself and the Not-I; i.e., the positing I is itself one of the two elements involved in this very interchange, and it is supposed to posit itself as the positing subject therein. As Fichte points out, moreover, such self-positing is possible only if the activity of the I is not entirely canceled by the *Anstoss*, for in that case it would not be able to distinguish this "externally imposed" limit from what might otherwise simply be the essential limits of its own nature. Put differently, if the I were *only* finite, then it would not be able to posit itself *as* an I—even as a finite I.[13] Consequently, the very concept of an I that posits for itself the occurrence of an *Anstoss*—that is, the concept of a subject conscious of its own finitude—implies that one and the same I must be simultaneously limited (with respect to the sheer occurrence of the *Anstoss*) and unlimited (with respect to the necessary positing thereof), or, in Fichte's somewhat hyperbolic language, finite and infinite at one and the same time.

The final result of Fichte's reflections upon the *Anstoss* (at least with respect to the theoretical capacities of the mind) is thus that the I cannot be infinite for itself without limiting itself and cannot limit itself unless it is also infinite.[14] The name for the remarkable power by virtue of which the I is able to accomplish this process of *Schweben*[15] between opposites is, of course, "productive imagination." Only by virtue of the productive imagination are we able to reconcile the infinity of the freely positing subject with the determinacy of the *Anstoss*. Part 2 of the *Grundlage* thus concludes with a deduction of an "original fact"[16] that must be present within the human mind (namely, the *Anstoss*), as well as with the deduction of a primordial "power" of productive imagination.

Important questions, however, still remain unanswered. Even if Fichte has succeeding in demonstrating the *necessity* of the *Anstoss* for the possibility of any consciousness, whether of "external objects" or of oneself, more remains to be said concerning precisely *how* such a determinate "check" or "impulse" presents itself to the I and concerning the sort of evidence that can be cited in support of the claim that such an *Anstoss* actually *does* occur. These questions are directly answered in the third, "practical" part of the *Grundlage*.[17]

Granted that the I itself, through its own spontaneous power, determines the precise mode and manner of its representations, it is nevertheless unable to produce representations on its own but is here dependent upon something beyond its control: namely, the *Anstoss*.[18] A further explication of the occurrence of such a "check" upon the infinitely outreaching activity of the I and of the manner in which this same occurrence serves as an "impetus" to the theoretical (or "objective") activity of the I would therefore require a detailed investigation of the various "activities" of the I and hence a theory of the drives and will of the same—which is precisely what Fichte provides in part 3.

Without even attempting to summarize the complex analysis of the I's activities that occupies such a large portion of part 3, one must still mention the remarkable manner in which Fichte's analysis of the practical powers of the I transforms the "external contradiction" between the activities of the I and the Not-I into a purely "internal" contradiction between the "infinite" and "finite" activities of the I itself. Indeed, the most noteworthy result of the practical part of the *Grundlage* is surely its convincing demonstration of the necessarily *divided* character of the self and its closely associated transformation of the "unity of consciousness" from a "simply posited" first principle into a practically demanded, albeit forever unachievable, *goal* of human striving.

In the course of this analysis of the practical powers of the I, we see how the two activities of the self discussed in part 2—namely, the infinite (self-reverting or "simply self-positing") activity of the I and its finite ("objective" or "representing") activity—presuppose an equally fundamental "practical" striving on the part of the I. Indeed, these two activities of the self presuppose an indeterminate striving to "fill out infinity," to overcome all external and internal hindrances, and to make itself totally independent of the same—in the words of the first principle of the practical portion of the *Grundlage*, to "determine the Not-I." It is this infinite, practical striving of the I that is particularly relevant to our present concern, since this is the activity that is "checked" by the occurrence of the *Anstoss*.

It must be emphasized that without the *Anstoss* not only would the I be unable to posit any objects at all (and hence would lack any consciousness whatsoever), but it would also be unable to posit itself—*and hence would not be an I at all.* Since there is some confusion on this point, and since Fichte states his own position quite unambiguously early in part 3, it is perhaps worth restating it: in order for the I to be an I at all it must not only "posit itself," but it must explicitly posit itself *for itself*—that is, it must posit itself "as self-positing." Thus it is simply not true, as Dieter Henrich has maintained, that the latter claim is not contained in the *Grundlage* and is instead developed only in the *Wissenschaftslehre nova methodo* and published only in the first chapter of the *Versuch einer neuen Darstellung der Wissenschaftslehre*.[19]

This point is of considerably more than pedantic interest, since it bears crucially upon the role of the *Anstoss* in the 1794/95 presentation. Because the I must posit itself for itself as self-positing, because all such explicit positing occurs according to what has been described above as "the law of the mediacy of positing," and because such reciprocal positing of the finite subject and finite object is possible only if an *Anstoss* actually occurs, the I, as such, is just as dependent upon the *Anstoss* as is the *Anstoss* upon the free self-assertion of the I. To be sure, the I must possess within itself a tendency to reflect upon and to posit itself, but it is quite unable to realize this tendency unless, as Fichte puts it, "there emerges within the I itself a disparity and thus something foreign."[20]

Thus *all* positing, whether of the I itself or of the Not-I, must presuppose and start with the positing of something that is "purely subjective" (since otherwise we would once again run aground on the reef of dogmatism) and, at the same time, is not produced by the activity of the I (since the I cannot "simply posit" its own limitations). The "something" in question, which has previously been designated by the abstract term "*Anstoss*"—a term that calls attention merely to a certain formal feature of theoretical consciousness—now receives a new name, one that calls attention to the actual *content* of the same, that is, to *what* we actually experience in the *Anstoss*.[21] This new name is *Gefühl*, or "feeling," which is nothing more nor less than the familiar name for that "original fact," which must be present to the human mind if any experience at all—and hence any self at all—is to be possible.

Feelings satisfy the two requirements mentioned above: they are subjective states of the I (and in this sense, all feelings are, at least originally, "*Selbstgefühle*"[22]) and they possess a determinacy that is not freely determined by the activity of the I. Hence they can also exercise the dual functions we have found to be essential to the *Anstoss*. First of all, feelings serve to *constrain* or to *check* the free, outward striving, practical activity of the I. Indeed, from the purely practical standpoint, this is the primary content of all feeling. Fichte asks, What does the I really "feel" when it "feels itself"? He replies that "the I feels itself to be limited; it is *limited for itself.*" All self-feeling (and hence, all feeling whatsoever) is, in the first instance, a feeling of limitation and constraint—of the I's own inability or *Nichtkönnen.*[23] Secondly, these same feelings serve to *stimulate* or to *set in motion* the objective, theoretical activity of the I. In that context they serve as the "original impetus," or "prime mover,"[24] as it were, for the reiterated acts of positing through which the intellect constitutes for itself a material, spatiotemporal world, at the same time that the I constitutes itself as a finite, embodied agent within this same world.[25]

It is a fundamental thesis of the Jena *Wissenschaftslehre* that all reality is posited reality and thus that reality is a "derived" category, itself based upon the prior activity of the I. Unfortunately, a corollary of Fichte's painstaking analysis of how such reality is "posited" by the I is less often noticed: viz., that such reality can be posited only in consequence of the occurrence of an *Anstoss*; that is, only if the requisite "feeling" is originally present within the mind (and is present as a determination not determined by the I) can the subject then proceed to "explain" this feeling to itself by positing some "reality" as the ground thereof. Thus, the familiar thesis that all reality is grounded in the free activity of the I must be supplemented by the insight, cryptically expressed in a note to the preface to the second edition of *Über den Begriff der Wissenschaftslehre*: whereas things are represented only as appearances, they are *"felt as things in themselves."*[26] This, of course, does not mean that we somehow "feel" independently existing things in themselves, but rather that the ultimate basis of our positing a realm of independent reality is precisely the presence within the I itself of a kind of determinacy for which the I is simply unable to hold itself responsible: namely, feelings.

Fichtean idealism must constantly be balanced by Fichtean realism, the core of which is precisely this same practical doctrine of feeling.[27] To be sure, we are no more conscious of such immediate "feelings" than we are conscious of the immediate unity of subject and object expressed in the *Tathandlung* with which we began our analysis. Both of these become objects of thetic consciousness only within philosophy, where they are abstracted from the full, rich context of lived experience, to which each makes an equally essential—if not equal—contribution.[28] Nevertheless, we can, through transcendental analysis of the sort exemplified by the *Grundlage*, easily convince ourselves that some such *Anstoss* or "original fact" is essential for the possibility of ordinary consciousness.

Philosophy itself, however, is no more able to demonstrate the *actual occurrence* of the *Anstoss* than it is able to prove the reality of freedom. From the standpoint of transcendental philosophy, both freedom and the occurrence of the *Anstoss* are simply presuppositions taken over from everyday life—within which alone they can be "demonstrated." The only proper response to anyone who wishes to challenge the reality of the *Anstoss* is not to urge him to read more philosophy, but rather to refer him to the testimony of his own inner experience.[29]

Anstoss and *Aufforderung* in the Later Jena *Wissenschaftslehre*

Before turning to a brief consideration of some of the more important implications of the doctrine of the *Anstoss* for Fichte's overall account of subjectivity, some mention, however cursory, must be made of a significant ambiguity in the use of this term in the 1794/95 presentation and of the problematic relationship of the same to the later, revised version of the Jena *Wissenschaftslehre*. In the *Grundlage* the doctrine of the *Anstoss* is presented at the greatest possible level of abstraction. All that we can say about the actual *content* of the *Anstoss* is that it is supposed to be identified with "feeling." But what *sorts* of feelings are actually capable of exercising upon the I the essential "checking" and "stimulating" roles assigned by Fichte to the *Anstoss*?

The most obvious answer to this question is: sense-impressions, that is, feelings or sensations such as "sweet," "hot," or "blue." And indeed, Fichte cites just such examples, both in the *Grundlage*, and in his 1795 elaboration of the "distinctive character of the *Wissenschaftslehre* with respect to the theoretical power."[30] He repeats this in his discussions of "feeling" qua "original limitation" of the I in the *Wissenschaftslehre nova methodo* and in the *Versuch einer neuen Darstellung* (where, incidentally, the term *Anstoss* does not occur at all, though the role of "original feeling" in the self-constitution of the I is explicitly reaffirmed, as is the necessity of a transcendentally underivable "original limitation of the I").[31]

Nevertheless, in Fichte's writings and lectures after 1795 it becomes increasingly apparent that, in addition to and alongside sensible qualia, there are present to the I immediate feelings of a radically different sort, feelings even better suited to the role assigned to the *Anstoss* in the *Grundlage*: our immediate feeling or sense of the freedom of others and of our own moral obligation to act in a manner that takes this freedom of others into account. Fichte's understanding of intersubjectivity, and especially of the evidence for the existence of other free, rational beings like ourselves, underwent a dramatic development between 1794 and 1796, when he published the first part of his *Grundlage des Naturrechts*, which commences with a justly famous demonstration that the very possibility of self-consciousness depends upon one's consciousness of oneself as an individual, which in turn depends upon one's free recognition of other free individuals—a recognition accomplished and signaled by voluntary self-limitation of one's own freedom out of respect for the freedom of others.

This new appreciation on Fichte's part of the role of mutual recognition in the constitution of consciousness had significant repercussions for the new presentation of the basic principles of the *Wissenschaftslehre* that he began expounding in his lectures on *Wissenschaftslehre nova methodo* and elsewhere. In this new presentation, as in the *Grundlage des Naturrechts*, it is clear that not only must the I contain within itself those "original limitations" that we have described above as sensible feelings, but it must also contain within itself an immediate awareness—a "feeling," if you will—of the freedom of other finite, rational beings. Such an immediate awareness is described by Fichte as an *Aufforderung*, a consciousness of being *externally summoned* to exercise one's freedom—more specifically, to exercise it through voluntarily *limiting* it.

This is not the occasion to explore Fichte's extraordinarily interesting account of intersubjectivity and of the role of the *Aufforderung* therein. However, no discussion of the *Anstoss* can completely ignore the intimate relationship between *Anstoss* and *Aufforderung*, especially in the post-1795 writings. This connection is emphasized by Fichte himself in a passage in § 3 of the *Naturrecht*, where he explicitly identifies the *Aufforderung* as a kind of *Anstoss*.[32]

Though some distinguished readers of Fichte, including Alexis Philonenko, have claimed to find this doctrine of the *Aufforderung* already present with the *Grundlage* itself,[33] my own view is that, while nothing in the *Grundlage* is inconsistent with such an interpretation of the *Anstoss*, this is nevertheless not what Fichte had specifically in mind in the 1794/95 presentation, though it is certainly present in the version of 1796/99. Though I cannot, on this occasion, provide any evidence for my own interpretation, I nevertheless maintain that in the revised Jena *Wissenschaftslehre* (the *Wissenschaftslehre nova methodo* and *System der Sittenlehre*) there are not one but two different types of *Anstoss* present to consciousness:[34] the original "system of feeling," thanks to which the I posits for itself an external, phenomenal world and posits itself as an internally and externally limited agent therein; and an immediately felt but non-sensible "summons" to exercise one's own freedom and to do so in a manner that respects and recognizes the freedom of others, thereby affirming one's place in the supersensible or noumenal realm—again, not as an "absolute I," but as a limited (in this case, to be sure, a "freely limited") individual. And, indeed, depending upon how one interprets Fichte's *Sittenlehre*, with its claim that the pure will has an original (moral) determinacy of its own, one might even cite this as a third type of *Anstoss*, inasmuch as such original determinacy both sets limits to the empirical willing of an individual moral agent and impels or stimulates that same agent to will morally in the first place.

Such suggestions certainly raise a number of important questions—concerning, for example, the precise relationship between the various sorts of *Anstoss*[35] or concerning the relationship between the phenomenal and noumenal realms or between "belief" and "knowledge"—not to mention a serious metaquestion concerning the possibility of satisfactorily answering such questions within the framework of the Jena *Wissenschaftslehre*. All such questions, however, must be postponed for some future time. All I wish to suggest on this occasion is that the doctrine of the *Aufforderung* by no means mitigates but merely reinforces the most important result of our detailed examination of the doctrine of the *Anstoss* as presented in the *Grundlage*: viz., the necessary finitude of all subjectivity and the unavoidable element of contingency—"facticity," if you will—at the heart of the Fichtean self.

The Finite Fichtean Self

1. The I can be an I only if it is limited and, moreover, only if it is limited for itself. An I that cannot posit (that is, reflect upon) itself is not an I at all. The I, however, can reflect upon itself only insofar as it reflects upon itself as a determinate object, and it can reflect upon itself as a determinate object only insofar as it relates itself to and indeed finds itself to be a part of a world of material objects related to one another in space and time. At the same time that the I posits itself as finite and determinate, it finds itself dissatisfied with this very determinacy and finitude, which conflicts with the I's own awareness of its own indeterminacy and "infinity"—an awareness present within ordinary consciousness not as any sort of philosophical thesis, but rather as a vague sense of "longing" to overcome the limits just posited, coupled with a categorical awareness of one's obligation to overcome those very limits and to determine rather than be determined by the facticity of the self and the world.

2. All of the above features of selfhood are ultimately dependent upon something beyond the control of the self; or rather, they are all dependent upon the presence, *within the I itself,* of an original determinacy that is not determined by the I's freedom but simply "is." This determinacy, which some later philosophers have described as the "facticity" of the I, is, I believe, precisely what Fichte means by the term *Anstoss*.

In the context of Fichte's transcendental idealism, however, the facticity of the I represents much more than a mere "check" or "limit" upon the pretension and projects of the I's practical striving—though, to be sure, it does represent this. Just as important, the *Anstoss* provides the essential occasion or "spark," without which neither the theoretical nor the practical activity of the I could be engaged and thus without which there could be no I at all.

To underscore a point already mentioned several times, the *Anstoss* is in no sense a "fact about the world" nor does it represent the effect upon the I of some external "thing in itself." If it is a "fact," it is, as Fichte puts it, a fact (*Factum*) about the mind itself, about the I, and not about the Not-I. Of course, as Fichte shows, it is also true that the intellect necessarily posits a Not-I in order to explain to itself this same "original fact"—and it does this in the same act in which it first consciously posits itself. Hence both I and Not-I are equally dependent upon the *Anstoss*, just as they are equally dependent upon the freedom and spontaneity of the self.

What this means for Fichte's philosophy in general and for his theory of the I in particular is that consciousness possesses an essential *openness* to the world. The task of somehow bridging the gap between the conscious self and the objective world is simply not a problem that can arise within the context of the *Wissenschaftslehre*, which considers the synthetic link between self and world, freedom and *Anstoss*, to be a fundamental condition for the very possibility of self-consciousness. This feature of Fichte's philosophy has, I believe, been widely neglected and has led to the quite unjustified dismissal of Fichte as some sort of "absolute solipsist." The truth, however, is precisely the opposite. The Fichtean self is a self that is always and inevitably *engaged* in a realm that it, to be sure, helps constitute as an object but which always escapes and eludes its ultimate control. In Fichte's words, "the I is supposed to encounter *within itself* something foreign, which must be encountered therein." Thus, "if any difference is ever to enter into the I, difference must already be originally present within the I itself; and indeed, this difference must be grounded in the absolute I as such."[36]

One of the few readers of Fichte to appreciate and to call attention to this aspect of his theory is Jean Hyppolite, who praises Fichte's philosophy precisely for its ability to answer the question "how is encounter possible?" without resorting to any sort of transcendent leap beyond the limits of consciousness. Like the self it describes, the Jena *Wissenschaftslehre* is a system that remains forever open to the "infinite richness of experience."[37] This is, at the same time, why the doctrine of the *Anstoss*, far from being some sort of dogmatic residue of dualism or vestige of the "reflective model of consciousness,"[38] is in fact absolutely central, not just to the *Grundlage*, but—under the name "feeling"—to the entire Jena *Wissenschaftslehre*.

Hegel, perhaps, can get along without an *Anstoss*, but not Fichte—indeed, this points to one of the central differences between transcendental idealism and speculative or absolute idealism. The former acknowledges the presence, within the I itself, of a realm of irreducible otherness, of absolute contingency and incomprehensibility. To be sure, we can, according to Fichte, explain a great deal about the world and ourselves through a combination of empirical research and transcendental analysis. But the question, Why does the empirical world have the experiential properties that it does?—i.e., Why does the I, and hence the world, possess the original determinacy that it possesses?—is a question that has no answer, and certainly no philosophical one.[39] Ultimately, not just Angelus Selesius's rose, but every *Anstoss* whatsoever *ist ohne Warum* (is "without a why"). Fichte's clear recognition of this point explains what I take to be the attractive *modesty* and *circumspection* of his project—at least in comparison with certain other philosophical projects of his era.

This is the point of Fichte's repeated insistence that, though philosophy can indeed derive the necessity of the *Anstoss* for the possibility of consciousness, it is utterly unable to derive or to demonstrate either the *actuality* or the *specific content* of the same.[40] Instead, the *Wissenschaftslehre* seeks to reconcile us to "the incomprehensible boundaries within which we simply find ourselves to be confined" by demonstrating that only *within* such boundaries can we possess either theoretical consciousness or practical freedom.[41] As for the boundaries themselves—facticity and freedom—whether we follow Fichte in employing abstract, figurative names like "*Anstoss*" and "*Tathandlung*" or, following Kant, prefer metonymies such as "the starry heavens above" and "the moral law within," the search for a ground, and hence all philosophical explanation, comes to an end at just these two extremes. And thus philosophy concludes with a reassertion of the "wonder" with which it so famously begins. The most that philosophy can do by way of "explaining" either is to show that each is presupposed as a condition for the possibility of the other. This is Fichte's most genuinely "original insight."

3. By now it should be clear that Fichte remains a dualist, albeit of a peculiar sort.[42] His dualism is not that of I and Not-I but is instead a dualism of finite and infinite activities of one and the same I. And just as his philosophy is ultimately dualistic, so is the self that it describes: the Fichtean self is a profoundly divided self. For Fichte, difference is not merely the opposite of identity: it is the condition for its possibility. The undifferentiated unity of consciousness—the congruence of the I with its own practical self-conception—can never be more than an infinite goal. Meanwhile, actual consciousness and self-consciousness remain, to adopt a familiar Hegelian expression, a "unity of identity and difference."

Just as Fichte explicitly recognized the reciprocal relationship between identity and difference, he also viewed the quest for unity—and hence the fact of contradiction—to be the moving force not only of systematic philosophy, but, more important, of both theoretical self-consciousness and practical self-activity. For this reason the "real-idealism" of the Jena *Wissenschaftslehre* might also be described as a *dialectical dualism*.[43]

This indeed is one of the main reasons why Fichte's conception of the self has proven so difficult to grasp. For self-consciousness is portrayed in this philosophy as a dynamic, unstable, and unending synthetic *process*, each moment of which refers us to every other moment. Thus, though we begin, as we are obliged to do for essentially practical reasons, with the assertion of the sheer freedom of the I, this freedom is no sooner posited than it becomes conditioned by something else—until ultimately it is revealed to be conditioned by a *Bestimmtsein*, an involuntary *Anstoss*, that would appear to be the very opposite of freedom. Fichte's point, however, is that it is precisely within the dynamic field produced by the tension between these "opposites" that all life and consciousness, all acting and knowing—in short, everything that pertains to what Fichte sometimes called the "circle of the functions of the I" ("*Kreislauf der Funktionen des Ich*")[44]—become possible.

In the technical language of the *Grundlage*, neither *Tathandlung* nor *Anstoss* can be reduced to the other, and thus neither can be "accounted for" in the transcendental sense of being "derived" from something higher. On the other hand, the *necessity* of each can be derived from the positing of the other. If I am to be free, then I must be a finite part of the natural world; if there is to be a world for me, then I must be free. Fichte often called attention to what he described as the "original duality" of the self and indeed concluded the *Grundlage* with an eloquent description of this same duality, there characterizing it as "the duality of striving and reflection" and noting that "the one is a necessary consequence of the other and the relationship between them is a reciprocal one."[45] Struggle as we may—and must—this original conflict within the self can never be eliminated, for the simple reason that the conflict itself is the condition for the very possibility of the self.[46]

In an early letter to Niethammer, Fichte expressed his belief that "pure philosophy is acquainted with only a *single* I, and this one I ought not to contradict itself."[47] Unfortunately—or rather, fortunately!—however, it always does. And, as Fichte came to see with greater and greater clarity, the I always *must* contradict itself, however much it may—and indeed *must*—struggle endlessly to overcome its own self-contradiction. In the end, the unity of the self is a necessary, infinite Idea of reason—nothing less, but also nothing more. Like the Sartrean "original project" of "striving to be God," which it so clearly anticipates, the original striving of the I is a striving after a self-contradictory goal.[48]

The answer to the question posed in my title has long since been clear: the *Anstoss* is indeed a "check" upon the original striving of the I to posit itself as comprising all reality, and as such it represents a *boundary* or a *limit* to the practical activity of the I. Yet it certainly represents no "checkmate" upon either the theoretical or the practical activities of the I. On the contrary, it is, as we have seen, the "prime mover," which stimulates and sets in motion the cognizing activity of the intellect and makes possible the practical striving to overcome this same limitation. Without such an "original impetus," which is originally not posited by the I, no activity of the I could be possible at all, and without activity there would be no self at all. To be sure, the self that becomes possible in this way is a self that remains radically open to and constrained by a realm beyond its own devising—a realm both of material things and of other rational individuals. Yet it is by no means wholly determined by its relationship to its other, but it constantly affirms and demonstrates its relative independence thereof as a freely self-determining practical agent—which is precisely what it means to be a "finite self."[49]

Notes

1. See, e.g., Emile Bréhier, *The History of Philosophy*, vol. 6, *The Nineteenth Century: Period of Systems 1800–1850*, trans. W. Baskin (Chicago: University of Chicago Press, 1968 [orig. French ed. 1932]), p. 118, where Bréhier, in line with his overall interpretation of Fichte's "absolute moralism," interprets the *Anstoss* as a mere self-limitation of the I, posited by the absolute I so that it will have something to test itself against. Thus, according to Bréhier, Fichte "deduces existence itself and the characteristics of nature from this very exigency [of acting in accord with duty]—like an ascetic who brings about a situation which will put him to the test and lead him to perfection."

2. See, e.g., Dieter Henrich, *Fichtes ursprüngliche Einsicht* (Frankfurt: Klostermann, 1967), p. 41; translated as "Fichte's Original Insight," in *Contemporary German Philosophy*, vol. 1 (University Park, Pa: Pennsylvania State University Press, 1982), pp. 15–53.

3. Pierre-Philippe Druet, "L'Anstoss' fichtéen: essai d'élucidation d'une métaphore," *Revue philosophique de Louvain* 70 (1972), pp. 384–92. To be sure, Druet notes that the term *Stoss* is more common in such contexts, though *Anstoss* is sometimes used as well, especially in contexts where the emphasis is upon the "originary" character of the force in question. "L'*An-stoss* est donc le choc premier qui met un système en mouvement: il est, pourrait-on dire, la création conçue méchaniquement." (p. 390) Druet thus maintains that the particle "*An*-" here has

much the same meaning as "*Ur-*" and asserts that Fichte, who used both *Stoss* and *Anstoss*, distinguished them in precisely this manner. In any case, it is clear that, for Fichte, the term *Anstoss* has a broader and more figurative meaning than the term *Stoss*.

4. Of course, there are passages in Fichte's writings where the term *Anstoss* is employed in a thoroughly unproblematic and nontechnical manner. Here, however, we will be concerned only with those usages that cast possible light upon Fichte's theory of the I. (According to Druet's study, the term occurs a total of 32 times in the I. H. Fichte edition of Fichte's writings, and most of these occurrences are indeed to be found in the *Grundlage*.) Fichte's writings are cited here according to the Critical Edition edited by Reinhard Lauth and Hans Gliwitzky, *J. G Fichte—Gesamtausgabe der Bayerischen Akademie der Wissenschaften* (Stuttgart-Bad Cannstatt: Frommann, 1964), abbreviated as *GA* and cited by series, volume, and page number. For the convenience of readers without access to *GA*, reference is also provided, wherever possible, to the edition of Fichte's writings edited by his son, I. H. Fichte, *Johann Gottlieb Fichtes sämmtliche Werke* (Berlin: Viet, 1845–46), abbreviated as *SW* and cited by volume and page number.

5. "Critical idealism, which governs our theory [that is, the "theoretical" portion of the *Grundlage*], has now been definitely established. It proceeds dogmatically against both dogmatic idealism and dogmatic realism in that it proves both that the mere activity of the I is not the ground of the reality of the Not-I and that the mere activity of the Not-I is not the ground of the passivity in the I. But the theoretical portion has still not answered the question, What grounds this presupposed interchange of activity and passivity in the I and the Not-I? And, with respect to this question, it confesses its ignorance and shows that the investigation of this question lies beyond the limits of theory. In explaining representation, the theoretical portion of the *Wissenschaftslehre* proceeds neither from an absolute activity of the I nor from an absolute activity of the Not-I, but rather, from a determinate being which is at the same time an act of determining, because nothing else is or can be immediately contained in consciousness. What might in turn determine this determination remains completely undecided within the theory, and it is this incompleteness which drives us beyond the theoretical into the practical portion of the *Wissenschaftslehre*" (Fichte, *GA*, vol. I/2, p. 328; *SW*, vol. 1, p. 178).

6. "The *mediacy* of positing (or, as will subsequently appear, the law of consciousness: *no subject, no object; no object, no subject*) is all that grounds the essential opposition between the I and the Not-I" (Fichte, *GA*, vol. I/2, pp. 332–33; *SW*, vol. 1, p. 183).

7. "Hence something must as such be present, wherein the active I traces out a boundary for the subject and consigns the remainder to the objective" (Fichte, *GA*, vol. I/2, pp. 351–52; *SW*, vol. 1, p. 206).

8. Fichte, *GA*, vol. I/2, pp. 354–55; *SW*, vol. 1, pp. 210–11.

9. See, e.g., George J. Seidel, *Fichte's Wissenschaftslehre of 1794: A Commentary on Part I* (West Lafayette, Ind.: Purdue University Press, 1993), p. 81: "This opposited non-self becomes Fichte's *Anstoss*."

The essential *difference* between the Not-I and the *Anstoss* (here identified as "feeling") is underlined in Fichte's *Grundriss des Eigenthümlichen der Wissenschaftslehre* (*GA*, vol. I/3, pp. 174–75; *SW*, vol. 1, p. 369): "Feeling is the most primordial interaction of the I with itself, and even precedes the Not-I, since of course a Not-I must be posited to explain feeling."

10. This indicates the inconvenience of the division of the *Grundlage* into a "theoretical" and a "practical" part. All too often, the natural development of the argument is impeded by this artificial division, which is precisely why Fichte dispensed with it in the 1796/99 presentation of the first principles of his system (in the so-called *Wissenschaftslehre nova methodo*). Even in the *Grundlage* itself he was occasionally forced to interject "practical" points into his presentation of the "theoretical" portion of the same—as, for example, at *GA*, vol. I/2, p. 355; *SW*, vol. 1, p. 211, where, in order to explain the sense in which the *Anstoss* is not a "determination" of the I, he has to look ahead to the subsequent identification of the *Anstoss* with "feeling" so he can explain that, "to be sure, a feeling is a determination of the I, but not of the I as intellect, that is, of the I that posits itself as determined by the Not-I, which is the only I we are here concerned with. Thus this task of determination is not the determination itself."

11. Fichte, *GA*, vol. 1/2, p. 356; *SW*, vol. 1, p. 212.

12. On "resistance" (*Widerstand*) as a synonym for *Anstoss*, see Fichte, *GA*, vol. I/2, p. 358; *SW*, vol. 1, p. 214. See also *Das System der Sittenlehre*, § 6: "The I can be posited only in opposition to a Not-I. But a Not-I exists for the I only if the latter acts efficatiously [*wirke*] and feels resistance in the course of its acting—a resistance that must nevertheless be overcome, since otherwise the I would not act at all. Only by means of this resistance does the I's activity become something sensible which endures through time; otherwise, it would be an activity outside of time—something that is for us quite unthinkable" (*GA*, vol. I/5, pp. 94–95; *SW*, vol. 4, p. 91).

13. "The conjoining [*Zusammenfassen*] or, as we can now call it more definitely, the positing of a boundary, is conditioned by a clash [*Zusammentreffen*]; or, since, according to what was said above, that which actively posits this boundary must itself—simply *as* active—be one of the clashing elements, it is conditioned by an *Anstoss* that occurs to the activity of this subject that posits the boundary. And this is possible only on the condition that the activity of this subject extends into the realm of what is unlimited, undetermined, and undeterminable, i.e, into the realm of the infinite. If this activity did not extend to infinity then it would by no

means follow from its being limited that any *Anstoss* would have occurred to its activity. The boundary in question could well be a boundary posited through its own sheer concept (which is what must be assumed within a system that simply posits a finite I)" (Fichte, *GA*, vol. I/2, p. 357; *SW*, vol. 1, p. 213).

14. "*No infinity, no limitation; no limitation, no infinity. Infinity and limitation are united in one and the same synthetic element*. If the activity of the I did not extend into infinity it could not itself limit its own activity, it could not posit any boundary of the same, which it is nevertheless supposed to do. The activity of the I consists in unlimited self-positing. Against this there occurs some resistance. If it yielded to this resistance, then the activity lying beyond the boundary of this resistance would be completely annihilated and canceled, and, to this extent, the I would not posit at all. Yet the I is nevertheless supposed to posit beyond this line. It is supposed to limit itself, i.e., it is to this extent supposed to posit itself as not positing itself; it must posit within this sphere the indeterminate, unlimited, infinite boundary . . . , and if it is to do this it must be infinite. Furthermore, if the I did not limit itself it would not be infinite. The I is only what it posits itself to be. To say that it is infinite means that it posits itself as infinite, it *determines* itself through the predicate of infinity: thus, it limits itself (the I) as the substrate of infinity. It distinguishes itself from its infinite activity (which is also in itself and is one and same with this substrate), this is how it must proceed if the I is to be infinite" (Fichte, *GA*, vol. I/2, p. 358; *SW*, vol. 1, pp. 214–15).

15. Usually translated as "to hover" or "to oscillate," *schweben* is another of Fichte's highly figurative technical terms and, like *Anstoss*, deserves more scrutiny than it has hitherto received.

16. "*ein ursprünglich in unserm Geiste vorkommendes Faktum*" (Fichte, *GA*, vol. I/2, p. 362; *SW*, vol. 1, p. 219).

17. "An I that posits itself *as* self-positing, i.e., a *subject*, is impossible without an object produced in the manner described (viz.: the determination of the I, its reflection upon itself as a determinate I, is possible only insofar as it limits itself by an opposite).—The sole question that cannot be answered is how and by what means the *Anstoss* that has to be assumed in order to explain representation occurs to the I, for this is a question that lies beyond the limits of the theoretical portion of the *Wissenschaftslehre*" (Fichte, *GA*, vol. I/2, pp. 361–62; *SW*, vol. 1, p. 218).

18. "To be sure, the I itself determines the *mode* and *manner* of representing as such, but *that* the I should engage in representing at all is, as we have seen, something that is determined not by the I, but by something outside of it. For we could in no way think representation to be possible at all, except on the assumption that an *Anstoss* occurs to an undetermined and infinitely outreaching activity of the I" (Fichte, *GA*, vol. I/2, pp. 386–87; *SW*, vol. 1, p. 248).

19. See Henrich, *Fichtes ursprüngliche Einsicht*, pp. 21 ff. To be sure, there are many respects in which the 1796/99 presentation represents an important advance upon the 1794/95 presentation; this, however, is simply not one of them.

20. "Es thut in ihm sich eine Ungleichheit, und darum etwas fremdartiges hervor" (Fichte, *GA*, vol. I/2, p. 400; *SW*, vol. 1, p. 265). For the explicit claim that the I must posit itself *as* the positing subject, see *GA*, vol. I/2, p. 399; *SW*, vol. 1, p. 264, as well as *GA*, vol. I/2, p. 406; *SW*, vol. 1, p. 274: "The I is supposed to posit itself, not merely for some intellect outside the I, instead, it is supposed to posit itself *for itself*; it is supposed to posit itself *as* posited by itself. Accordingly, just as surely as the I is an I at all, it must possess the principle of life and of consciousness purely within itself. And thus, just as surely as it is an I, it must contain within itself, unconditionally and without any ground, the principle that it must reflect upon itself."

To employ the technical language of part 3, though the I, by virtue of its very nature, always strives to reflect upon itself, it cannot do so unless it is able to distinguish its "centripetal" from its "centrifugal" activity, which, in turn, it is unable to do unless "the infinitely outreaching activity of the I is checked [*angestossen*] at some point or another and driven back into itself" (*GA*, vol. I/2, p. 408; *SW*, vol. 1, p. 276). "The I contains within itself a constant tendency to reflect upon itself as soon as the condition of all reflection—viz., a limitation—is present [*eintritt*]" (*GA*, vol. 1/2, p. 430). This same point is restated in the *Grundriss*: "The I cannot reflect without being limited, but it cannot limit itself" (*GA*, vol. I/3, p. 169; *SW*, vol. 1, p. 362).

21. "In the theoretical part of the *Wissenschaftslehre* we dealt solely with *the act of cognizing* [*das Erkennen*]; here [in the practical part] we are dealing with *what is cognized* [*das Erkannte*]. There the question was, *how* is something posited, intuited, thought, etc.? Here the question is, *what* is posited? Thus if the *Wissenschaftslehre* were to possess a metaphysics, as an alleged science of things in themselves, and were such a metaphysics demanded of it, then it would have to refer to the practical portion of the system. As will become increasingly apparent, it is this practical part alone that speaks of an original reality" (Fichte, *GA*, vol. I/2, p. 416; *SW*, vol. 1, pp. 285–86).

22. "Feeling is entirely *subjective*. For an *explanation* of feeling, which is an act of theorizing, we certainly require *something that limits*. This, however, is not required for a *deduction* of feeling insofar as it is supposed to be present within the I" (Fichte, *GA*, vol. I/2, p. 419; *SW*, vol. 1, p. 289). "The I never feels an object, but only itself. . . . Yet the I cannot produce any feeling within itself" (*GA*, vol. I/2, p. 433; *SW*, vol. 1, p. 306). See also *GA*, vol. I/2, pp. 427–29; *SW*, vol. 1, pp. 298–301.

23. "To feeling there pertains: a feeling of a force that is not yet expressing itself; an object of this feeling, which likewise does not express itself; and a feeling

of compulsion, of inability—and this is the expression of feeling that was supposed to be deduced" (Fichte, *GA*, vol. I/2, p. 426; *SW*, vol. 1, p. 297).

This point is elaborated in the *Grundriss*, as follows: "When the I finds itself to be limited at a certain point it finally "becomes able to reflect upon itself. It discovers itself; it feels *itself.*" Only subsequently is this original self-feeling reposited as a feeling (sensation and/or intuition) of external things. Moreover, "in this reflection the I discovers itself for the first time; it first comes into being *for itself*" (*GA*, vol. I/3, p. 167; *SW*, vol. 1, p. 359). Note, however, that at this point the I is present to itself only passively: it feels itself but is not yet aware of its own activity as underlying and making possible this very feeling of constraint.

24. "What is opposed to the I merely serves to set the I in motion in order to act, and without such a prime mover [*erstes bewegendes*] outside of itself the I would never have acted, and, since its existence consists entirely in acting, it also would not have existed. But nothing more pertains to this mover than the fact that it is a mover, an opposing force, which, as such, can only be felt" (Fichte, *GA*, vol. I/2, p. 411; *SW*, vol. 1, p. 279).

25. Dieter Henrich first raised the charge, reiterated by Manfred Frank, that even though Fichte was the first to challenge successfully the dyadic, reflective model of self-consciousness, he failed to remain true to this insight and again and again falls back into the discredited position that separates the subject and object of consciousness—the act of self-positing from the I's consciousness of this act—and is therefore guilty of reifying the I as a quasi-substantial "ego." One might reply that it is not *Fichte* who is guilty of this dualism and reification so much as it is *the conscious I itself*! For what the Jena *Wissenschaftslehre* demonstrates is that a free subject cannot posit itself as such except as materially *embodied* and spatiotemporally situated—and, in this sense, "reified." And, of course, no sooner does it do this than it inevitably *distinguishes itself* as a freely self-positing subject from this bodily "ego." See, e.g., Manfred Frank, *Die Unhintergehbarkeit von Individualität* (Frankfurt: Suhrkamp, 1986), p. 34.

26. Fichte, *GA*, vol. I/2, p. 109 n.; *SW*, vol. 1, p. 29 n. "Here is the basis of all reality: Reality—whether of the I or of the Not-I—is possible for the I only through the relation of feeling to the I, as we have now shown—something that is possible only through *the relation of a feeling*, without the I being conscious or being able to be conscious, *of its own intuition of this feeling*, and *which therefore appears to be felt*, is *believed. A belief* is all that we have regarding reality as such, whether of the I or of the Not-I" (*GA*, vol. I/2, p. 429; *SW*, vol. 1, p. 301).

27. "The *Wissenschaftslehre* is thus *realistic*. It shows that the consciousness of finite natures simply cannot be explained unless one assumes the presence of a force that is independent of them and completely opposed to them, upon which they themselves depend for their empirical existence. However, it asserts no more

than this: that there is such an opposed force, which is not cognized but only felt by the finite creature in question" (Fichte, *GA*, vol. I/2, p. 411; *SW*, vol. 1, p. 280).

28. "According to the *Wissenschaftslehre*, therefore, the ultimate ground of all reality for the I is an original reciprocal interaction between the I and something or other outside of the I—of which we can say only that it must be completely opposed to the I" (Fichte, *GA*, vol. I/2, p. 411; *SW*, vol. 1, p. 279).

29. This is precisely what Fichte does on several occasions in the *Grundlage*, where he notes, for example, that the emergence within the I itself of the sort of "disparity" signaled philosophically by terms such as *Anstoss* and *Gefühl*, is simply not something that can be demonstrated a priori. Instead, "*that* this happens is something that everyone can establish [*darthun*] for himself only within his own experience" (*GA*, vol. I/2, p. 400; *SW*, vol. 1, p. 265).

"It is simply certain that every act of positing that is not a positing of the I must be a positing of the Not-I; but that there is any such positing is something everyone can establish for himself only through his own experience. For this reason the argumentation of the *Wissenschaftslehre* is valid purely a priori, for it establishes only such propositions as are certain a priori. Reality, however, is something that these same propositions first obtain only within experience. The entire science would have no content for someone who could not become aware of the postulated fact—and one can know with certainty that this will not be the case with any finite being" (*GA*, vol. I/2, p. 390; *SW*, vol. 1, p. 253). See also, *GA*, vol. I/2, p. 408; *SW*, vol. 1, p. 275.

30. See, e.g., Fichte's *Grundriss* (*GA*, vol. I/3, p. 155; *SW*, vol. 1, p. 344), where the *Anstoss* is identified with "sensible impressions" [*Eindrücke*] affecting the I. See also *GA*, vol. I/2, pp. 437–46; *SW*, vol. 1, pp. 311–12.

31. See § 6 of the "Second Introduction" to Fichte's *Versuch*, where we are reminded that, "just as certainly as I posit myself at all, I posit myself as limited, and this occurs as a consequence of my intuition of my own act of self-positing. I am finite in virtue of this intuition.

"Since this limitation of mine conditions my positing of myself, it constitutes an original limitation. . . .

"As we can see, the necessity *of some limitation of the I* has been derived from the very possibility of the I. The *specific determinacy* of this limitation is, however, not something that can be derived in this way; because, as we can also see, such determinacy is itself what provides the condition for the very possibility of all I-hood. Consequently, we have arrived at the point at which all deduction comes to an end. The determinacy in question appears to be something absolutely contingent and furnishes us with the *merely empirical* element in our cognition. It is because of this determinacy, for example, that I am, of all possible rational beings, a *human being*, and that, of all human beings, I am this *specific* person, etc.

"The determinate character of my limitation manifests itself as a limitation of my practical power (this is the point where philosophy is driven from the theoretical to the practical realm). This determinate limitation is immediately perceived as a *feeling*: sweet, red, cold, etc. (I prefer the name 'feeling' to Kant's 'sensation,' for it becomes a sensation only when it has been related to an object by means of an act of thinking.)

"Forgetting to take into account the role of original feeling leads to an unfounded transcendent idealism and to an incomplete philosophy which is unable to account for the purely sensible predicates of objects" (*GA*, vol. I/4, pp. 242–43; *SW*, vol. 1, pp. 489–90). For further elaboration of this point, see, above all, the discussion of the "system of feeling" in § 8 of Fichte's *Wissenschaftslehre nova methodo*, ed. Erich Fuchs (Hamburg: Felix Meiner, 1982).

32. In the preceding section of the *Grundlage des Naturrechts*, self-consciousness has been shown to be possible only if the conscious subject is able to perceive its own free self-activity. But how is such a synthesis of objectivity and self-activity possible as an object of consciousness? Fichte's answer is as follows:

"Both are completely united when we think of a *subject's being determined to determine itself*, that is, when we think of a summons [*Aufforderung*] to the subject to decide to act efficaciously.

"Insofar as what is required is an object, it must be given to sensation, and indeed to *outer* sensation. . . .—But this object is not comprehended otherwise, and cannot be comprehended otherwise, than as a mere summons of the subject to act [*eine blosse Aufforderung des Subjeks zum Handeln*]. As certainly, therefore, as the subject comprehends this object, then it just as certainly has a concept of its own freedom and self-activity—and indeed, as a concept given to it from outside. It receives the concept of its free efficacy, not as something that *exists* in the present moment, for that would be a true contradiction, but as something that *ought to* exist in some future moment.

"(The question was: how is the subject able to discover itself as an object? In order to discover *itself*, it must discover itself only as self-active, otherwise it does not discover *itself* . . . In order to discover itself as the *object* (of its own reflection) the subject cannot discover itself as *determining* itself to self-activity (how the matter may be, in itself, viewed from the transcendental standpoint, is not the question here, but only, how it must appear to the subject which is to be investigated); instead, it must discover itself as determined to self-activity by an external *Anstoss*, which must nevertheless leave him his full freedom for self determination, since otherwise the first point would be lost and the subject would not discover itself as an I.

"In order to make the last point clearer I will take for granted some things to which we will return in the future. The subject cannot discover itself to be required actually to act, even in a general sense, for then it would not be free, nor would it be an I. Should it decide to act, it can even less discover itself to be required to act in this or that determinate way, for then, once again, it would not be free, nor would it be an I. How then and in what sense is it determined to efficacy, in order to discover itself as an object? Only insofar as it discovers itself to be something that *could* act efficaciously on this occasion, something that is summoned [*aufgefordert*] to act efficaciously, but which can just as well not act)" (*GA*, vol. I/3, pp. 342–43; *SW*, vol. 3, pp. 33–34).

33. Reinhard Lauth, Alexis Philonenko, and Thomas Hohler all find the doctrine of intersubjectivity, and hence the interpretation of the *Anstoss* as *Aufforderung*, to be at least implicit in the "deduction of representation" in part 2 of the *Grundlage*. See Lauth, "Das Problem der Interpersonalität bei Fichte," in *Transzendentale Entwicklungslinien von Descartes bis zu Marx und Dostojewski* (Hamburg: Felix Meiner, 1989), pp. 180–95 (esp. pp. 184–87); Philonenko, *La liberté humaine dans la philosophie de Fichte* (Paris: Vrin, 1966), p. 328; and Hohler, *Imagination and Reflection: Intersubjectivity. Fichte's Grundlage of 1794* (The Hague: Martinus Nijoff, 1982), pp. 68 ff. I must confess that, despite Fichte's assertion (*GA*, vol. I/2, p. 337; *SW*, vol. 1, p. 189), *"kein Du, kein Ich; kein Ich, kein Du,"* I am unconvinced by their arguments and evidence. For an interpretation that supports my own, see Claudio Cesa's discussion of this point in his essay "In terma di intersoggettività," in *Difettività e fondmento*, ed. A. Masullo (Naples: Guida editori, 1984), pp. 39–60, esp. pp. 52–57.

34. To be sure, the term *Anstoss* is almost completely absent from this revised presentation (occurring only once in the "Halle transcript" of the lectures on *Wissenschaftslehre nova methodo* and twice in the "Krause transcript" of the same). Instead, Fichte talks simply about *Gefühl* and *Aufforderung*. The few occurrences of the term *Anstoss* that do occur in the *Wissenschaftslehre nova methodo*, however, simply confirm the interpretation of *Anstoss* as signifying the *Gebundenheit* or "constrained condition" of the I's real and ideal activity. See *GA*, vol. IV/2, p. 68 and *Wissenschaftslehre nova methodo*, pp. 73 and 126.

35. It is perhaps worth calling attention, even if only in passing, to a recently published and little-known note of Fichte's from the winter of 1794/95 or 1795/96 which seems to have a direct—if problematic—bearing on the relation between the various senses of *Anstoss*: "Even the philosopher explains this production [of representation by the productive imagination] by referring to an *Anstoss*. As we have seen, my *activity* is *limited*. This original limitation is a limitation that occurs through a duty. Every other limitation is, in turn, only a *sensible* presentation [*Darstellung*], by means of the imagination, of this original limitation" (*GA*, vol. II/4, p. 360).

36. Fichte, *GA*, vol. I/2, p. 405; *SW*, vol. 1, p. 272. "As was also required, we have thereby discovered within the I itself the ground of the possibility of some influence of the Not-I upon the I. The I posits itself purely and simply, and thereby it is self-contained [*in sich selbst vollkommen*] and closed to all outside influences. But if the I is to be an I, it also has to posit itself as posited by itself, and it is by means of this new positing, which refers to an original positing of the I, that the I opens itself, if I may so express myself, to external influence. Simply through this repetition of positing it posits the possibility that there could also be something in the I that is not posited by the I. Both types of positing are conditions for the possibility of an influence of the Not-I: without the former positing there would present no activity of the I which could be limited; without the second, this activity

would not be limited for the I and the I would not be able to posit itself as limited. Consequently, the I, qua I, stands in original reciprocity with itself and it is this that makes possible an external influence" (*GA*, vol. 1/2, pp. 408–09; *SW*, vol. 1, p. 276).

37. See Jean Hyppolite, "L'idée fichtéene de la doctrine de la science et le projet Husserlien," in *Figures de la pensée philosophique*, vol. 1 (Paris: Presses Universitaires de France, 1971): "Fichte wishes to preserve absolute, apodictic knowledge, which provides the very exigency for science, and, at the same time, the *open* character of incomplete experience. He wishes to establish that openness to experience that is *encountered* within absolute knowledge itself. . . Thus, absolute knowledge would not be the historical end of knowledge, but rather, the justification of its openness. If one asks, 'how is experience possible?' this amounts to asking, 'how is encounter possible without, so to speak, implying an absolute transcendence?' We comprehend only what we encounter and we only comprehend what we encounter. Encounter and comprehension mutually condition each other: this is the profound theme that Fichte presents abstractly. But its significance cannot escape us: the encounter with the other is the condition for comprehension and comprehension is the condition of the encounter with the other. . . . Absolute knowledge, knowledge within immanence, is not opposed to the infinite richness of experience. It shows how such richness is possible. The closure of absolute knowledge does not exclude the openness of experience. This Fichtean conception seems to us particularly remarkable. It justifies precisely what one expects from experience—namely, the *encounter*—without falling into either empiricism or scepticism. This conception grounds the very possibility of such encounter within immanence itself. As a transcendental science, a science of the conditions of experience, this philosophy justifies experience itself. One could almost say that the transcendence of encounter within experience finds its guarantee in the integral immanence which is posited at its foundation. This is what is signified by the transcendental" (p. 177).

38. See Henrich, *Fichtes ursprüngliche Einsicht*, p. 41.

39. Only a complete neglect of the doctrine of the *Anstoss* and an ignorance of the implications of the same can explain how a philosopher as astute as Josiah Royce could have criticized the *Wissenschaftslehre* for its failure to answer such questions as "Why do I create a world that has a belt of asteroids between the orbits of Mars and Jupiter?" Royce, *The Spirit of Modern Philosophy* (Boston: Houghton, Mifflin, 1892), p. 167. Of course, Fichte himself must bear some of the blame for this misunderstanding, to the extent that he sometimes expressed himself in an incautious manner that could all too easily lead to such neglect.

40. "*That* this [*Anstoss*] occurs, as a fact [*Factum*] is something that simply cannot be derived from the I, as we have often mentioned. However, it certainly can

be shown that it must occur *if* any actual consciousness is to be possible" (Fichte, *GA*, vol. I/2, p. 408; *SW*, vol. 1, p. 275).

41. "The world is nothing more than our own inner acting (qua pure intellect), made visible to the senses in accordance with comprehensible laws of reason and limited by incomprehensible boundaries within which we simply find ourselves to be confined" (Fichte, "Über den Grund unseres Glaubens an eine göttliche Weltregierung," *GA*, vol. I/5, p. 353; *SW*, vol. 5, p. 184). For a discussion of the "reconciling" function of the Jena *Wissenschaftslehre* see my "Philosophy and the Divided Self: On the Existential and Scientific Tasks of the Jena *Wissenschaftslehre*," *Fichte-Studien* 6 (1994), pp. 1–29.

42. Thus Schelling, after calling attention to the absolute indispensability, within the context of Fichte's theory of the I, of "a theoretically incomprehensible *Anstoss*," is quite correct to conclude that "the characteristic feature of this philosophy is to have given a *new form* to the ancient duality" ("Über das Verhältniss der Naturphilosophie zur Philosophie Überhaupt" [1802], in Schelling, *Schriften von 1801–1804* [Darmstadt: Wissenschaftliche Buchgesellschaft, 1976], pp. 427, 431).

43. On the profoundly "dialectical" character of the Jena *Wissenschaftslehre*, as well as the ineradicable dualism implicit in Fichte's conception of the finite I, see Reinhard Lauth, "Der Ursprung der Dialektik in Fichtes Philosophie," in *Transzendentale Entwicklungslinien*, pp. 209–26.

44. "Here one can see even more clearly that the I must be finite and limited. No restriction, no drive (in the transcendent sense); no drive, no reflection (transition to the transcendental); no reflection, no drive, and no limitation, and nothing that limits, etc. (in the transcendental sense): so runs the circuit of the functions of the I and the intimately linked reciprocal interaction of the I with itself" (Fichte, *GA*, vol. I/2, p. 423; *SW*, vol. 1, p. 294).

Thus there is a noncoincidental isomorphism between the inescapable circularity of all transcendental derivation and the equally inescapable circularity of the freely self-positing I's relationship with its own finitude. The I must both take itself to be absolute (that is to say, ungrounded in its free choosing) and, at the same time, recognize itself to be limited. Similarly, it must posit the independent existence of its various "objects," at the same time that it recognizes that all objectivity is immanent within (posited by) subjectivity. As Fichte writes: "This fact, namely, that the finite mind must necessarily posit something absolute outside of itself (a thing in itself) and yet must recognize, from the other side, that the latter is present only *for it* (is a necessary noumenon), constitutes that circle which the finite mind can infinitely expand but from which it can never escape. . . . Indeed, it is only this circle that limits us and makes us finite beings" (*GA*, vol. I/2, p. 412; *SW*, vol. 1, p. 281). On this "necessary circle" of finite selfhood, see too *GA*, vol. I/2, pp. 414–16, 420; *SW*, vol. 1, pp. 283–85 and 290–91, as well as *GA*, vol. I/3, pp. 166–69; *SW*, vol. 1, pp. 358–61.

Note the similarities between Fichte's description of this circle of the selfhood and Hegel's description, in the introduction to the *Phenomenology of Spirit* of how "consciousness examines itself," as well as the similarities of Fichte's doctrine to Sartre's account, in *Being and Nothingness* (part 2, chap. 1), of "the circle of selfhood." Significantly, Fichte's account is closer to Sartre's than to Hegel's, inasmuch as neither Fichte nor Sartre hold out the possibility of ever escaping from this "circle"—of moving, with Hegel, from "the standpoint of consciousness" to the nondualistic "standpoint of spirit."

45. Fichte, *GA*, vol. I/2, p. 423; *SW*, vol. 1, p. 294. See also, *GA*, vol. I/2, p. 432; *SW*, vol. 1, pp. 304–05.

46. Note that, since this conflict depends upon something more than the productive activity of the I (inasmuch as it presupposes the equally "groundless" presence within the I of the *Anstoss*) it is misleading of Henrich and others to attribute to Fichte a "production theory" of the I. The claim that the Fichtean I "produces itself" has also been challenged, albeit from a somewhat different direction, by Reinhard Hiltscher in his "Stellt Fichtes Theorie vom 'Ich' in der WL von 1794/95 eine Produktionstheorie des 'Ich' dar?" *Fichte-Studien* 5 (1993), pp. 107–16. Against the "production theory of the I" Hiltscher too notes that even though "reason provides an a priori foundation for the *possibility* of the *Anstoss*, it nevertheless no longer grounds the *fact* thereof (p. 115).

47. Fichte, letter to F. I. Niethammer, December 6, 1793 (*GA*, vol. III/2).

48. "The combination 'infinite' + 'objective' is a self-contradiction. What applies to an object is finite, and what is finite applies to an object. The only way this contradiction could be removed would be for the object to be eliminated altogether, which would happen only in a completed infinity. The I can extend the object of its positing to infinity, but if it were extended to infinity in any particular moment then it would cease to be an object, and the Idea [*Idee*] of infinity would be realized—which, however, is itself a contradiction.

"Nevertheless, the Idea of an infinity to be thus completed hovers before us and is contained in our innermost nature. It requires us to resolve a contradiction the solution of which we cannot even conceive to be possible. . . .

"The nature of the I is henceforth determined in this manner, insofar as it can be determined at all, and the contradiction therein is resolved, insofar as it can be resolved at all: The I is infinite, but only with respect to its striving: it strives to be infinite. But finitude is already contained within the very concept of striving, since that to which there is no *counterstriving* is no striving at all. If the I were more than a striving, if it possessed an infinite causality, then it would be no I; it would not posit itself, and therefore it would be nothing. But if it did not possess this endless striving, then again it could not posit itself, since it could not posit anything in opposition to itself; thus it would also not be an I in this case, and hence it would be nothing" (Fichte, *GA*, vol. I/2, pp. 403–04; *SW*, vol. 1, pp. 269–70).

49. For interpretations of Fichte that emphasize the essential *finitude* of the Fichtean self, see, in addition to Philonenko's seminal *La liberté humaine*: Luigi Pareyson, "La deduzione del finito nella prima dottrina della scienza di Fichte," *Filosofia* 1 (1950), pp. 13–40; Thomas P. Hohler, "Fichte and the Problem of Finitude," *Southwestern Journal of Philosophy* 7 (1976), pp. 15–33; and Frederick Neuhouser, *Fichte's Theory of Subjectivity* (Cambridge: Cambridge University Press, 1990).

7

Original Duplicity: The Ideal and the Real in Fichte's Transcendental Theory of the Subject

Günter Zöller

Fichte's work on the *Wissenschaftslehre* from his Jena period (1794–99) centers around the role of the subject as the principle of consciousness and its objects. Taken as a doctrinal concept, the *Wissenschaftslehre* amounts to a systematically radicalized Kantian transcendental idealism according to which all objects of possible experience, and indeed all objects in general, are necessarily conditioned by some nonempirical activity of the subject. Notoriously, Fichte eliminates the transcendental-realist remnants of Kant's formal idealism, viz., the things in themselves, in favor of a complete transcendental idealism, which has the matter as well as the form of all objectivity originate entirely in the subject and its transcendental acts.

It is not surprising, then, that the *Wissenschaftslehre*, taken as a disciplinary concept, shares the amphibious status of Kant's transcendental philosophy. With its examination of the grounds and conditions of knowledge (*Wissen*), the *Wissenschaftslehre* seems an epistemology (*Erkenntnistheorie*) *avant la lettre*.[1] Yet its idealism regarding objects of all kinds gives the *Wissenschaftslehre* a decidedly metaphysical appearance. And it is no accident that the beast called "*Wissenschaftslehre*" should seem so much at home both in the old waters of metaphysics and on the new land of epistemology. In its very conception, transcendental philosophy, whether in Kant or in Fichte, undercuts neat disciplinary divisions in favor a comprehensive account of the conditions and objects of consciousness. In the manner of a true "first philosophy," the transcendental science is about everything, to be precise, or about the principles or grounds of everything.

With its ambition toward a systematic theory of consciousness, the *Wissenschaftslehre* takes on the difficult task of accounting for the unity among consciousness and its objects, while preserving the diversity and divisions that make up the complex structures of mind and world. Given the foundational role of the subject in the *Wissenschaftslehre*, the delicate balance between unity and difference concerns most importantly the nature of the subject itself. Fichte refers to that unity-within-duality and duality-within-unity by the nominalized pronoun of the first-person singular, "I" (*Ich*), and coins for it such paradoxical terms as "subject-object" and "subject-objectivity."

The most advanced expression of Fichte's reflections on the complex unity of the subject is to be found in the writings of the second or "new presentation" of the Jena *Wissenschaftslehre* (1796–99), which comprise the rudimentary *Versuch einer neuen Darstellung der Wissenschaftslehre* (*Attempt at a New Presentation of the Wissenschaftslehre*; 1798/99)[2] and two independent student lecture transcripts of Fichte's lectures on the *Wissenschaftslehre* according to the new method ("*nova methodo*"; 1796/99).[3] Unlike the forbiddingly terse, highly condensed initial presentation to be found in the *Grundlage der gesamten Wissenschaftslehre* (*Foundation of the Wissenschaftslehre*; 1794/95),[4] the new presentation features detailed explanations of the procedure, goals and nature of Fichte's enterprise that accompany the Fichtean text almost like a running commentary. Moreover, the new presentation of the *Wissenschaftslehre* employs a number of conceptual distinctions that are particularly well suited to articulating the complex, yet unitary deep structure of the subject—chiefly among them the concepts of the ideal and the real and the related distinction between thinking and willing. Tracing the intricate relations between those notions will show the extent to which the subject in Fichte is both irreducibly complex and indicative of some ultimate reality that emerges at the heart of even the most radical transcendental idealism. The following critical reconstruction of Fichte's account of the subject and the ultimate reality it presupposes is based primarily on the recently discovered transcript of Fichte's lectures on *Wissenschaftslehre nova methodo* from the winter semester 1798/99 authored by K.C.F. Krause (of Krausismo fame) and will proceed in four sections, dealing with the ideality of philosophy, the ideal and real activity of the subject, the relation between ideal and real thinking, and the relation between thinking and ultimate reality.

The Ideality of Philosophy

Fichte's project of a fundamental philosophy, presented under the programmatic title "*Wissenschaftslehre*," takes up Kant's systematic investigation of the nature of finite rational beings in the three *Critiques*. Like

Kant, Fichte presents an account of the theoretical or cognitive dimension of human existence that is systematically linked to the practical and affective dimensions of being human. Yet while Kant treats the distinction between the theoretical, the practical, and the reflective employment of finite reason as a given that is beyond further analysis, Fichte seeks to elucidate the very origin of the principal divisions that make up the basic structure of finite rational beings. This leads Fichte to a highly integrated account of finite rationality, in which the transcendental theory of experience and the transcendental theory of freedom are thoroughly intertwined.

To be sure, the distinction between theoretical and practical reason, along with its associated divisions, is not simply replaced by some undifferentiated generic conception of reason. Such a move would leave the subsequent differentiation unexplained and indeed inexplicable. Rather, the deep structure of the finite rational being must be such that the later, overt disjunctions are already, latently prefigured. Hence the originary structure of the finite rational being is itself complex rather than simple. However, the elements that make up the core of finite rationality do not exist independent of and prior to their unification. Otherwise, the unity of the subject would be merely derivative, even accidental, and the original structure of subjectivity would be a disjointed plurality. Fichte's own model for the mutual dependence of elements and whole in the constitution of the finite rational being is the living organism, understood along the lines of Kant's philosophical biology in the *Critique of Judgment*.

Given these requirements, the *Wissenschaftslehre* has a twofold task. It must elucidate the original, yet complex deep structure of finite rational beings and it must relate that originary structure to the overt distinctions and differentiations of human mental life. In the first presentation of the *Wissenschaftslehre* the former task is assigned to the short and highly condensed first part, which presents the three principles of the entire *Wissenschaftslehre*, while the latter task is carried out in the remaining second and third parts of the work, which contain the Foundation of Theoretical Knowledge and the Foundation of the Science of the Practical, respectively. The new presentation of the *Wissenschaftslehre* provides a further step toward a unified theory of finite rational beings. The principles are no longer presented separate from the derivations of the principal forms of rational mental life, and the basic forms of theory and practice are presented together in order to bring out their original unity.

The numerous methodological reflections that accompany the doctrinal core of the *Wissenschaftslehre nova methodo* attest to the fact that the philosophical presentation of the structure of finite rational beings is a highly artificial undertaking, dependent on the successful and sustained employment of a number of technical devices. Neither the original unity of the finite mind nor its articulation into the principal forms of mental life are empirically given data. Rather, they are the very ground of any experience, and as such they elude all observation.

The investigations of the *Wissenschaftslehre* demand disregarding what is merely empirical in experience ("abstraction")[5] and focusing on the nonempirical conditions that underlie all experience ("reflection").[6] Fichte mobilizes the term "intellectual intuition" to designate the peculiar nonsensible awareness required for grasping the non-sensible nature of the finite rational being.[7] Yet intellectual intuition as such does not establish any insight or knowledge. The latter requires that the material provided by the philosopher's intuition be thought. Now all finite, human thinking is discursive, i.e., a synthesis of elements that are taken up successively and subsequently united.[8] Hence in the *Wissenschaftslehre*, the original, holistic structure of finite rationality is subjected to the necessary conditions of discursive thinking. The dimension of time, and specifically temporal succession, thus introduced into the account of finite rationality is a reflection of the philosopher's own finite mind. The *Wissenschaftslehre* provides a discursive representation (*Darstellung*) of the original nondiscursive constitution of the human mind.

Fichte conveys the peculiar status of philosophy and its objects by resorting to the term "ideal."[9] The philosophical representation of the nature and operations of the finite mind is certainly not real, if reality is equated with sensorily observable, empirical reality. But neither does the philosophical account of human mentality capture the nonempirical, absolute reality of the mind, which after all eludes all discursive thinking. Fichte also expresses the ideality of philosophy in general, and the *Wissenschaftslehre* in particular, by likening it to an experiment with its characteristic artificial setup.[10] The idealist, experimental reconstruction of human mentality can be seen as a cognitive approximation of the absolute nature of the human mind under the conditions of finite thinking. In fact, Fichte's never-ceasing work on the project of the *Wissenschaftslehre* suggests that the process of approximation can never be completed. Philosophy as the supreme self-comprehension of the human mind is the endless struggle of the mind against its own limitations—a struggle that has to take place within those very limitations. That Fichte considered this struggle worthwhile attests to an idealism of yet another kind on his part.

The ineliminable tension between the philosophically reconstructed finite mind and the finite mind itself finds expression in the paradoxical, highly speculative descriptions of the mind that form the very core of Fichte's *Wissenschaftslehre*. The complex, organic structure of the mind involves a part-whole relation whose representation strains the capabilities of discursive thinking. What is called for is uniting the thought that the whole precedes the parts with the opposite thought that the parts precede the whole. More specifically, those two thoughts must be thought as belonging together and supplementing each other rather than contradicting each other. The only logical form in which this task of thinking can be achieved is that of the circle (*Zirkel*). Fichte's main effort in the *Wissenschaftslehre nova methodo* consists in not having the inevitable circularity of philosophical presentation deteriorate into a fallacious circle.[11]

Ideal and Real Activity

At the basis of Fichte's transcendental philosophy of the human mind in the second Jena *Wissenschaftslehre* lies the insight that the subject of consciousness is its own immediate object.[12] Fichte argues that all consciousness of objects requires a subject that is conscious (*Bewusstseiendes*). Now in order to be conscious of itself, the subject of consciousness itself must be an object of consciousness. Yet this would require a further subject of consciousness for which the first subject is object, and so *in infinitum*. Fichte sees only one way to avoid the fallacious regress and to account for the fact that there is indeed consciousness of the subject of itself or self-consciousness: the subject of consciousness is its own object without the mediation of any further acts and entities of consciousness, i.e., immediately.

The *Wissenschaftslehre* elucidates the structure of original, immediate self-consciousness and relates it to the structure of all consciousness. Fichte seeks to show that all consciousness of other objects is conditioned by immediate self-consciousness and, more important, that immediate self-consciousness is possible only in a being that is conscious of things and human beings other than itself. On Fichte's account, immediate self-consciousness is not an independently existing state of consciousness but rather the necessary ingredient or the ground that makes all other consciousness possible. It is not an instance of consciousness but its principal form.

In the *Wissenschaftslehre nova methodo* the peculiar relation between the subject and the object of consciousness in immediate self-consciousness and, a fortiori, in all other consciousness is articulated through the distinction between the mind's ideal and real activities. Fichte resorts to the generic characterization of the mind as "activity" in order to capture the radical difference between things that are for minds and minds that are for themselves and other minds (*Fürsein*). More precisely, the activity or agility of the mind is one of transition or passing-over (*Übergehen*) from the undetermined (*Unbestimmtes*) to the determined (*Bestimmtes*).[13] The activity of the mind is spontaneous in that it occurs absolutely or unconditionally. Once spontaneously initiated, though, the mind's activity follows strict laws that reflect its finitude.[14] The spontaneity of the mind is thus limited to the absolutely free beginning of series that then continue according to fixed laws.

Fichte identifies the subjective side of consciousness with ideal activity and its objective side with real or practical activity.[15] The real activity consists in the absolute transition from the undetermined to the determined, which Fichte understands as an activity of self-affection.[16] By contrast, the ideal activity is bound by the real activity and consists in internally imitating (*nachmachen*) and imaging (*abbilden*) the real activity.[17] Fichte also uses the term "positing" for the ideal activity, thereby linking the latter to reflection and awareness.[18] The ideal activity of the mind in the *Wissenschaftslehre nova methodo* thus continues the theory of the positing I from the *Wissenschaftslehre* of 1794/95. Both doctrines are concerned with the cognitive, or rather the proto-cognitive, aspect of the mind. By contrast, the real activity introduced in the *Wissenschaftslehre nova methodo* takes up the theory of the striving I from the *Wissenschaftslehre* of 1794/95, with its emphasis on the practical, self-determining nature of the mind.

It must be kept in mind that the real and the ideal activities are not independently functioning instances of consciousness, but moments that only together make up consciousness. Fichte proposes an experimental, "ideal" isolation for the methodological purpose of reconstructing the origin of consciousness.[19] On his view, consciousness involves an original division of mental life into an object of consciousness that takes the form of the mind's absolute but finite real activity and a subject of consciousness that takes the form of capturing the real activity in an image. Drawing on the etymological connection between "idea" and "sight" or "vision," Fichte contrasts the two essential moments of consciousness as "seeing" and "acting."[20]

While the occurrence of consciousness depends on the original separation, or rather separateness, of ideal and real activities, it is equally necessary that the two activities be connected—and that the connection take place right at the point of origin (*gleich ursprünglich*).[21] No subsequent unification of separates would do.[22] Fichte refers to the relation between real and ideal activity as one of "identity."[23] That term should not be taken to refer to some predisjunctive primal oneness in consciousness, but to indicate the ultimate proximity of the distinct moments that make up consciousness. Real and ideal activities mutually require each other.[24] In particular, the real activity of consciousness is in need of ideal activity in order to be for consciousness and thus for itself, and the ideal activity is in need of real activity in order to have something to be posited. Thus the real or practical activity is always already posited, and the ideal or positing activity is always already positing some real activity. Hence Fichte's basic characterization of the human mind in its ideal-real unity as "practical intelligence."[25]

The relationship of mutual requirement between the real and the ideal activities of the mind threatens Fichte's account of the mind with a fallacious circle.[26] On Fichte's account, the real activity stands for the practical, productive feature of the mind, while the ideal activity stands for the mind's cognitive, reflecting side. The mutual requirement of real and ideal activity thus translates into the mutual requirement of practice or action and theory or cognition. But that way the point of origin for consciousness remains elusive. It seem that consciousness would never come about, for want of a cognition that is not in need of some prior action or an action that is not requiring some prior cognition.

Fichte's solution to the dilemma of a mind that cannot be practical without being cognitive and that cannot be cognitive without being practical structurally resembles his earlier postulation of immediate self-consciousness. He introduces an original unity of theory and practice in which the practical is already theoretical and the theoretical already practical. The postulated theoretico-practical unity is introduced as pure, pre-deliberative willing (*Wollen*).[27] Such a willing is theoretical insofar as it is expressive of an insight which takes the form of the recognition of an ought (*Sollen*). It is practical insofar as it involves a self-determination or self-affection in accordance with that ought. The stipulation that the willing in question be independent of any deliberation is designed to avoid the regressive presupposition of some knowledge that is prior to the pure willing itself.

Fichte's postulation of a predeliberative willing that is under the command of some absolute ought is obviously modeled on Kant's conception of a pure will (*reiner Wille*) dissociated from choice (*Willkür*) and extrinsic motivation. Yet Fichte insists that the ought in question is not yet the specifically moral ought of the categorical imperative.[28] Rather the pure willing in question is the generic, transcendental condition of all theory and practice, moral and otherwise.

As in the case of immediate self-consciousness, it is imperative not to hypostatize pure willing into an independently functioning state or instance of consciousness. Fichte is even apprehensive about using the related noun, "will," to designate the original unison of the theoretical or ideal and the practical or real. He regards pure willing as the "mere form of willing" (*blosse Form des Wollens*).[29] Pure willing as the transcendental form or condition of theoretical as well as practical consciousness is never experienced as such. Its closest representation in actual consciousness is the moral ought of the categorical imperative.

In the postulated pure form of consciousness, immediate self-consciousness, and its volitional counterpart, the pure form of willing, the real and the ideal activities of the mind are united almost to the point of fusion. And yet in each case the original unity of the ideal and the real is also and equally originally their division. Without original unity, there would be no unity to the mind and hence no mind in the relevant sense. Without original division, there would be no consciousness to the mind and thus no mind either. Fichte's further efforts in the *Wissenschaftslehre nova methodo* are geared toward an account of that mental activity that is responsible for the simultaneous occurrence of unity and division in consciousness.

Ideal and Real Thinking

At the core of Fichte's transcendental theory of the subject in the *Wissenschaftslehre nova methodo* lies a theory of finite, discursive thinking. On Fichte's understanding, the activity or agility characteristic of human mental life is fundamentally the activity of thinking. In thinking the mind spontaneously brings about a determination (*Bestimmtheit*). The activity of determination (*Bestimmung*) follows strict laws that govern the way in which the spontaneity of thinking is exercised in finite minds. The basic law of thought (*Denkgesetz*) is the law of reflection concerning opposites (*Reflexionsgesetz des Entgegensetzens*).[30] According to this law, all determination proceeds by way of opposition. In particular, the law states that determination can only be brought about by opposing or op-positing in one's thinking something undetermined (*Unbestimmtes*) but determinable (*Bestimmbares*) against the background against which the act of determination (*Bestimmung*) takes place. Fichte here draws on Spinoza's principle that all determination is by way of negation (*omnis determinatio est negatio*) and Kant's discussion of the contrast between the determinable and the determined under the heading of the concepts of reflection (*Reflexionsbegriffe*), matter and form.[31]

A crucial element of Fichte's account of the oppositional nature of all thinking is the status of the undetermined-determinable. The latter is "discovered alongside" (*mitgefunden*).[32] Strictly speaking, it is added through thinking (*hinzugedacht*)[33] and thus a product of thought—a byproduct, to be precise, given that the primary product of thinking is the determination brought about through the act of thinking. Yet the ideal, thought-produced status of the determinable is not always properly recognized. On the contrary, the undetermined but determinable basis for determination typically appears as something found and not made, as something existing prior to and independent of thought, as something real.[34]

On the surface, the law of reflection regarding opposition seems to introduce contrast and division into the life of the mind. Yet when considering the ideal nature of the determinable and the relation of mutual requirement of determination and determinable, the law in question is as much the law concerning the unity of the opposites. What is opposed belongs together; nothing is an opposite all by itself. Fichte goes even further than that. He maintains the identity (*Identität*) of the opposites, arguing that the opposites are the same viewed from two different sides.[35] The identity claimed for the opposites is thus the identity of different, even opposed sides or aspects of one and the same ("identical") entity or state of affairs. On Fichte's account, the opposed views of the same entity or state of affairs are inseparable (*unzertrennlich*). The complete nature of the entity or state of affairs only shows itself in the joint consideration of the opposites. Fichte repeatedly refers to this internally oppositional, yet unitary basic structure of the human mind as its "original duplicity" (*ursprüngliche Duplizität*).[36]

For Fichte the primordial case of the identity of opposites is the I (*Ich*) in its originary structure as subject-object.[37] All other oppositions, including that between I and Not-I, must be regarded as the unfolding of the basic opposition in the I between the subjective or ideal and the objective or real. Consciousness in all its forms and shapes, along with the world to which it relates through cognition as well as volition, is the subject-object *writ large*.

The opposition of the real and the ideal introduced into human mentality under the basic form of subject-objectivity shows itself as a fundamental opposition within thinking itself. Fichte contrasts the thinking involved in the cognition of objects and the thinking involved in the formulation of ends.[38] The point is not to propose the independence of one form of thinking from the other. Rather, Fichte seeks to elucidate the complicated relationship of mutual requirement between the thinking of an object and the thinking of an end.

In a perplexing terminological move, Fichte casts the opposition between of the two basic forms of thinking as the opposition of real and ideal thinking.[39] The latter distinction is a distinction within thinking and must not be confused with Fichte's distinction between real and ideal activity. The term *ideal*, as used in the locution *ideal thinking*, refers to the thinking of some ideal, yet-to-be-realized object. The image involved in "ideal thinking" is not the copy of some prior reality, as in the ideal activity of positing some real activity, but the design of something that is yet to be realized. The primary sense of "ideal" has shifted from that of an "after-image" (*Nachbild*) to that of a "fore-image" (*Vorbild*).[40]

The term *real* undergoes an analogous change in the move from "real activity" to "real thinking." The "real" in "real *activity*" refers to some actual activity that is then posited by the ideal activity. By contrast, "real *thinking*" refers to the activity of having one's thought determined by how the object is in actuality. In a complete reversal of terms, the *ideal* activity ("copying") is being reconceptualized as *real* thinking (thinking of the real), while the *real* activity ("self-determination") is being reconceptualized as *ideal* thinking (thinking of the ideal). Alternatively put, the feature of production—as opposed to mere reproduction—is no longer associated with the real (in "real activity") but with the ideal (in "ideal thinking").[41] The true, "real" activity of the I is its ideal activity of formulating and pursuing ends, i.e., the thinking involved in willing.

The upshot of the conceptual reorientation in Fichte's usage of the terms *ideal* and *real* is that the real or practical activity of the mind is now understood in decidedly idealist terms. Willing is no longer something real that then becomes the object of some ideal activity or positing. Rather, willing itself is now something ideal, i.e., something thought. Yet unlike the ideal activity of positing, willing is not the thinking of something already made, but the thought of something to be made, of something that ought to be. The real, as reproduced in positing, comes about as the product of thinking and willing the ideal. Thus, the primacy of the ideal over the real in the *Wissenschaftslehre nova methodo* provides a reformulation of the doctrine of striving and the associated primacy of practical reason from the first presentation of the *Wissenschaftslehre*.

Thinking and the Real

In the *Wissenschaftslehre nova methodo* the activity of thinking occupies the central position in the constitution of consciousness and its objects. Both in ideal and real thinking, some determination is brought about spontaneously, and this in such a way that something undetermined but determinable is presupposed by thought as a basis or substratum for the act of determination. Fichte's generic term for the intellectual activity of introducing the determinable along with the determination is "synthesis," and the thinking in question is called "synthetic thinking."[42]

The joining of the determining and the determinable is not some external piecing together of two separate things. Rather, the two belong together *ab origine*. One cannot be what it is without the other. According to Fichte, the synthesis involved in synthetic thinking points to the original identity of what is to be synthesized. In fact, it is the very act of thinking that first introduces nonidentity or manifoldness through some act of analysis that is just as original as the synthesis.[43] Thinking as the mind's primary activity is as much unifying as it is diversifying, and it must be both in order to be either.

Fichte traces the operation of synthetic-analytic thinking through the two series (*Reihen*) of ideal and real thinking. Real thinking (theoretical cognition) involves the presupposition of a realm of determinability in the form of the empirical world. Real thinking produces or generates the representations of this world. Moreover, it is characteristic of real thinking that in it those spontaneously produced representations are taken as existing independently of the mind's activity. To real thinking, the products of thought appear as found objects.

By contrast, ideal thinking (the thinking and willing of an end) carries with it the presupposition of a realm of determinability in the form of an intelligible world. Fichte refers to the objects of this world of ideal beings as "objects of thought" or "noumena."[44] The noumenal realm is comprised of other rational beings. The *Wissenschaftslehre nova methodo* contains a detailed theory of intersubjectivity in which the constitution of subjectivity presupposes the activity of other subjects that call upon the subject to realize its potential for independent existence.[45]

The contrast between the sensible and the intelligible system of determinability is based on Kant's distinction between phenomena and noumena.[46] In Kant, though, the concept of an intelligible object is merely a limiting concept (*Grenzbegriff*), designed to trace the confines of sensible knowledge by demarcating an open conceptual space possibly inhabited by objects of pure reason. For Fichte, on the other hand, every act of ideal, volitional thinking involves the thought of a noumenal substratum of determinability. To Fichte, (ideal) thinking as such opens up the noumenal realm.

The noumenal realm also functions as the condition or ground for the empirical world.[47] For Fichte, our bodily existence in the spatiotemporal world comes about by having our intelligible being subjected to the laws of discursive thinking. That diremption from noumenal to phenomenal existence is unavoidable and is a reflection of human finitude. To be sure, the pre-empirical, pre-embodied existence is not an actual experience but a necessary thought on the part of the subject, which thus interprets its own dual existence as noumenal and phenomenal being. The only thing that can be thought as belonging to the elusive noumenal pre-existence of the I is the pure will, understood as a timeless activity of self-determination.[48]

The pure will thus takes on the function of the ultimate determinable for discursive thinking. Fichte distinguishes two degrees of determination with respect to the pure, "absolute" will: first, the subjection of the will to the limiting concept of individuality, resulting in individual will; and second, the concrete empirical determinations of the will to particular, empirical volitions.[49] Fichte also characterizes the ultimate determinable of all willing as the "absoluteness of reason in its entirety" (*Absolutheit der gesamten Vernunft*),[50] thus suggesting a distinction between the finitizing thinking of the discursive intellect and some nondiscursive, undetermined, thus indefinite, realm of pure reason. It should be emphasized that Fichte's introduction of the notion of absolute reason is very much part of his transcendental inquiry into the conditions of finite consciousness and not some extraneous piece of speculative metaphysics.

The distinction between pure, pre-individual willing and finite, individual willing and the identification of pure will with absolute, indefinite reason lead Fichte to claim a unique status for the pure will.[51] On his account, particular acts of individual willing are themselves modes of thinking. They are instances of determined, resolved thinking and hence affected by the finitizing conditions of discursive thought.[52] By contrast, the pure will is considered to be "the originally real" (*das urspüngliche Reale*).[53] Paradoxically, it is the most intelligible of entities, viz., the sheer determinable, that is here accorded the status of ultimate reality, while everything else is merely a product of thought, either of real or of ideal thinking. It must be asked, though, whether the pure will qua sheer determinable is not itself significantly affected by discursive thinking. After all, the pure will is presupposed by finite thinking in the process of its activity of determination. Fichte himself seems to have realized this point. For in his popular treatise on the definition of humanity (*Die Bestimmung des Menschen*, usually translated as *The Vocation of Man*), which was begun in early 1799 and published in 1800, the ultimate reality of pure will or absolute reason is no longer an object of thought and knowledge (*Wissen*) but of faith (*Glaube*). Moreover, the later versions of the *Wissenschaftslehre* (after 1800) are so many further attempts to develop the thought of the ultimately real in the context of a transcendental theory of consciousness. The proper relation between the duplication and indeed the multiplication involved in all forms of consciousness and some original, absolute reality remained the focus of Fichte's thinking on the subject.[54]

Notes

1. On the history of the post-Kantian origin of the discipline called "*Erkenntnistheorie*," cf. Klaus Christian Köhnke, *The Rise of Neo-Kantianism: German Aca-*

demic Philosophy Between Idealism and Positivism, trans. R. J. Hollingdale (Cambridge: Cambridge University Press, 1991).

2. Johann Gottlieb Fichte, *Versuch einer neuen Darstellung der Wissenschaftslehre*, second, improved edition, ed. Peter Baumanns (Hamburg: Felix Meiner, 1984).

3. The *Hallesche Nachschrift* was first published in Fichte, *Nachgelassene Schriften*, vol. 2, ed. H. Jacob (Berlin: Ducker & Dünnhaupt, 1937), pp. 341–612, and was reedited in *J.G. Fichte-Gesamtausgabe*, 4th ser., vol. 2, ed. R. Lauth and H. Gliwitzky (Stuttgart: Frommann-Holzboog, 1978). The *Krause Nachschrift* was discovered in 1980 and published as *Wissenschaftslehre nova methodo: Kollegnachschrift K. Chr. Fr. Krause 1798/99*, ed. E. Fuchs (Hamburg: Felix Meiner, 1982). For a compilated edition of the two transcripts, cf. Fichte, *Foundations of Transcendental Philosophy. (Wissenschaftslehre) Nova Methodo (1796/99)*, ed. and trans. D. Breazeale (Ithaca: Cornell University Press, 1992). Cf. also my review of that edition in *Philosophical Review* 103 (1994), pp. 585–88.

4. Fichte, *Grundlage der gesamten Wissenschaftslehre*, ed. W. G. Jacobs (Hamburg: Felix Meiner, 1970).

5. Fichte, *Wissenschaftslehre nova methodo*, p. 25.

6. Ibid., p. 14.

7. Cf. Fichte, *Versuch einer neuen Darstellung der Wissenschaftslehre*, p. 43.

8. Fichte, *Wissenschaftslehre nova methodo*, pp. 8 f.

9. Ibid., p. 23.

10. Ibid., p. 21. On Fichte's experimental reconstruction of the I, cf. my "An Eye for an I: Fichte's Transcendental Experiment," forthcoming in *Figuring the Self: Subject, Absolute, and Others in Classical German Philosophy*, ed. D. Klemm and G. Zöller (Albany: State University of New York Press).

11. The inevitable circle of presentation in Fichte's theory of subjectivity is not to be confused with the deficiently circular "reflection theory" of self-consciousness diagnosed by Dieter Henrich in "Fichte's Original Insight," in *Contemporary German Philosophy*, vol. 1 (University Park, Pa: Pennsylvania State University Press, 1982), pp. 15–53. Original German edition, *Fichtes ursprüngliche Einsicht* (Frankfurt: Klostermann, 1967).

12. Fichte, *Versuch einer neuen Darstellung der Wissenschaftslehre*, pp. 106 f.

13. Fichte, *Wissenschaftslehre nova methodo*, p. 32.

14. Ibid., pp. 50, 60.

15. Ibid., p. 63.

16. Ibid., p. 49.

17. Ibid., p. 46.

18. Ibid., p. 50.

19. Ibid., p. 67.

20. Ibid., p. 54.

21. Ibid., p. 84.

22. Ibid., p. 62.

23. Ibid., p. 182.

24. Ibid., p. 48.

25. Ibid., pp. 53 f.

26. Ibid., p. 138.

27. Ibid., p. 142. On Fichte's theory of the will, cf. my "Bestimmung zur Selbstbestimmung: Fichtes Theorie des Willens," in *Fichte-Studien* 7 (1995).

28. Fichte, *Wissenschaftslehre nova methodo*, p. 143.

29. Ibid., p. 142.

30. Ibid., p. 38.

31. Cf. Immanuel Kant, *Critique of Pure Reason*, trans. N. K. Smith (New York: St. Martin's Press, 1929), A266–68/B322–24 (pagination of the first/second German editions).

32. Fichte, *Wissenschaftslehre nova methodo*, p. 39.

33. Ibid., p. 18.

34. Ibid., p. 38.

35. Ibid., p. 42.

36. Ibid., pp. 185, 227.

37. Ibid., p. 42.

38. Ibid., p. 182.

39. Ibid.

40. Ibid., p. 53.

41. Ibid., p. 218.

42. Ibid., p. 146.

43. Ibid., pp. 184, 186.

44. Ibid., p. 124.

45. Ibid., pp. 176 ff. On Fichte's theory of intersubjectivity in the *Wissenschaftslehre nova methodo*, cf. Ives Radrizzani, *Vers la fondation de l'intersubjectivité chez Fichte. Des Principes à la Nova Methodo* (Paris: Vrin, 1993). Cf. also my review of that edition in *Philosophischer Literaturanzeiger* 47 (1994), pp. 366–68.

46. Fichte, *Wissenschaftslehre nova methodo*, pp. 124, 131 f.

47. Ibid., p. 124.

48. Ibid., pp. 134, 167.

49. Ibid., p. 176.

50. Ibid.

51. Ibid., p. 167.

52. On the relation between intellect and will in Fichte, cf. my "Thinking and Willing in Fichte's Theory of Subjectivity," in *New Essays on Fichte*, ed. D. Breazeale and T. Rockmore (Lanham: Humanities Press, forthcoming); and "Geist oder Gespenst: Fichtes Noumenalismus in der *Wissenschaftslehre nova methodo*," presented at the Congress of the International J. G. Fichte Society, Jena 1994.

53. Fichte, *Wissenschaftslehre nova methodo*, p. 167.

54. Work on this essay was supported by a Fellowship for University Teachers from the National Endowment for the Humanities and carried out during a research stay at Queens College, Oxford. I would like to thank these institutions, as well as Wolfson College, Oxford.

8

Individuality in Hegel's *Phenomenology of Spirit*

Ludwig Siep

"In the present work, the aim which I have in mind is to break the stranglehold which a number of dichotomies appear to have on the thinking of both philosophers and laymen. Chief among these is the dichotomy between objective and subjective views of truth and reason."[1] This is not one of Hegel's formulations but rather the opening lines of Hilary Putnam's *Reason, Truth and History*. If we put aside for a moment all the differences in ontology and methodology between these two thinkers, this quotation from Putnam could well characterize the program of Hegel's philosophy. As is well known, in his first publication, the *Differenzschrift*, Hegel takes as his starting point the "need of philosophy" to overcome the opposition of "mind and matter, body and soul, belief and understanding, freedom and necessity." The development of thought, in Hegel's view, brought these oppositions to the "universal concept" of "absolute subjectivity and absolute objectivity."[2] Of course, Putnam would not aim at an ontological or conceptual synthesis of such pairs of opposites in the Hegelian sense. However, his attempt to expose as untenable the split between subject and object, science and morality, and the true and the good shows that these oppositions which, according to Putnam, lead to fruitless, "ideological" disputes, have become entrenched once again.

As is well known, Hegel's first great attempt to realize his plan for the overcoming of the dualistic oppositions in traditional philosophy is the *Phenomenology of Spirit*. This work was conceived not only as a philosophical system, but it was also supposed to help the spirit of the age reach that level of consciousness which it had attained in the great breakthrough of the political revolutions—above all in France—as well as in the subjectification of art, religion and philosophy. This meant above all a new relationship of individuality to community and of subjective reason to public laws. With respect to this point as well, we might be standing at a similar turning point: the ideological struggles between individualism and collectivism seem to have lost their acuteness and political significance. However, what the theoretical result of overcoming both extremes is supposed to look like still remains unclear from both the philosophical and the political perspective. Perhaps Hegel's attempt to overcome this dualism can help us to gain some clarity here. In what follows, I would like to discuss Hegel's "phenomenological" conception of a form of individuality that is not separated from the "objectivity" or "universality" of the social sphere. My emphasis is on the "practical" rather than the ontological side of this synthesis.

My discussion is divided into three parts. In the first section, I investigate the relation of the self-*understanding* of the individual to that of the community primarily as it is treated in the "Self-Consciousness" chapter of the *Phenomenology*. In the second section, I am concerned with the relation of individual self-*realization* to social-historical reality—a relation that Hegel investigates in the "Reason" chapter of the *Phenomenology*. Finally, in the third section, I discuss the synthesis of individual conscience and public ethical life (*Sittlichkeit*), i.e., morality, law and religion, as it appears in Hegel's "Spirit" chapter.

I

Human individuals have consciousness. Groups, institutions, laws and states do not. This is an ontological difference which nonspeculative philosophers up until the present have considered insurmountable. But what is consciousness? Whoever has consciousness has representations of states of affairs, both real and desired, and representations of himself. What is it that he is conscious of when he is conscious of himself? At the simplest and most rudimentary level, it seems to be his pleasant and unpleasant sensations and perceptions. Sensations and perceptions are interconnected. Whatever hampers or threatens our pleasant sensations is perceived as something fearful and to be avoided; whatever preserves or increases them is perceived as something to be sought. Just as immediately, one perceives one's own pursuit and avoidance of these objects. One is conscious of wanting and being able to adjust one's condition and that of the perceived thing according to one's longing for pleasure. *Actually* subjecting the perceived thing to'one's own pursuit of pleasure (and not merely *wishing* to do so) is what Hegel calls "desire" (*Begierde*). Yet desire is a reflexive and self-developing consciousness. Desire is immediately conscious as a reaching out and a capacity: a capacity to appropriate something else, something lacking. This capacity, however, remains dependent not only on the individual's own ability to act but also on the objects of desire. The dependence is itself perceived as unpleasant and as a limit to one's ability. This limit is extended when the object of desire is not used up but rather renews itself. The partner of pleasure or the objects of use, provided and prepared by servants, are such "objects."

But pleasure, even in animals, is a two-sided feeling; it involves both self-renunciation and self-confirmation—self-confirmation because one is desired by the other. This desire itself is perceived and, at least by human beings, desired.[3] Self-confirmation is perceived and sought via the passions of the other and also in the pleasure of domination: even the other's fear and dependence on me is an acknowledgment of my capacity to appropriate. Therefore, my feeling of self as being capable of satisfying my desires is dependent upon a fusion with the other's desires and his feeling of self. But one tries is to bring this under control too. The other has to confirm my feeling of self, if need be under compulsion. This confirmation becomes an end in itself.

The analysis of desire in the *Phenomenology* abstracts from the fact that humans live in groups and that we, like other primates (as we know today), occupy a place in a social hierarchy. Hegel's analysis begins in a quasi-solipsistic manner, but this abstraction is only methodological. He usually analyzes complex phenomena into various cross sections representing different perspectives and then recombines them. From the original social perspective, one can perhaps even more easily demonstrate that the satisfaction of desire is bound up with social dominance, or at least with a stability of roles, and vice versa that the confirmation of my role and my self-understanding is itself desired. However, only in the social history of humans does there emerge such a desire and such a capability to determine the way one wants to be regarded by oneself and others. This is a necessary step in the genesis of individuality. And since man learns that he is capable of subordinating all his natural drives, including the drive for self-preservation, this self-determination is for Hegel also a step towards "spiritual existence."

Nevertheless consciousness cannot attain the desired independence in this way. It overlooks the fact that the confirmation of a feeling of self presupposes both a self-renunciation and a merging and coming together of spontaneous feelings. Spontaneity and noncompulsion are required for the emotional agreement as well as for rationally controlled social relations: confirmation by means of fear and dependence is unstable and makes the feared individual dependent—since all the know-how remains on the side of the bondsman. Moreover, this asymmetry is not what the demand for confirmation by the other was trying to attain. Human beings in society seek, as Aristotle said, not merely pleasure or benefit but also community and company for its own sake. To act in a communal fashion and to see oneself through the eyes of the other means to be more active and to see more correctly. Since life is the conscious performance of human abilities, it also means to live more intensely.[4]

According to Hegel's originally "solipsistic" perspective, the demand for sociality is reconstructed in the following way: I want to see my independent self-understanding confirmed by another independent agent. This, however, is not possible in an asymmetrical partnership or in domination, whether it is natural or results from a struggle. Rather, it comes about only in free agreement or consensus. The lasting and stable form of agreement is always a legal relation whose interpretation is secured against private bias. As long as everyone is a judge of his own affairs, right, like honor, remains a private assertion that, lacking a neutral adjudication, must be decided by a struggle. The recognition of the individual as a legal subject is the new common self-understanding that replaces the private self-definition of honor. This is clearer in the *Realphilosophie* than in the *Phenomenology* in which a long series of experiences of consciousness lies between the struggle, the attainment of right, and ethical life.[5] Nevertheless, it is not accidental that stoicism, which follows "Lordship and Bondage," is the basis of Roman law.[6]

The legal relation must preserve the character of free and spontaneous agreement. It should not become merely a nonviolent strategy for appropriation. How this is possible remains to be seen.

To summarize the experience of self-consciousness: an individual who is conscious of his spontaneous but enduring and controlled appropriation of his environment discovers his dependence upon social agreement. A stable individual self-understanding must at the same time be a common social understanding. In principle, it must be a symmetrical relation that, as is well known, Hegel calls "mutual recognition." All "rational" social institutions rest on this common self-understanding and the will to realize its conditions. Even the irrational and historically outdated institutions presuppose some degree of mutual recognition—if only in an asymmetrical way.[7]

And what about the problem of the ontological difference between individuals and the community? Hegel claims that individual self-understanding is dependent upon a communal understanding—a consciousness of right, for example. He doesn't claim that institutions or impersonal organizations like the state have their own consciousness in the sense of having subjective representations. However, he *does* think that the common self-understanding must manifest itself not only in "normal" but also in special individuals who in their own subjective representations are inspired and permeated by the values and goals of a community. I will return to this point below.

The ontological condition for both is that individual consciousness and rational communal spirit are structured by a conceptual system that has the form of a self-individualizing whole of meanings. This is not only shown in Hegel's *Logic* but also is demonstrated in the *Phenomenology* as the underlying structure of the history of the experience of consciousness. I will not discuss this conceptual development here—for instance of the concepts of infinity, difference, life, etc. I will also skip over the history of the experience of consciousness in the first three chapters of the *Phenomenology*. As regards questions of method, I have assumed that in the "Self-Consciousness" chapter, Hegel is discussing not only examples of conceptual relations but also actual "phenomena" of human emotion and understanding, as well as paradigmatic configurations taken from actual social history.[8] This seems to me legitimate, since Hegel discusses similar phenomena in his *Philosophy of Nature* and his *Anthropology*, his *Encyclopaedia* "Phenomenology" and in the *Philosophy of History*.[9] In the course of a justification of speculative logic vis-à-vis traditional ways of knowing, the emphasis lies on the implicit theses about the truth of such phenomena. But given a contemporary interest in Hegel's conception of individuality, it seems justified to focus on his analysis of social phenomena. However, the ultimate basis of the synthesis of individual and communal consciousness lies in Hegel's ontological logic.

II

An approach "from the phenomena" is much more difficult when we turn to the second theme: the self-*realization* of the individual in society. In the "Reason" chapter, Hegel's subject matter is a developed understanding of individuality. In addition, the text is complicated by his references to the various forms of individualism in the philosophy and literature of the seventeenth and eighteenth centuries. For our purposes the basic question is as follows: How does Hegel treat the actualization of individual intentions vis-à-vis social reality and to what degree does the individual actualize himself in this social sphere? To these questions as well, there seems today to be an easy answer: social reality is in large measure independent of the individual's intentions and the representations of the good and the right. History passes over the intentions of most individuals without mercy. Moreover, even in processes whose special aim is to bring the opinion of individuals to bear on public decisions and actions, the contribution of the individual becomes qualified and weakened beyond recognition. This is a common experience both in political campaigns and in economic processes aggregating "consumer decisions." Nevertheless, the basic concepts of law, morality and religion in the modern age rest on the claim that individuals may act according to their own rationally determined convictions and that the social institutions respect these convictions. Action based on this foundation is what Hegel in the "Reason" chapter calls "The Actualization of Rational Self-Consciousness Through its Own Activity."

Hegel discusses three basic forms of this actualization in the manner of a history of experiences. The first starts with the search for "true" reality in the Faustian enjoyment of the "full human life" (*das volle Menschenleben*).

The second is the experience of the bona fide revolutionary who wants to establish a law securing everyone's spontaneous activity. It turns out that the reasons for this "law of the heart" cannot be made explicit and comprehensible to others. Hegel gives a critical twist to Pascal's dictum "*le coeur a ses raisons, que la raison ne connait pas*"[10] at a time when, through the influence of Rousseau and the sentimental literature, the heart—that is, the intuitive and emotional knowledge of the morally right—was played off against the Enlightenment cult of reason.

The third form is individuality that sacrifices itself for the betterment of the world, or the "virtue" that wants to help historical reason to its ultimate success. This form of individuality must campaign against the evil reality that the egoism of oppressors and the avaricious creates and maintains. Hegel may have Robespierre's concept of virtue in mind.

According to Hegel, the self-actualization of rational individuality fails in all three of its forms. It cannot succeed in principle, because the opposition between individual action and universal objective reason cannot be overcome. None of these views of practical reason disposes of a conception of individual self-actualization in the "life of a free people" and its institutions. The positive background for the account of this failure is always, for Hegel, the Greek *polis* in which the individuals could "reach their determination" in public roles. But in Greece this took place in a sort of world-historical naiveté that was not yet clouded by the self-reflection of individuals discovering their own spontaneity and absolute value. The modern subject still has to reestablish this unity. But this does not come about either through the "pursuit of happiness," as through the self-realization in unfolding one's talents, or through the confused convictions about universal spontaneity. The lived customs of a people cannot be replaced by abstract programs for the well-being of humanity directed against egoism and oppression. However, Hegel leaves open what precisely these programs consist in. For his analysis of the "Law of the Heart," one might think of Enlightenment programs for the free development of natural human "drives,"[11] even though the concept of the "heart" seems rather to refer to the *critics* of the Enlightenment (Rousseau, Jacobi, et al.).[12] In his discussion of the virtuous betterment of the world, Hegel refers to the development of human "talents, abilities and powers."[13] In all three forms, the issue apparently concerns only the liberation and actualization of individual claims and not the institutions in which a common consciousness and a universal will can develop beyond the private interests of the individuals. Universal reason only has the function of confirming the independence and importance of individual consciousness. But this attempt collapses into a phenomenological reversal: the first form falls prey to an uncontrolled and incomprehensible fate, and in the latter two forms of consciousness the results reverse the concepts and intentions of the individual. Either they are not accepted by those to be liberated or they are spoiled by their own ideas of the good. In truth, behind these conceptions of the good, what is sought is only the "action and drives of the individual . . . the use of forces, the play of their expression."[14]

This goal becomes explicit in those forms of self-actualization that Hegel treats in the third part of the "Reason" chapter. These forms no longer assume that the unity of individual reason and reality has yet to be brought about. Rather they suppose an individual who is real "in and for itself" and only "presents" and "expresses" itself in the social world. "The manifestation of itself,"[15] the immediate unity of self-relation and external, causal necessity, is also the meaning of the category of "actuality" in the *Logic*.

In the third part of the "Reason" chapter, Hegel discusses again three basic forms of this self-representation. The first is an account of the creative nature of the individual, who achieves his fulfillment in a work of art or a public "cause." Then there are the two forms of Kantian moral reason that Hegel distinguishes here: the consciousness of autonomous, lawgiving reason and the testing of maxims and positive laws according to the idea of a noncontradictory universal law.[16] In both forms, the individual believes he knows immediately what is demanded by practical reason and thus expresses its own essence in the social world.

None of these three forms does justice to the given historical situation or to the manifold mutual dependencies among interacting individuals. No work by itself can express the individuality of its creator if he abstracts from the expectations and interpretations and thus from the forms of life, beliefs and knowledge of his contemporaries. No contribution to the actualization of a good cause will be effective that is not in contact with the public ideas and the individual contributions of others. And the individual procedures for the application of the ethical law, which apply the "test of universalizability" to given maxims and laws, abstract from the historical situation and the systematic order of legal systems. As the test for property rights shows, only a specific order of rights, duties and institutions can balance the conflicting claims of both private and public property: the equal claim of each person to use things according to his needs and the claim of the self-conscious individual to dispose permanently of his means of action. It must be noted, however, that in his critique of Kantian "abstractions," Hegel does not take into account the systematic development of legal and moral systems in Kant's or Fichte's systems of ethics.

To return to the general question of the self-actualization of individuals in social action and judgment—what is Hegel's answer in the "Reason" chapter? He seems at first to acknowledge the correctness of the sceptical position: individual self-actualization fails when it uses as its starting point its own convictions about the good and the right either for itself or for everyone. In a concrete society, this self-actualization is always bound up with the intentions and actions of others, with the effects of law and customs, the effect of social forces, etc. But Hegel, as is well known, does not think that there are only collective forces or that only systems are real. It remains true for him that individual action is what makes the social world real. But the individual himself can be "real" only when he understands the meaning of the social order and manifests it in his own social role. This does not demand rigid role playing. For Hegel, a mechanical social order is dead, whereas a living culture demands creative individual interpretation of social roles. As long as it remains comprehensible to others, this interpretation can be innovative, reforming or—under certain historical circumstances—even revolutionary. Moreover, the individual must fulfill his role with conviction and with the approval of his sovereign conscience. How does this square with the independence of public laws and institutions from individual opinions about the common good? Hegel tried to overcome this "hardest" opposition of individuality and the social order in the "Morality" section of the "Spirit" chapter.

III

Both of the sections of the "Spirit" chapter prior to "Morality" contain a sort of short "world history" of ethical consciousness, from the complete identification of the individual with its religion and its community up to the skeptical disintegration of all moral rules in the French Enlightenment (Diderot). This sovereignty of the enlightened mind is reversed by the violent assimilation of the individual in the abstract universal will in the French Revolution, especially during the Jacobin terror. Hegel presents this process as the history of the experience of consciousness whose criteria of truth prove to be internally contradictory in the spiritual reversals of the epochs. These contradictions come about through the isolation of (logical and ontological) concepts that in truth form a holistic system of mutual "semantic" dependence and of complementary explication. This concerns once again the logical aspect of the *Phenomenology*.

In this development, the highest level of legal and political integration of the individual in the community that Hegel treats in the *Phenomenology* is reached even before the "Morality" chapter. After the freedom of the universal will from all privileges and also from all special roles, functions and hierarchies proved to be pure compulsion and even the destruction of every particularity,

> [the] organization of spiritual 'masses' or spheres to which the plurality of individual consciousnesses are assigned . . . takes shape once more. These individuals who have felt the fear of death, of their absolute master, again submit to negation and distinctions, arrange themselves in the various spheres, and return to an apportioned and limited task but thereby to their substantial reality.[17]

The fear of death brings the individuals back to the consciousness of their finitude and particularity. Only in particular social functions and groups (classes) can they actualize themselves and simultaneously express a common "spirit." Rosenzweig already correctly suspected that Hegel was here referring to the Napoleonic constitution of Italy of 1805, in which the rational result of the French Revolution had, for him, taken form.[18] Since 1805, constitutional monarchy and the organization of society according to professional classes constituted, for Hegel, the heart of a rational constitution. In the *Philosophy of Spirit* of 1805–6, he presented his doctrine of classes as a process of individualization. While the agricultural class is characterized by its "unindividualized trust, having its individuality in the unconscious individual, the earth," the citizen knows himself in his work and in his property "as recognized in his individuality."[19] Through his skill he makes himself into what he wants to be and what he wants to count as. With this Hegel already indicates the free choice of profession and class that is so important in the *Philosophy of Right*. Individualization demands education and universalization: the individual has his "substantial reality" in the professional competence and uprightness ("*Rechtschaffenheit*") of a class. As such, the individual contributes to the ethical life of a community and the cooperative pursuit of its goals. Without this integration into the appropriate habits of groups that perform the necessary functions in the "organization" of a community, the political views of an individual remain mere opinions.

On the other hand, it is the function of morality and religion to liberate the individual from the particular perspective of his social class. This is

Hegel's view after 1803. In his moral judgment the individual is not restricted by his social group and may not be exposed to any civil compulsion with respect to questions of conscience. As a religious being, he knows himself to be of the same value and rank as the highest member of a society—he is "the equal of the prince."[20]

But how can a community have an enduring, let alone necessary, common will when it is composed of such individual sovereign judges of the morally good and evil? How can it remain a "collective individual" capable of action? Didn't Rousseau already see the gap between "ancient" republicanism and the modern morality of conscience?[21]

Hegel's chapter on "Morality," and above all the last section titled "Conscience, The Beautiful Soul, Evil and its Forgiveness," clearly does not treat all the problems of conscience. The legal aspect of the freedom of conscience is only marginally discussed, and the problem of the religious contents of conscience is not mentioned at all. For these questions we must include considerations from the *Philosophy of Right* and the *Encyclopaedia*.[22] In the *Phenomenology*, the conceptions of morality in Jacobi, Fichte and the romantics play the key role. Hegel establishes a systematic connection among them that is hardly fair to the individual positions and that often makes the references difficult to trace. Since I am concerned with the *systematic* aspects of the criticism of conscience, I will limit myself to the "reconciliation" of conscience with the community as it appears in the last section of the chapter.[23]

Hegel first of all unfolds the inner oppositions of the moral point of view, which recognizes the conscience of each individual as the highest authority in any decision about dutiful action. The assertion of the dutifulness of an action implies its universal character and its right to recognition by every self-conscious agent. However, at the same time the individual's conscience is supposed to decide what his duty is even in concrete cases. This knowledge is an intuitive act: conscience knows immediately and without an examination or weighing out of individual duties what it is enjoined to do. "In the simple moral action of conscience, duties are lumped together in such a way that all these single entities are straightaway demolished, and the sifting of them in the steadfast certainty of conscience to ascertain what our duty is, simply does not take place."[24] Even the "consciousness" of the analysis of the situation has its limitations: The claim cannot be redeemed that "requires that the actual case before it . . . be viewed unrestrictedly in all its bearings, and therefore that all the circumstances of the case . . . be accurately known and taken into consideration."[25] The situation simply cannot be surveyed adequately since "reality is a plurality of circumstances which breaks up and spreads out endlessly in all directions, backwards into their conditions, sideways into their connections, forwards in their consequences."[26] This is also valid—one may add with respect to the contemporary discussion of utilitarianism—for results of an action in regard to the balance of pleasure and pain for the concerned parties. Hegel discusses a version of this in the universal maxim: "action for the general good is to be preferred to action for the good of the individual."[27] Such a maxim contradicts the distance of conscience from the public laws since their "substance" and goal is, according to Hegel, precisely the common good.

Unshakable, intuitive self-certainty and rising above the public rules are constitutive of the concept of conscience presented in the *Phenomenology*. Moreover, conscience is not only the concrete application, but also the very ground of morality and right. Such a concept of conscience can be found in some passages from Jacobi's novel *Woldemar* and in Novalis's *Heinrich von Ofterdingen*.[28] In *Woldemar*, however, the superiority of conscience over right and law, and the identification of the moral genius with the artistic genius, is criticized by Jacobi himself.[29] Only Novalis unconditionally attributes to conscience the "divine power of creation" of which Hegel speaks.[30] I do not want to pursue these references further here since they have already been discussed by Emmanuel Hirsch and Otto Pöggeler.[31] But the general problem that any decision may be based on a claim of conscience that cannot be proved by an intersubjective argument is independent of Hegel's criticism of his contemporaries. In the contemporary discussion in ethics, for instance, J. L. Mackie has treated this issue.[32]

Hegel discusses this problem in a second step that concerns the relation of the individual agent of conscience (*Gewissenstäter*) to the common moral consciousness of his group. The group is supposed to recognize the individual conscience and the freedom of the agent from publicly valid rules. Since this claim is grounded on nothing but a private conviction, it cannot be acceptable for a universal public moral consciousness but must be judged as evil. "Others, therefore, do not know whether this conscience is morally good or evil, or rather they not only cannot know, but they must also take it to be evil."[33]

Whoever places his will above the universal will is evil also according to the Kantian definition. In order to reject a claim of conscience, the motives of the agent are given a new interpretation. One attributes to him self-interest, the desire for fame or honor—an explanation that is grounded no less well or badly than the claim of the agent of conscience.

A resolution of this opposition is possible only by means of a concession from each party, which appears internally necessary from a philosophical point of view but which demands moral performance from each party. From the point of view of philosophical reflection, both are equally one-sided: the acting consciousness sets its own dissenting decision of conscience against universally valid customs, and the judging consciousness cannot make its moral criteria concrete and therefore does not want to compromise their universality through any sort of application. As is well known, Hegel sees this judging form of consciousness as embodied in the "beautiful soul," a concept and literary figure that was also introduced into the literature and philosophy of the Goethe period by Jacobi.[34] Such a consciousness becomes inactive for the sake of the universality of moral ideals and refuses "to let his own *inner* being come forth into the *outer* existence of speech."[35] Both sides defend a universal claim that is supposed to be recognized by the other. But this is possible only by a mutual backing down: the individual who insists upon his conscience must acknowledge the one-sided nature and possible error of its decision. Likewise, the universal moral consciousness must, for its part, recognize individual decision as a necessary moment of spirit, even in its nonconformity and wickedness: "The word of reconciliation is the *objectively* existent Spirit, which beholds the pure knowledge of itself of *qua universal* essence, in its opposite, in the pure knowledge of itself qua absolutely self-contained and exclusive *individuality*—a reciprocal recognition which is *absolute* Spirit."[36] Conscience and universal lawfulness are thus two moments of a single spirit, which makes itself concrete in an individual decision, through which it enriches and perfects itself and at the same time either fits the individual decision within the common order of right and life or cancels it.

In the *Phenomenology* Hegel did not develop the concrete forms of this reconciliation. But the reference in the final chapter to the correspondence between this form of morality and the last level of revealed, Christian religion leads us to suppose that he sees the reconciliation at work above all in the forms of rational religious morality. The religious community is the medium for the mutual correction of public morality and private conscience. In it outsiders are recognized and integrated—possibly even with the correction of accepted common criteria.

Certainly, there are also forms of legal and political integration of the "outsider" that are discussed in the *Philosophy of Right*: for instance the direct appeal to the highest decision-maker of the state who can correct legal procedures and administration or can pardon criminals, i.e., make their act "undone."[37] The ultimate "political" decision of the sovereign is in itself necessarily individual. What the *Phenomenology* says ontologically about spirit is, according to the *Philosophy of Right*, also legally and practically valid for "objective spirit": it is a universal individualizing itself. The constitution, laws and culture of a community must be expressed not only in the action of its citizens but also in special representatives. The individuality of objective spirit must be embodied in the rational willing of a natural individual, the monarch.

The "wickedness" of the decision of conscience, on the other hand, is minimized in various ways: for instance, by the subjection of the agent of conscience to public laws, by the education of conscience through law and professional virtue, and finally—as the *Encyclopaedia* says—by the justification of the constitutional state in religious conscience.[38] This, however, requires enlightened religion and speculative philosophy.

But is the problem completely solved with this answer? Can "substantial ethical life" characterized by the performance of a functional role in the life of a people, be united in this way with the sovereign decision of conscience? Isn't this unification a matter of chance as long as the final decision about good and evil remains with the individual in the religious conscience—even the decision about the truth of the ultimate grounds for justification? Hasn't Hegel, in fact, mitigated the opposition between private conscience and public ethical life?

IV

Let us first summarize the conception of individuality developed in the *Phenomenology*: according to the "Self-Consciousness" chapter, the self-understanding of an individual itself and its feeling of self as a desiring being already presuppose an agreement with other self-conscious agents. My self-understanding, as acting in some relation with other agents, is not possible without their confirmation, and this confirmation must be spontaneous, if it is not to be dissembled. Free, mutual agreement is, however, possible only in communities in which the members mutually recognize each other in their claims and roles. Individual self-understanding participates in a common self-understanding in which both sides condition each other mutually. A developed common self-understanding must also leave room for a certain distance of the individual from all social convention, i.e., for his free self-reflection and truth testing.

On the other hand, the self-actualization of an individual in the community has to "translate" itself into the community's behavioral patterns and conventions. Communication presupposes social habits and undisputed rules, but rigid conformism sacrifices the spontaneity of the self to a blind social mechanism. The community itself must be understood as an individual with its own self-understanding and behavioral patterns that can be changed only "organically." For this, the historical developments leading to more individual freedom and to more collective ability to act must be understood. The highest individual form of unification of rational universality and intuitive situatedness is conscience. But an agent acting from his own conscience does not do justice to his social environment if he cannot justify his decisions with reasons belonging to a common rationality.

For Hegel, unlike Locke, a legal procedure for resistance based on reasons of conscience is unthinkable.[39] The addressee of the ultimate appeal to justice cannot be the voice of God in conscience (Locke's "appeal to heaven") but rather the individual incarnation of the spirit of the constitution, the monarch. For Hegel, revolutions in the established order of a state can be justified at best in view of the spirit of history if they find agreement among contemporaries and bring forth a new, "organic" and viable order. However, if a state finds itself in its essentials at the high point of the culture of its time—as was the case, according to Hegel, for the states of Europe influenced by the Enlightenment and Protestantism—then there is no rational reason for a fundamental revolution. In this European culture, specifically in its constitution and law, art and religion, science and philosophy, there is expressed not merely a certain degree of development and perfection but truth itself. This truth can be reconstructed in a conceptual system in such a manner that little room for development and plurality is left. For Hegel, even this conceptual system is like the individual and the community, a self-individualizing whole, in which every determination contains the whole in varyingly developed forms right up to the most comprehensive and most concrete concentration in the "personal" apex. In this apex, the self-reflecting *logos* is the whole of its determinations in a pure self-relation of its movement of thought, or "method."

Since Hegel considers the truth-claim of a specific culture to be philosophically redeemable, in the final analysis he runs the risk, as I have already indicated, of mitigating the opposition between individual conscience and communal spirit. But if neither the *Logic* nor the *Phenomenology* can completely convince us of the truth of speculative philosophy in Hegel's sense of the term—and furthermore, if a philosophical proof of the truth for any given religion is no longer possible—then a lasting agreement between decisions of conscience and public customs cannot be expected. Certainly Hegel is right in his view that decisions of conscience cannot be legally sacrosanct. An exception to the laws would represent a legal privileging of convictions or even an acknowledgment of the validity of private lawgiving. Rationally, the most that can be expected is a renunciation of any sort of compulsion of conscience and a hope for agreement in the ways of thinking and acting in the common culture of a people.

But how much hope can we put in the integrating effect of a common moral and legal culture while we live in "multicultural" states with radically different views of the freedom of conscience, individual rights and communal tasks? The violent attempt to establish ethnic monocultures shows a desperate return to the commonalities of language, religion, and history. Of course, in Hegel's view as well this is incompatible with the universal rights and moral freedoms of the modern subject. But, on the other hand, one does not have to abandon the supporting force of common moral and legal traditions. Particularly in a society that has overcome rigid class distinctions, institutions are necessary in which specialized knowledge, appropriate and fair ways of dealing with others, and a qualified perspective about the task of the community have to be developed. Moreover, a culture of civil friendship must be developed that, along with other social virtues, unifies mutual respect, even for outsiders, and public engagement and willingness to renounce one's own self-interest. Here we can still learn from the Aristotelian tradition, without its metaphysical presuppositions. Certainly, some of the present renewals of the Aristotelian doctrine of virtue, for example in MacIntyre,[40] have an anti-individualistic tendency that could be criticized even from Hegel's perspective as a return to a premodern "village morality." And against Hegel's and Aristotle's insights, virtues in a technologically developed society are becoming more and more private: they can no longer be understood as the optimal performance of ever scarcer socially necessary roles, but rather only as humanly admirable individual forms of comportment in changing contexts.

Today the common self-understanding of a people or a state can no longer rest on an absolute truth-claim. On account of this, individuals must be granted more latitude in their conception of a private morality. However, this conception should be understandable as a contribution to the development of the moral culture of a community. Individual perfection as the expression of a common moral culture designates perhaps a realizable inheritance of Hegel's *Phenomenology*. Against prevailing liberal conceptions, this means, however, that morality, right, and political culture should not merely prevent or regulate conflicts between private preferences. They must, like art and science, pursue an ideal of perfection without ever claiming to have reached it.[41] Instead of the technical perfection of inner and outer nature, we should be concerned with an aesthetic and political culture that does justice to humans and nature—in accordance with our best available knowledge at a given time. About such a cultural perfection, the various cultures and traditions can enter into competition with each other. Not the closed, fundamentalist cultures, but rather the open, pluralistic, even eclectic ones, will have the best chances in such a competition. This, at least, seems to be what history teaches us.

Notes

1. Hilary Putnam, *Reason, Truth and History* (New York: Cambridge University Press 1981), p. ix.

2. G.W.F. Hegel, *Gesammelte Werke*, vol. 4, *Jenaer Kritische Schriften*, ed. H. Buchner and O. Pöggeler (Hamburg: Felix Meiner, 1968), p. 13.

3. This desire for the desire of the other is of crucial importance in the famous interpretation by A. Kojève, *Introduction to the Reading of Hegel*, trans. J. Nichols Jr. (New York: Basic Books, 1969).

4. Cf. Aristotle, *Nicomachean Ethics* 1069 b 20 ff.

5. Cf. my "Der Kampf um Anerkennung. Zur Auseinandersetzung Hegels mit Hobbes in den Jenaer Schriften" *Hegel-Studien* 9 (1974), pp. 155–207.

6. Cf. Hegel's hints at the realization of stoicism in Roman Law in the chapter on the state of law (*Rechtszustand*). Cf. Hegel, *Phänomenologie des Geistes*, ed. H.-F. Wessels and H. Clairmont (Hamburg: Felix Meiner, 1988), pp. 316 f. Quotations follow the translation by A.V. Miller: Hegel, *Phenomenology of Spirit* (hereafter *PS*) (Oxford: Clarendon Press, 1977).

7. Hegel's theory of mutual recognition is discussed in my *Anerkennung als Prinzip der praktischen Philosophie* (Freiburg/München: Alber, 1979); and recently in Robert Williams, *Recognition: Fichte and Hegel on the Other* (Albany: State University of New York Press, 1992); and in Axel Honneth, *Der Kampf um Anerkennung. Zur moralischen Grammatik sozialer Konflikte* (Frankfurt: Suhrkamp, 1992).

8. Otto Pöggeler argues against a social-historical interpretation of the *Phenomenology*. He understands the task of the book primarily as an exercise in the use of the categories of speculative philosophy. See his *Hegels Idee einer Phänomenologie des Geistes* (Freiburg/München: Alber, 1973), pp. 235, 259 and the postscript to the second edition, 1993, p. 413.

9. Cf. Hegel, *Enzyklopädie der Philosophischen Wissenschaften im Grundrisse* (1830), ed. F. Nicolin and O. Pöggeler (Hamburg: Felix Meiner, 1959). pp. 369, 396, 397, 430–36; Hegel, *Philosophy of Right*, trans. T. M. Knox (Oxford: Clarendon Press, 1952), pp. 35, 57.

10. Blaise Pascal, *Pensées*, ed. L. Lafuma (Paris, 1951), vol.1, series II, fragm. #423.

11. Hegel, *PS*, p. 238.

12. The editor's note in the 1988 German edition of the *Phenomenology* suggests a reference to Thomas Paine, *Rights of Man* (1791/92). But Paine's concept seems by far too rational and elaborate for a vague "law" of general spontaneity. Hegel may rather have Jacobi's novel *Woldemar* in mind (F. H. Jacobi, *Werke*, vol.

5, ed. F. Roth and F. Köppen [Darmstadt: Wissenschaftliche Buchgesellschaft, 1968], pp. 91, 115; cf. Jacobi's critique of "*Eigendünkel*," p. 382). He also refers to this novel later in his discussion of virtue and conscience. Regarding Hegel and Jacobi, see O. Pöggeler, *Hegels Kritik der Romantik* (Diss. Bonn, 1956), pp. 39 ff., 52 ff.

13. Hegel, *PS*, p. 259.

14. Ibid.

15. Hegel, *Enzyklopädie*, § 142.

16. For a general evaluation of Hegel's critcism of Kant's practical philosophy, see C. Cesa, "Tra moralità e Sittlichkeit. Sul confronto di Hegel con ka filosofia pratica die Kant," in *Hegel Interprete di Kant*, ed. V. Verra (Napoli, 1981), pp. 147–78.

17. Hegel, *PS*, p. 361.

18. Franz Rosenzweig, *Hegel und der Staat* (Munich/Berlin: R. Oldenbourg, 1920; reprint Aalen: Scientia, 1962), vol. 1, pp. 193, 219.

19. Leo Rauch, *Hegel and the Human Spirit: A Translation of the Jena Lectures on the Philosophy of Spirit, 1805–06* (Detroit: Wayne State University Press, 1986), pp. 163, 165.

20. Rauch, *Hegel and the Human Spirit*, p. 177.

21. Cf. R. Spaemann, *Rousseau—Bürger ohne Vaterland* (Munich, 1980), pp. 29 f.

22. Cf. my *Praktische Philosophie im Deutschen Idealismus* (Frankfurt: Suhrkamp, 1992), pp. 225 ff., 324.

23. Hegel's treatment of conscience in the *Phenomenology* is carefully discussed in M. d'Abbiero, *Le ombre della comunità* (Genoa: Marietti, 1991), pp. 165 ff.

24. Hegel, *PS*, p. 386.

25. Ibid., p. 389.

26. Ibid.

27. Ibid., p. 392.

28. Jacobi, *Woldemar*, pp. 87, 217. However, the crucial concept in Jacobi's concept of the moral genius is virtue, not conscience. Conscience is the central moral and even theoretical concept in Novalis, *Heinrich von Ofterdingen*, ed. J. Hörisch (Frankfurt, 1982), pp. 167 ff.

29. Jacobi, *Woldemar*, pp. 379, 469.

30. Novalis, *Heinrich von Ofterdingen*, p. 169.

31. See Eli Hirsch, "Die Beisetzung der Romantiker in Hegels Phänomenologie," in *Materialien zu Hegels Phänomenologie des Geistes*, ed. H.F. Fulda and D. Henrich (Frankfurt: Suhrkamp, 1973; first published 1924), pp. 245–75; Pöggeler, *Hegels Kritik der Romantik*.

32. Cf. J. L. Mackie, *Ethics: Inventing Right and Wrong* (New York: Penguin, 1977), p. 124.

33. Hegel, *PS*, p. 394.

34. Jacobi, *Woldemar*, pp. 14, 281, 375, 419; J. W. Goethe, *Wilhelm Meisters Lehrjahre*, bk. 6, in *Bekenntnisse einer schönen Seele* (*Werke*, Weimarer Ausgabe, Abt. I, Bd. 22).

35. Hegel, *PS*, p. 405.

36. Ibid., p. 408.

37. Cf. Hegel, *Philosophy of Right*, pp. 282, 295.

38. Cf. ibid., pp. 140, 220; *Enzyklopädie* (1830), p. 552.

39. John Locke, *Two Treatises of Government*, ed. P. Laslett (New York: Cambridge University Press, 1988), pp. 422, 445 (Second Treatise, pp. 209, 241 f.).

40. Alasdair MacIntyre, *After Virtue*, 2nd ed. (Notre Dame, Ind.: University of Notre Dame Press, 1984), pp. 255 ff. I am not clear in which way MacIntyre's concept of "local forms of community" characterized by a moral life in the tradition of Aristotle and St. Benedict (p. 263) can avoid the danger of an oppressive "village morality."

41. As to the idea of perfection, cf. Iris Murdoch, *The Sovereignty of Good* (London: Routledge, 1970), especially chap. 1, "The Idea of Perfection."

9

Hegel's Ethical Rationalism

Robert Pippin

I

Hegel is a well-known defender of what he regarded as a distinctly modern notion of "right" (*Recht*): justice and law in a political sense, rightness or even righteousness in a more broadly ethical sense. Modern institutions conform to *the* criterion of right: freedom.[1] This already sets Hegel apart from those who think happiness, or the perfection of the natural qualities of the soul, is the human good, but it would be fair to say he has provoked the most debate among those moral and liberal theorists dissatisfied with his interpretation of that criterion, not with his elevation of the notion to supreme status.

This dissatisfaction is provoked by Hegel's claim that participation in certain modern social institutions is constitutive of freedom; to live freely *is* to participate in these institutions, to *be* a social and political being of a certain sort.[2] This already sounds dangerously conformist and anti-individualist and Eurocentric to many. But many also would hold that the position slips from dangerous romanticism to deep obscurity with the defense Hegel gives for such a claim. For Hegel clearly takes the side of Rousseau and Kant before him and strongly links the possibility of free agency with a kind of practical rationality. Being a modern ethical being (*sittliches Wesen*) is to act on rational norms and thereby to have realized (or actualized, *verwirklicht*) freedom, and *this* is what turns out to require a certain social existence. In the following, I want to propose one way of seeing the links between these questions.

Two familiar characterizations of Hegel's case, however, have impeded a full consideration of his argument. First, the nature of Hegel's ethical rationalism has been obscured by his own spirited critique of moral rigorism, dualism of all kinds, the general "*Zerrissenheit*" of modern life and so forth. Inspired by such passages, and what they might mean for Hegel's own account of moral motivation, some commentators classify Hegel as a romantic, along the lines of Schiller's position, and so try to equate a practically rational life with some sort of sensuous harmony with "the whole," or with *The Rational*, "what there truly is." This has the effect of rendering Hegel, to use his own classification, a premodern rationalist in ethics and so conflicts with his own enthusiastic modernism. (*My* reasons for acting, "my subjectivity," seem lost in any such account of *being* in harmony with, reconciled with, actuality.) Second, since Hegel's account of ethical life is an historical one, it is often assumed that Hegel's argument for the power of modern ethical ideals, his claim that the rational is now "actual," must rely on a sweeping, highly implausible historical theodicy, that the rationality of our participation in ethical practices stems from something like the divine rationality of history itself and its resolution or culmination in modern institutions. I want to propose an alternative, although preliminary, reading of Hegel's general case for the rationality of ethical life.

II

It should first be noted that Hegel does not argue that such sociality is all there is to an ethically worthy life. In his *Elements of the Philosophy of Right,* he sides with those who argue that all human beings are bearers of "abstract rights." In his account too, it is simply by virtue of being free agents that we are universally entitled to the ownership of some property and to the rights of transfer and exchange that this entails.[3] He also argues that responsibility may be attributed to free agents only by reference to their individual intentions and purposes and that we all stand under universal moral obligations to all other individuals, whether another person is a member of our ethical community or not.[4]

However, the claims of right and morality are also argued to be "incomplete," and this is where the controversy begins. For example, "The sphere of right and that of morality *cannot exist independently* [*für sich*]; they *must* have the ethical as their support and foundation."[5]

This sort of claim not only expresses a reservation against believing that the question of a fully free and so worthy life can be *exhausted* by the protection of rights and the avoidance of moral harm, as if a fuller, more active and purposive collective pursuit of ethically worthy ends is also important.[6] Hegel is clearly maintaining that "the ethical" is the "*support and foundation*" of rights-based and moral sanctions, that it is only within certain social institutions that the nature, implications, and bindingness of other sorts of normative claims can be fully made out. He is especially claiming that it is only in being so linked that I can actually *be* an individual, a rights-bearing, morally responsible individual.[7]

Ethical life, then, these "laws and institutions which have being in and for themselves," comprises what is called the "objective sphere of ethics," which is said to "take the place of the abstract good" and so to constitute "the living good" for human beings.[8] Hence, too, the familiar question: Why does Hegel believe that such social interaction is so essential to the human good and that it is the "basis and support" of all other aspects of a worthy life?

III

I begin with Hegel's own formulations of the claim for the rationality of ethical life. The decisive criterion is clearly expressed in the preface of the *Philosophy of Right*. We cannot be content, Hegel writes, to stop at what is merely given as public law and public morality,

> whether the latter is supported by the external positive authority of the state or of mutual agreement among human beings, or by the authority of inner feeling and the heart and by the testimony of the spirit which immediately concurs with this.[9]

The task is rather to grasp what is "rational" in such institutions, so that it "may also gain a rational form and thereby appear justified to free thinking." A modern social norm "demands to know itself as united in its innermost being with the truth."[10]

It is more widely conceded now than it used to be that such a claim is not based on an a priori justification of whatever happens in history, at least if the justification is supposed to mean that everything is deducible or derivable with necessity from the unfoldings of some World Spirit.[11]

This is a simple point, but it needs to be vigorously stressed. In the *Philosophy of Right*, Hegel never argues for the rationality of modern institutions simply by describing them and then insisting that, whatever they are, they must be rational because we know a priori that history is rational. However one interprets and defends the claim that "history" has produced these rational institutions, one is independently committed to some interpretation and defense of the claim that the institutions are rational. Indeed, unless we are able to describe independently in what sense such institutions *are* practically rational, any claim that some process of historical change produced them or even had to produce them, won't have accomplished very much. More generally, it is very hard to see how any theoretical claim about the rationality of history could count for me as a reason to act, as *my* reason to participate in the institution. Since Hegel believes there are reasons to act, we shall have to look elsewhere.[12]

But then the problem arises: What else could it mean to suggest that modern institutions are rational, can be "justified to free thinking"? A natural assumption would be that Hegel means to affirm only those "laws and institutions" that are in some sense "what all participants would rationally will." Only thereby could such institutions actually comprise the "objective sphere of ethics." Modern institutions simply happen to meet such a criterion.

This response raises a problem. Hegel clearly does maintain that modern ethical life is rational and that one distinctive feature of modern ethical life is that this rationality is the basis of both the normative claims for allegiance implied by such institutions and for the actual participation and continued allegiance of participants. In the modern "ethical world" it is "reason" (not tradition or sentiment or religion) which has "power and mastery"; the science of right will "conceive and present the state as something in itself rational." And, "In right, man must meet with his own reason."[13]

Such passages, together with Hegel's spirited attacks on sentiment, or national feeling and the like, in accounting for ethical and political allegiances, do appear to support the view that by calling modern ethical institutions rational, he is simply appealing to the widely shared modern notion that they are the institutions that any individual would will, were she to will rationally. But it also does not help much in our attempt to understand his claims for the centrality and priority of ethical life. In such readings, it would be hypothetically rational individuals who are "prior," with ethical life as a consequence. And this simply cannot be right.[14]

So, to avoid resting everything on some contractarian view of the rational will, or on the *List der Vernunft* thesis, we need to begin instead with Hegel's general theory of practical rationality—what, for him, makes some consideration, desire, social convention, and so forth a justified *reason to act*—and then move to a case showing that a commitment to and participation in modern social existence, the family based on personal love, modern market societies, and republican regimes, are defensible, are rational, in that sense.

IV

Although Hegel has a great many things to say about the considerations that lead him to a social view of rationality (to the claim that reason is essentially a social norm), there are also a number of levels and strategies in Hegel's large *Encyclopedic* presentation, and it is possible to understand his defense of the claim for the priority of ethical life and the rationality of modern social institutions in more limited ways, ways that derive from his general account of practical rationality.[15] That case begins with an account of agency itself and, following Kantian suggestions, the "conditions" of agency. Since, as we shall see in more detail, Hegel agrees with Kant that agents are agents by subscribing to norms, he proceeds immediately to the question of the norms constitutive of agency itself and then to the question of what really subscribing to them would involve. As he proceeds it becomes clearer what he thinks, and a little clearer why. To be an agent, to be free, is to subscribe to norms of a certain sort, and both the content of such norms and their possibly being mine (their motivating power) require certain sorts of social institutions and my participation in them.

In line with this approach, consider first the more limited question of what it is for human conduct to be governed by a *norm*. Now Hegel's theoretical approach to the question on freedom is different than Kant's,[16] but both agree that it is practically necessary that, when I act, I act "under the Idea of freedom," as Kant put it.[17] (All this need mean for the moment is: I cannot act as if, say, my acts were determined unless *I* determine that I shall; unless even such a principle becomes my norm.) And for both, this requirement cannot be satisfied if I act arbitrarily or wantonly. If the act comes about because of my determining that it should, then I am acting for some reason or other, some reason that it should occur. I am acting under a self-imposed norm. For Hegel, the question of the possibility of such a norm is the same as the conditions under which a principle or goal or claim could play some role in an agent's justification of, reasons for, an action (and so in any third-person explanation of the action).[18] As in many philosophical accounts, if the question is an explanation of why some agent did what she did, or "what motivated agent A to Ø," a necessary component of the answer has to be "what reasons justified the act for A." We need to know what A thought she was doing, and why she thought Ø should be done, or we will not know what action is being performed.

Now this situation immediately gets complicated because there is obviously a difference between someone's own "personal reasons" (sometimes glossed as simply "motives") for doing something and genuinely justifying "reasons."[19] (People still have "their own reasons" for acting even when they act against their own interests, or irrationally, or imprudently, when there is no good reason in any sense to do what they do.) But if we assume that anyone's individual reasons for acting, in order to be reasons for that person, must fit into some overall structure of justification, or that no one could have reasons for acting that weren't regarded by that person as sufficiently justifying (even if, from her own point of view, mistakenly), then we are entitled to look for the explicit or implicit justificatory claim implied in people's acting as they do.[20] This is what it means to say that their actions presuppose a commitment to some norm, whether acknowledged or not. (For the moment we can remain neutral on whether such a norm could ultimately be wholly "subjective" or personal.[21])

Hegel is quite explicit about a number of conditions necessary for a norm to be a norm in this sense. For example, for something to function as a norm, it must be *self-imposed*. In one sense, his theory of "objective spirit" just is an account of the possibility of those human activities and interactions that are what they are *because* constrained by such self-imposed norms in certain ways, constituted by such self-conscious norm following. An action *is* the fulfillment of a contract, the punishment of a criminal, a promising, an inheriting, and so forth only because the participants in the relevant institutions "take themselves" to be participating in institutions governed by certain rules and view these rules as norms, reasons, as in some sense justifiable. Said more speculatively, human beings are "in themselves" what they are "for themselves," or are collectively self-forming creatures. (This has nothing to do with what they individually believe or the contents of their mental history. Such self-construals can be implicit, dispositional, revealed more in deeds than statements, and so forth. But that is another story.) The main point is: were individuals to perform the same body movements without taking themselves to be following such norms, or if they took themselves to be conforming to other norms, the actions would not be those actions.

Said perhaps more directly: there are and can be no straightforwardly natural or divine norms, no facts about the natural world, or revelations about God's will, or intuition of nonnatural properties, which, just by *being* such facts or revelations, thereby constrain or direct my conduct. They could be norms only if they could count as reasons for me to act, and nothing about what nature is like or what God said, etc., can show that.[22]

V

Thus far, such reference to a generally Kantian direction in Hegel's reflections do not yet distinguish his position much. By a Kantian direction I mean, so far, only: the considerations Hegel is interested in defending, as a subject's reasons to act, are not reasons because based on perceptions of objective goods, or benefits, or values, but are evaluations and esteemings (*conferrings* of value) whose *justifications* have a certain character.[23] Certain sorts of relations in which persons stand to their own activities are what is decisive in "actions being valuable."

So far, however, all we know is that actions are those events that are explicable by reference to a subject's reasons for acting, that such reasons always presuppose certain norms for action, and that such norms can be norms only as self-imposed, as conferring value on a course of action for a subject, and so cannot be understood in what has come to be called some strictly "externalist" sense.[24] What we have said so far, though, is still compatible with someone acting because he wanted to very badly and because his general norm is to do whatever he most feels like doing.

Now, as indicated, Kant argued that this sort of norm could not be fully self-imposed (or ultimately justifying) because such a subscription must itself be motivated by considerations not fully self-imposed, dispositions and desires true only of the individual and which Kant called constitutive only of heteronomy, not autonomy. Only one sort of norm could be self-imposed and so could constitute what it is for an act to be rationally motivated and so freely performed: his famous categorical imperative.

Hegel's objections to this possibility begin to reveal the direction of his own analysis of what could count as practical reasons. He objects, that is, to the claim that an action is fully justifiable to all others, and so morally worthy, only if it is governed by a certain kind of norm, the categorical imperative. On the Kantian account, this means that an action is morally worthy only if performed "from duty alone," or only if I act in recognition of, and am motivated by, the bindingness of this norm. If I act because of a fear for my reputation, or to secure my individual well-being, or to satisfy an emotional need to act benevolently, I might end up doing what a purely rational agent would do because of the constraints of universal justifiability, but I get no moral credit. In such a case, my reasons for action—what Kant calls my maxim—express a principle which I have no reason to expect that others could share or find justifying except under contingent circumstances. (They just happen to want what I want or fear what I fear, etc.) I thus could not expect my reasons to act to count as reasons for them.

Hegel famously claimed first that the categorical imperative, or the general principle to do only what all other rational agents could will to do, cannot be action guiding because so formal. It fails, as a norm, to rule in or rule out, with sufficient determinacy, kinds of actions or policies. It is empty.

I am not concerned with that objection here. But Hegel also claims that the criterion of moral worth is *rigoristic*, that no one *could* act as Kant demands. And that claim brings out what seem to be Hegel's implicit assumptions about the conditions under which a principle could serve as a norm and so should point the way to the most important issues in his theory of the rationality of ethical life.

There are two *loci classici* for such claims, one in chapter 6 of the *Phenomenology of Spirit* and the other in the account of the moral point of view in the *Philosophy of Right*. In the former, Hegel argues that Kant's own moral system reveals that he himself acknowledges that

> The moral consciousness cannot forego happiness and leave this element out of its absolute purpose. The purpose, which is expressed as pure duty, essentially implies this individual self-consciousness; individual conviction and the knowledge of it constitute an absolute element in morality.[25]

But, Hegel argues, Kant's response to this recognition of the inevitably interested and individual character of our relation to any principle of action is, on the one hand, to condemn us as radically evil, incapable of ever fully realizing, but only at best striving for, what reason demands, and, on the other hand, to concede that human beings could not sustain the moral enterprise, could not fully make sense of its demands, unless it were also possible to believe in an all-powerful moral judge, an immortal soul, and eternal reward and punishment.

This condemnation of our unworthiness and this concession about "Postulates" reveals, according to Hegel, that in such a point of view, we are not "serious" about what morality requires, that we "dissemble," or shift inconsistently from what we say we are requiring of ourselves to what we concede we are able to do, and so we promote a kind of hypocrisy, a feature of Christian moralism that Hegel considers essential to it, not incidental.[26] "Duty for duty's sake," Hegel charges,

> is an unreality; it becomes a reality in the deed of an individuality, and the action is thereby charged with the aspect of particularity. No man is a hero to his valet; not, however, because the man is not a hero, but because the valet is a valet, whose dealings are with the man, not as a hero, but as one who eats, drinks, and wears clothes, in general, with his individual wants and fancies. Thus, for the judging consciousness, there is no action in which it could not oppose to the universal aspect of the action, the personal aspect of the individuality, and play the part of the moral valet towards the agent.[27]

Clearly, Hegel's proposition is that playing the rôle of this moralistic valet is pointless, that there is no point in formulating a view of the right that could not count for any real individual as a reason to act. And finally:

> the right of the subject's particularity to find satisfaction or—to put it differently—the right of subjective freedom, is the pivotal and focal point in the difference between antiquity and the modern age. This right, in its infinity, is expressed in Christianity, and it has become the universal and actual principle of a new form of the world.[28]

I am not here concerned with the obvious problem of whether all of this amounts to a fair criticism of Kant. One might dispute whether Kant's position relies on the Postulates in the way Hegel claims, and one might insist that nothing Hegel says undermines Kant's considered or full argument to establish how pure practical reason can motivate action (perhaps, chapter 3 of part 1 of the *Critique of Practical Reason*). I want to focus attention only on what these remarks reveal about Hegel's own position and the general structure of his reasoning in support of it.

This is especially important because there are two different ways of drawing implications from these sorts of considerations, and Hegel's formulations often suggest what I think is the most misleading and ultimately un-Hegelian. On one interpretation, what Hegel is saying is that human actions can be shown to presuppose a certain motivational structure and that once we understand these constraints, we will be able to see that no recognition of what practical reason requires of us could fit such constraints; no consideration of what an impartial agent, motivated by no motives particular to him, would do could ever be on its own a motivating factor in action. Presumably, we can show that human beings could only be motivated by desire for their own happiness and well-being and so could be motivated to subscribe to norms only on this condition. On this reading, the standard for a justifiable reason is a principle that makes no reference to any particular desires or ends and the question is, Why should I care about such a principle, how could I come to see such a view of a purely rational agent *as a reason for me to act*? The answer is: I could not. Kant's own fuller position, so goes such a reading, shows this, since he concedes we could not and either reminds us that we just are radically evil or looks around for motivational support for that which could not on its own motivate (the Postulates).

This sort of an objection is a familiar one in attacks on rationalist conceptions of ethics and is most familiar in Hume's attacks on the possibility of any practical rationality. If we see Hegel's attacks on Kant in this light, and keep in mind our question about sociality, then Hegel begins to emerge, somewhat surprisingly, as sympathetic to these Humean concerns but as substituting a kind of historical sociology for Hume's naturalistic psychology in accounting for the true wellsprings of human motivation. It is our affective and emotional dispositions, or our basic interest in our own well-being, or, say, our status (our "being recognized"), that motivates what we do, but we are far more malleable than Hume realized. We can come to understand our own much-desired happiness or status in certain ways, by seeing that well-being or status as essentially linked to others and so subscribing to norms that others could fully share, but all this only in certain sorts of societies, with certain sorts of socially formative, desire-shaping institutions.

As we have been seeing throughout, however, this *cannot* be the right conclusion to draw from Hegel's attack on Kant's rigorism. He is manifestly a rationalist in ethics and stresses this himself even when criticizing the moral point of view:

> the assertion that human beings cannot know the truth, but have to do only with appearances, or that thought is harmful to the good will and other similar notions, deprive the spirit both of all intellectual and of all ethical worth and dignity. The right to recognize nothing that I do not perceive as rational is the highest right of the subject, but by virtue of its subjective determination, it is at the same time, formal; on the other hand, the right of the rational—as the objective—over the subject, remains firmly established.[29]

This must mean, contrary to the obvious readings, that Hegel is not denying that rational considerations can be motivating on their own (can count for an agent as reasons) or that *any* position that maintains this is positivistic or rigoristic. He must be objecting to the *kinds* of rational considerations that Kant thinks are compelling. (In other words, the claim is that it is Kant's version of an unconditionally overriding or categorical imperative, or his own formulation of an exclusive and singular principle of free action, that creates the rigoristic dualism between my core or autonomous self and the entirety of my contingent attachments. The appearance Hegel creates, that he is celebrating what Kant is decrying, self-love, hedonism, egoistic motivation, is what is misleading. Ultimately, Hegel is objecting to this characterization of nonmoral motivation.)

Yet the results thus far are still puzzling. As we have seen, whatever Hegel believes about the content of norms, they are not binding simply because of who we are and what we happen to desire or who we have become historically, and so because of what we cannot, as a matter of fact, help but esteem, but, still, they are binding because of what it is rational to esteem. Yet when Kant demands that we subscribe to norms that can be rationally self-imposed, norms that are even abstractly "social" (in all acts we must take the other into account, as in the idealized Kingdom of Ends), Hegel complains that Kant is hardhearted, ascetic, and that his account could not explain how we could be motivated to act on such principles, could count the categorical imperative as a reason to act.[30]

VI

Hegel is clearly no antirationalist, "whatever-my-community-says-is-OK" conventionalist. To understand his case for this better, we need to put the passages we have been quoting into some sort of perspective. That is, we need to recall some classificatory issues. As the passages we have been quoting indicate, Hegel clearly believes that the *possibility of motivation* is a crucial condition for a norm's possible status as a norm. He does not, that is, believe that some consideration could count as a norm, and so a compelling reason for me to act, even if it could be shown that I could never be *motivated* to act on such a reason. Indeed, this is the very sort of language he uses to introduce his notion of ethical life. He claims that it is "in ethical existence" (*an dem sittlichen Sein*) that self-consciousness has its "basis in and for itself" *and* its *motivating purpose* (*bewegenden Zweck*).[31]

Said more abstractly, Hegel accepts as a general constraint on the possibility of a norm the principle P:

> For some fact, or state, or consideration to be able to count as a reason for S to do A, S's acceptance of, or having of, such a consideration must be able to motivate him to do A.[32]

Now, as already noted, such a principle is most common in antirationalist and skeptical accounts. Philosophers who accept P are often Humeans, moral sense theorists, egoists, or emotivists. Given this, it can look like the general debate is between those who, on the one hand, want to keep ethical considerations pure by keeping them strictly normative. The good *is* simply, say, the greatest happiness for the greatest number, even if the best of human beings, because of their selfishness and irrationality, could never act for the sake of such a good, or the good is some nonnatural property in the world that we can apprehend but could bring ourselves to realize and promote only if prompted by some view of our own self-interest. On the other side are those who find it hard to understand any view of the human good, or moral value, that was not originally oriented from some consideration of what human beings want and need or oriented from what would have to be compelling reasons for persons to act. The former camp worries that we are thereby trimming our ethical norms to fit our commonest natures; the latter worries that we are spinning tales of ethical perfection that not only take no account of our common humanity but betray a kind of ascetic hostility to it.[33]

But this would all be too narrow a way of viewing the categories. As we have been seeing, plenty of rationalists in ethics believe in P and would never concede that they have trimmed their moral sails to fit our corrupt needs. Kant is one, and Hegel is another.[34] It would be a long digression to explore theses options in any detail. But it should at least be noted that, in the case of Hegel, one result of viewing the matter from this perspective is that it now helps clarify his famous denial that normative theory is about what merely ought to be and so his celebration of the rationality of the actual. We can now see, I hope, that what is important in such formulations is what he is denying: that rational, normative principles could be considered norms apart from any demonstration of how and why they could be actual reasons for persons to act, or that some inspection of a quality or a good could function as a norm apart from such a demonstration of my "taking it up" and justifying "imposing" it on myself as a norm. To say that the rational is actual is just to say that some reasons *could not but be motivating,* that no person could be presumed to be "actually" indifferent to what they require. And to make such a claim is to attack any view of moral theory (like many religious views) that ignores such a consideration.

So, finally, the decisive question is why Hegel believes *this*, a question that is one of the two decisive ones in our inquiry. The other is why he thinks only his version of "ethical norms" could satisfy this condition.[35]

VII

The most general result of trying to view Hegel as a rationalist can now be formulated. In a phrase, Hegel's concerns are, manifestly, not Schiller's. He is not portraying the problem as *primarily* one of psychic harmony, integration, or an inner alienation, as if what is originally wrong with the moral point of view is that it requires me to detach myself from all that I have come to care about, all that makes me "me." The question he is raising, *together* with Kant, is whether what you have come to care about really does reflect "you" as a *subject*, or is about the conditions of *attachment* in the first place, such that these attachments truly reflect your subjectivity.[36] Kant thinks this is so if they pass the test of moral permissibility, are at least not *contrary* to what a spontaneous will could legislate. Hegel thinks this an excessively limiting and unsatisfying view, and that the norms you must be committed to, such that any such attachments could come to reflect you and your subjectivity (such that you could be acting "under the idea of freedom"), involve social and institutional conditions wherein you can "meet with" your own reason.

The decisive issue in his case, read this way, turns on quite a general consideration. As we have seen, Hegel's interest in the role of motivational possibility in ethical theory does not amount to a claim that we must find room for hedonic or egoistic concerns in order to explain such motivation. He accepts the normative link between justification and autonomy and then begins to look for some account of a *kind* of justification that would explain "*its* own" motivational force.[37] In his somewhat romantic language, finding such a consideration, one that does not *need* extrarational support, ensures that we have found "ourselves," that freedom as "*bei sich selbst sein*," "being-with-self," can be assured. Like many others, his account comes down to what reasons could be given by a rationalist or, for that matter, by any "internalist" in satisfying such a motivational constraint.

This issue is complicated in Kant's case by the fact that the question of practical rationality is a question of imperatives, not "reasons" to act in the general sense. So what reason recognizes in Kant is that we stand unavoidably under a universal moral law, a requirement that we must act in a certain way. We experience the "fact of reason," that by acting intentionally at all we are bound by such a norm. (He then goes on to show what happens to us sensibly in recognizing this obligation, how we come to feel the pain of denying the priority of self-love and the esteem he calls "respect.") But it is in showing *that there is this obligation* that Kant, to his mind, shows that we could not be indifferent to what reason commands, could not possibly ask "why should I care, want to do, what pure reason requires?" If he can show what he claims, we have already been given the answer to such a question. Hegel will not agree that practical reasons are primarily imperatives, and he obviously thinks that Kant has formulated the inescapably compelling character of reason in an inadequate way, but the structure of this argument is what is important here.

That structure involves considerations in Kant and Hegel that are unavoidably metaphysical, at least in the general Kantian sense of a "metaphysics of the person."[38] It is at this level, I want to suggest, that Kant and Hegel are mostly disagreeing and that the distinctiveness of Hegel's position begins to emerge. The common question is: What must be involved in acting "under the Idea of freedom?" and this is understood to mean: What principle must govern the self-imposition of norms by such a freely acting agent? This sounds like it is asking about some putatively timeless event, "when" someone would, on purely rational grounds, impose such a principle ("self-love," or "lawfulness itself"). But the question asks rather: What principles are we already and unavoidably committed to just by virtue of acting under the Idea of freedom? (This would mean: such that, imagining what it would be to repudiate such a consideration and still "act under the Idea of freedom" would be incoherent.) To know what such a consideration is (or must be), we have to know what it must be to be such an agent. All the weight of the case for any principle (or for the social norms of ethical life) comes down to that sort of a consideration. (It is quite important to stress that the same would be true for a skeptic, like Hume or Williams, who wants to say: *given who we are, only* considerations relativized to what we already want, or are motivated to pursue, *could* count as reasons to act. And the same would be true of a strict contractarian, whose views on what could be justified to, or accepted by, another must be driven by some consideration of what could not but be compelling for anyone, given "who we are.")

We argue, in other words, that conceding that someone could be indifferent to some sorts of considerations, whether commands of reason or the goal of self-realization, would be tantamount to postulating a being wholly unrecognizable as us, someone who could not act on reasons at all. Because of this, such considerations could not be unmotivating (at least where all this means is prima facie motivating; I could not be indifferent to them and still be me.)

The same sort of account is visible in many other rational accounts, although with wide variations. Plato too argues that what pure reason determines to be the best social and political arrangement could not be such a norm, unless it could also be shown that "justice pays," that individuals could be motivated to subscribe to such a norm. Given "what it is to be a human being," and what the fulfillment and happiness of such a creature amounts to, no one could help but be motivated to subscribe to the *Republic, if* (and here the decisive, massive "if") they could come to understand their own "good" or psychic health. They cannot, of course, and so we end up with the peculiar position (peculiar to moderns) that masses of people are as happy as they could be, if they live in the *Republic*, even if, subjectively, *they* might disagree and prefer, imprudently, to live in a democratic regime.

And so on in Kant. Here the considerations rest on the metaphysics of agency itself, the "fact" that no one could deny that she is a free, responsible agent and so could not possibly be indifferent to what is a priori required of any such agent. To deny that would be to try to deny that one is free—something that one must be free to be able to do. (It is, in all such arguments, supposed to be *impossible* to concede "I see what there is good reason for me to do" and still ask, "Why should I do what there is good reason for me to do?")

The parallel claims in Hegel are terminologically idiosyncratic, but the general strategy is still recognizable, as in the general account of *Sittlichkeit* found in *Die Vorlesungen von 1819/20 in einer Nachschrift*.

> In so far as individuals are in such an ethical unity, they attain their true norm [*ihr wahrhaftes Recht*]. The individuals attain their norm in that in such a manner they acquire their essence. They would achieve thereby, as one says, their destiny [*ihre Bestimmung*]. . . In that the ethical is actual in individuals, it is their soul in general, the universal mode of their actuality.[39]

And, "The common ethical life of a people is their liberation [*Befreiung*]; in it they come to an intuition of themselves."[40]

VIII

I have argued that we can locate Hegel roughly in this rationalist camp and as broadly sympathetic to many aspects of the Kantian approach. In Hegel's account such justifications are rational in that they cannot merely appeal to or "deliberate from" elements of "my motivational set."[41] This is because the evaluative issue at stake for a subject is precisely the bindingness or justifiability, as reasons to act, *of* any such element. It is only by means of the possibility of such an evaluative "elevation" and "purification" of my own motives that any such element could be said truly to belong to me, to be mine.[42] The basic Hegelian point is: this desideratum is not a condition I can achieve individually, by trying to "put out of play" all my attachments.

Accordingly, a summary of the points made thus far would look like this. My argument has been that the core of Hegel's account of *Sittlichkeit* consists in a theory of practical rationality, or an account of what sorts of considerations count for Hegel as reasons to act, i.e., count as considerations that could confer value on one course of action over another. (And again, what Hegel is aiming for is: only within certain sorts of social arrangements could various considerations count for me as such reasons.) This is the crucial question because Hegel clearly believes that only a practically rational agent is a free agent, and he is trying to identify an ethically worthy life with a free life. As just noted, it is a controversial position because Hegel also believes that only a certain sort of social being (a "*sittliches Wesen*") can be a "practically rational" and so free being.

Traditionally the question of the rationality of action has been limited to views like: a course of action is rational if it is the most efficient means to some end; or it is rational if conducive to an end unavoidable in *any* worthy or free life (some "human good"); or a course of action is rational if required by a principle no one could be presumed exempt from.

Hegel's general theory of action is teleological; all action is purposive, or for the sake of some end. But Hegel does not believe that such a premise commits him to any Humean account of motivation (where ends are set by "the passions") or an Aristotelian theory of the human good (of essential ends). In Hegel's account, to pursue an end is to subject oneself to a norm; I pursue an end for a reason, a reason I take to have justifying force. This then raises the central question of the conditions under which my attachment to any such ends, any conferring of value, could be expressive of rational agency, "reasons we could share," to borrow a recent phrase.[43] It is these conditions that are argued to be unavoidably social and historical, although a formal and general account of the adequacy of modern institutions in meeting such criteria can also be given. (All we have done to motivate such a direction thus far is to explore what Hegel assumes is involved in trying to meet these constraints by an account of an individual, abstracting from all particular, contingent attachments, and thereby finding himself subject to a moral law. He is trying to suggest that we could defend such a Kantian way of justifying action or conferring value only by a metaphysics of personhood that must make some implausible and question-begging assumption.) And Hegel is clearly trying to move in just the opposite direction: only *within* certain social conditions could individual attachments to a plurality of possible ends be established "non-idiosyncratically," *in* consideration of others and their attachments. Therefore I am a rational agent and so in that sense free only within *those* (rational) institutions.

If this much of at least the framework for the problem is accepted, the basic problem then comes down to how to determine the relevant conditions or constraints on any such attaching or conferring—especially against Kantian suspicions. Since, I have been trying to suggest, much of Hegel's case is best seen in the light of and as opposed to that Kantian position, let me risk redundancy and state these suspicions again in the sharpest way.

The largest Kantian suspicion about this direction is the most obvious. It is extremely important for Kant to be able to maintain that freedom is simply a capacity all rational agents share. (It is a noumenal predicate in his infinitely misleading language.) This is what entitles everyone to universal respect, whatever social arrangements they live in. And it is what allows us to expect that anyone, slave or free, abused and destitute or loved and nurtured, be held equally and unqualifiedly responsible in any circumstance for failing to do the right thing.

Stated just this way, I see no evidence that Hegel would want to deny any of these claims. He too defends the idea of universal moral respect and some sort of universal moral responsibility. What he dismisses with such frustration is the view that the kind of moral freedom that could be so universally ascribed and the kind of obligations consistent with it could be said to exhaust our ethical lives, as if doing no moral harm in this sense qualifies us as ethically worthy, or as if truly being a subject of one's deeds could be exhaustively understood as such moral subjectivity, or as if the place of such a moral ideal within a complex ethical life could be dismissed by insisting that subscribing to such an ideal is all there is to an ethically worthy life. (Indeed, only within a particularly alienated and fragmented ethical community would such a moral ideal come to have its supreme and exclusive motivational force.) (He would have the same impatience with the claim that politics, religion, and the virtues should all be seen merely as enabling us to reach such a standard.) A Kantian case could be made that someone must come to "see" her own agency, truly being a subject, in such a narrow, moralistic sense (with everything else heteronomy), and so be unavoidably compelled, bound by the moral law, only by appeal to a ludicrously narrow practical metaphysics of the person—a position created, Hegel implies, only to secure, not genuinely to support, the moral position.

There is no doubt, in other words, that we could abstract from everything that is particular and contingent to arrive at a conception of ourselves thin and uncontroversial enough to justify those sorts of considerations that no one could be presumed indifferent to. We assume that the rationality condition requires that we ask ourselves what an impartial agent having no attachments or commitments, or relying on, as it is said, no agent-relative reasons, could justify. This, though, would be the opposite mistake of thinking that such deliberation and justification must be based on some particular, contingent set of interests and desires or projects, on who we contingently are. That view is wrong, but it is equally wrong to conclude that we must adopt a criterion of justification based on so neutral and impartial a notion of a subject as to be quite problematically related to a real life of attachments, commitments, desires, and projects. In Kant's view the obligations that derive from so considering ourselves are supposed to be unconditional, to trump all other practical considerations, what might otherwise seem for us practical necessities. In Hegel's view, this could be shown (and so the motivational condition met) only by showing that all aspects of our lives not connected with such a core self, or set of obligations, could simply be "indeterminately negated," were mere appearances, "*not*" who "we are."

Admittedly, thus far such considerations merely get us to a "neither the one nor the other" position, an affirmation that there is some reflective, deliberative condition necessary for our attachments and projects to be genuinely "ours" (for us to be "subjects," to act "under the Idea of freedom"), but a denial that this can be satisfied by a merely prudential deliberation, or by the strict demands of moral rationality. It would be necessary, to complete the picture, to show how some worked-out view of the fundamental or unavoidable character of our social attachments determines the character of this reflective or rationality condition.

But it is not difficult to imagine how such an account looks for Hegel. In the simplest terms, individuals all have parents, can reproduce the conditions of their existence only cooperatively, and are invariably subject to, or the subjects of, decisions about the common good or the exercise of some sort of political power. We are not simply one agent among many, or all alike in being agents who can act on reasons. We are, but even in being able to recognize and act on such considerations, we require others, such that the socially formative and educational institutions that make possible such recognition and its realization are effective.[44] Or, while there are moral considerations in an ethical life, they are not unconditionally overriding considerations. In trying to determine if and when such obligations may be superseded (as when a spy lies) we bring to bear on judgment the unavoidably formative and motivational priority of ethical life as sketched here.[45]

IX

Hegel claims a number of things about modern ethical life. Modern institutions are said to embody the differentiated normative requirements of modern social life and so to provide a rich content-laden answer to the question of what we ought to do. And he also claims that in modern ethical roles, there is no gap between the objective demands of right and what he terms the subjective, what I have called the motivating, aspect of such demands. These claims open up a number of questions. Our interest has been to explore a foundational issue: what Hegel means by insisting that such an ethical existence is normatively prior in any worthy life and that participation in such roles is rational.

These questions have obviously turned out to be linked. Among other things the priority claim means that being a family member, and a cooperative, dependent member of some norm-governed, ecumenically complex civil society, and having an unavoidable stake in some political whole, are not relations to others I could be said to have imposed on myself as the putative result of the requirements of rational individuality *überhaupt*. However these predeliberative attachments and formative involvements do not represent merely our tradition, community, or *Volk*. Their claim on us can be redeemed by their public claim to legitimacy, as making possible and sustaining a social culture of subjects who act on reasons, who can and do "move" within the "space of reasons."

That is, to summarize another way, if we try to classify Hegel's position more carefully, it becomes possible to see how his defense of the rationality of modern social institutions relies on quite common and indeed necessary strategies in any rationalist ethics. He accepts the condition that reasons for action must be able to motivate a subject to act and tries to consider such possible reasons in the light of the general features of personhood and possible agency. What he adds is a simple but decisive insistence that whatever we are, we are not autonomously self-forming creatures. Everything, he argues, about both the content and motivating force of reasons to act changes dramatically when we take account of this fact at some significant level. Such a realization shifts the focus of ethical issues away from two traditional areas and toward a third. It denies the priority or even the presumed ultimacy of "dispositions," "passions," or "ground projects" in our esteemings and evaluatings, raising large questions about what could be said to make up an "individual's *own*" inclinations, such that they could be decisive. But Hegel's ethical point of view does not do so under the assumption that the only condition which will realize such self-determination is some kind of radical detachment, a pure, individual moral self-legislation, or a reflection coming from, and leading to, "nowhere."

Notes

1. In Hegel's introduction to the *Philosophy of Right*, the "system of right" is said to comprise the "realm of actualized freedom, the world of spirit produced from within itself as a second nature" (§ 4; *GPR*, p. 28; *PR*, p. 35). And in § 29, "Right is therefore in general freedom, as Idea" (*GPR*, p. 45; *PR*, p. 58). For the most part, references to the *Philosophy of Right* will be first to the *Grundlinien der Philosophie des Rechts* (hereafter *GPR*) (Hamburg: Felix Meiner, 1955) and where possible will refer to the paragraph number or Remark (R) to the paragraph. Page numbers will be followed by reference to the English translation of H.B. Nisbet, *Elements of the Philosophy of Right* (hereafter *PR*), ed. A. Wood (Cambridge: Cambridge University Press, 1991), which I have relied on but occasionally altered. For the original of Gans's *Zusätze*, or the Additions translated by Nisbet, I have consulted volume 7 of the *Jubiläumsausgabe in zwanzig Bänden* (hereafter *GPR*2) ed. H. Glockner (Stuttgart: Frommann Verlag, 1952) and the relevant volume of Ilting's edition of the lectures, as quoted below.

2. The reference to modernity in this claim is not an idle modifier. In his *Phenomenology*, to cite one of many such references, Hegel makes very clear that an ethical community as such (one constitutive of freedom) is a distinctly modern, Western European accomplishment. It is not merely the "universal substance of all

individuals (*die allgemeine Substanz aller Einzelnen*"); rather, "ethical" or "true" spirit is a substance "known by these individuals as their own essence [*Wesen*] and their own work." It is not like some "essential light" that swallows up such individuals (in the manner of readings of Hegel's own account of the "divinity" of the state) but is the "free *Volk*" in which "custom [*Sitte*] makes up the substance of all, whose actuality and existence each and everyone knows as his own will and deed." *Phänomenologie des Geistes* (hereafter *PhG*), in *Gesammelte Werke*, vol. 9 (Hamburg: Felix Meiner, 1980), p. 376; *Hegel's Phenomenology of Spirit* (hereafter *PS*), trans. A.V. Miller (Oxford: Oxford University Press, 1979), pp. 424–25.

3. Hegel also argues, contrary the contractarian or natural right tradition, that our being capable of mutually recognizing each other as equally rights-bearing, morally responsible individuals is itself a historical achievement, that such claims are relevant to modern agents, and so his defense of property entitlement is, by classical liberal standards, idiosyncratic. He recognizes too what his historical argument will sound like, and he hastens to try to show that he is not thereby "excusing" past injustices with respect to right, as the important Addition to *PR* § 3 makes clear.

4. The general purpose of Hegel's practical philosophy is to describe the conditions for the possibility of being a free subject, or of "agency," and the results of that account are: (i) be a "person" and respect others as persons (don't violate another's rights; respect legitimate claims of non-interference, above all with respect to property); (ii) be a "subject," or be morally responsible for what you do and regard others, all other human beings, as morally responsible beings; and (iii) be an ethical being, affirm and sustain certain ethical institutions. Or in the conventional language: act legally, act morally, act ethically; respect rights, do what is morally obligatory, and do what is ethically good.

5. This is from Hotho's *Zusatz* to § 141, *GPR*2, p. 225; *PR*, p. 186. Right and morality are said to have "*das Sittliche zum Träger, zur Grundlage. . .*" For the original notes, see Hegel, *Vorlesungen über Rechtsphilosophie 1818–1831* (hereafter *VRP*), vol. 3, ed. K. Ilting (Stuttgart-Bad Cannstatt: Frommann-Holzboog, 1974), p. 478.

6. I also don't mean by this that Hegel has in mind by such collectivity a common attempt to bring about substantive benefits or goods. Ethical life in general is not what Oakeshott has called an "enterprise" association, but a "civil" association. Cf. Michael Oakeshott, "On the Character of a Modern European State," in *On Human Conduct* (Oxford: Clarendon Press, 1975), pp. 257–63. The ends we pursue consist of the arrangements of our relations to each other such that any end might be pursued in certain ethically appropriate ("self-chosen") ways. The point being made here is that even such a "civil" ethical end involves much more than rights protection and the avoidance of moral harm, or more than institutions that guarantee the former and take account of the latter. Such an end requires a

kind of civic life or political culture. What that might consist in and why it is the "rational" support and foundation of all "right" are the issues in Hegel's *Rechtsphilosophie*.

7. His best-known reasons in support of such a claim for the priority of ethical life have to do with a broad, systematically based *animus* against what he regards as merely "formal" or wholly "negative" normative principles. Those considerations are quite important, but I shall be reconstructing a version of Hegel's case here without direct reliance on such logical issues.

8. Hegel, § 144; *GPR*, p. 142; *PR*, p. 189. § 142; *GPR*, p. 142; *PR*, p. 189.

9. Hegel, *GPR*, pp. 5–6; *PR*, p. 11.

10. Hegel, *GPR*, pp. 5–6; *PR*, p. 11.

11. This consensus has been strengthened recently by the edition and publication of Hegel's 1819/20 lecture notes, where the rationality of the actual is said much more cautiously, without such theodocical implications. Cf. Hegel, *Philosophie des Rechts. Die Vorlesung von 1819/20 in einer Nachschrift* (hereafter *VPRN*), ed. D. Henrich (Frankfurt: Suhrkamp, 1983), p. 51, and Henrich's remarks, pp. 13–17. In the *Berlin Encyclopedia*, Hegel also describes objective spirit not only as a world "brought forth" by spirit, but "to be brought forth by it." *Enzyklopädie der philosophischen Wissenschaften III*, in Hegel, *Werke: Theorie Werkausgabe* (Frankfurt: Suhrkamp Verlag, 1970), § 385. Cf. the discussion by Allen W. Wood, *Hegel's Ethical Thought* (Cambridge: Cambridge University Press, 1990), pp. 10–11.

12. This is not at all to suggest that Hegel's account of historical change is hopeless or that it plays no role in a full case for the rationality of modern institutions. The twin claims (1) that agents, by acting at all, are implicitly committed to the realization of freeedom and (2) that when such a norm is unrealized, institutions and practices cannot be sustainable (that this normative failure is a good historical explanation of breakdown and transition) are worth more rigorous attention than they have been given. I am only claiming here that it would be a gross oversimplification to collapse or reduce all dimensions of Hegel's claim for the rationality of modern *Sittlichkeit* into a general claim about the rationality of history. As we shall see later, Hegel will come to link the possibility of a rational norm, as well as the "actuality" of such a norm (which I shall interpret as its possibly motivating force) with a historical narrative. But he is also out to show the inescapability of such a historical self-consciousness in any ethical account, and that transcendental case needs to be clarified and analyzed first.

13. The first two quotations are from Hegel's preface to the *Philosophy of Right*, *GPR*, p. 7; *PR*, p. 13; and *GPR*, p. 15; *PR* p. 21. The last remark is from Hotho's additions, *VRP*, p. 96; *PR*, p. 14. And, for Hegel, modern man is said to

"meet his own reason" in a particularly enthusiastic, affirmative way. Such an ethical world, presumably in its rationality, "is not something alien to the subject. On the contrary, the subject bears spiritual witness to them as to its own essence, in which it has its self-sentiment and lives as in its element which is not distinct from itself—a relationship which is immediate and closer to identity than even faith or trust" (§ 147; *GPR*, p. 143; *PR*, p. 191).

14. Moreover the enthusiastic passages which begin the last section of Hegel's *Philosophy of Right* do not appeal to what a subject would approve were she rational in some hyper-idealized state of nature, but to what "modern subjects" actually "find" in modern "actual" ethical "self-consciousness," i.e. "its own substantial being" (Cf. §§ 146 and 147). And then there are also the famous claims in the preface to the *Philosophy of Right* that philosophy does not propose "a world beyond which exists God knows where," and that philosophy "must distance itself as far as possible from the obligation to construct a state as it ought to be. . ." (*GPR*, pp. 14–15; *PR*, pp. 20 and 21).

15. In any full account of his position, one would have to include and assess his claim that the characteristics that define any possible individuality, or the various ways persons could understand themselves to be "bounded off" from and distinct from others, are historically distinct possibilities, and are necessarily results of what he called a "struggle for mutual recognition." As both a phenomenological and logical issue, Hegel's claim is that self-definition is necessarily self-definition in relation to and even in unavoidable struggle with an other and that no account of such a possible relation and result can ignore the inevitable problem of power inherent in such a relation. We cannot figure out what it is rational for anyone to do by pretending that life begins with relatively self-transparent, self-owning, determinate, adult, self-sufficient individuals. The ultimate Hegelian claim is that the problem of self-definition or identity is a problem of social power, not metaphysical truth, and that this process has a certain "logic" to it, and it is a book-length topic in itself.

Also part of any full picture would have to be Hegel's denial that "being rational" (which he agrees is the foundation of any possible agency or freedom) involves only the proper use of a faculty or competence. To be rational in this ultimate sense is to "fit into" the rational structure of the whole, to live "in truth," in the light of how "things in the broadest sense of that term hang together in the broadest sense of that term." The phrase is of course Wilfrid Sellars's, not Hegel's. See "Philosophy and the Scientific Image of Man," in *Science, Perception and Reality* (London: Routledge & Kegan Paul, 1963), p. 1. Cf. also the helpful remarks by Ludwig Siep, *Praktische Philosophie im Deutschen Idealismus* (Frankfurt: Suhrkamp, 1992), p. 308, and my discussion in "Horstmann, Siep and German Idealism," *European Journal of Philosophy* 2 (1994) pp. 85–96.

16. See my "Idealism and Agency in Kant and Hegel," *Journal of Philosophy* 88 (1991), pp. 532–41.

17. *Groundwork of the Metaphysic of Morals*, trans. H. J. Paton (New York: Harper & Row, 1964), p. 448 of *Kants gesammelte Schriften*, vol. 4 (Berlin: Königliche Preussische Akademie der Wissenschaften, 1900–22). Cf. Henry Allison, "Morality and Freedom: Kant's Reciprocity Thesis," *Philosophical Review* 95 (1986), pp. 393–425; and Christine Korsgaard, "Morality as Freedom," in *Kant's Practical Philosophy Reconsidered*, ed. Y. Yovel (Dordrecht: Kluwer, 1989), pp. 23–48.

18. Cf. Bernard Williams, "Internal and External Reasons," in *Moral Luck* (Cambridge: Cambridge University Press, 1981), p. 102: "If there are reasons for action, it must be that people sometimes act for those reasons, and if they do, their reasons must figure in some correct explanation of their action. . . . "

19. This issue has played a large role in the many contemporary discussions of duties, reasons to act, and "motivation." Cf. W. D. Falk's exploration of the ambiguities in "pure" oughts, and "formal-motivational" considerations in "'Ought' and Motivation," in *Ought, Reasons, and Morality* (Ithaca: Cornell University Press, 1986), pp. 21–41.

20. For a discussion of how Hegel argues for the claim that any "natural will" (or any policy that seeks only to satisfy natural inclinations) itself commits a subject to a "fully free" or rational will (ultimately understood as embodied in collectively self-forming institutions), see my "Hegel, Ethical Reasons, Kantian Rejoinders," *Philosophical Topics* 19 (1991), pp. 99–132. For a discussion of Hegel's objections to prudential notions of rationality, see my "You Can't Get There from Here: Transition Problems in Hegel's *Phenomenology of Spirit*," in *The Cambridge Companion to Hegel*, ed. F. C. Beiser (Cambridge: Cambridge University Press, 1993), pp. 52–85.

21. Compare the controversial denial that they could be, by Thomas Nagel, *The Possibility of Altruism* (Princeton: Princeton University Press, 1970), Chapters 10–13. And see his qualification and, to some extent, withdrawal of such a claim in *The View from Nowhere* (New York: Oxford University Press, 1986), p. 159.

22. "*Die Rechtsgesetze sind Gesetztes, herkommend von Menschen*." ["Laws of right are posited, made, something stemming from human beings."] Hegel, *VRP*, p. 93.

I should also acknowledge here that much of my summary of Hegel could be challenged on interpretive grounds. I've only space here to claim that I think my approach—to claim that (a) Hegel's defense of the rationality of social norms, or modern *Sittlichkeit*, (b) can be derived from an analysis of the possibility of agency, (c) once we recognize what is involved in trying to show that the norms constitutive of such agency must be shown to be motivating or "internal"—is well supported in various texts from very early in his writings.

23. There is a useful discussion of the ambiguities in Nagel on this score in

Christine Korsgaard, "The Reasons We Can Share: An Attack on the Distinction between Agent-Relative and Agent-Neutral Reasons," in *Altruism*, ed. E. F. Paul, F. D. Miller Jr. and J. Paul (Cambridge: Cambridge University Press, 1993), pp. 24–51.

24. In Williams's formulation: "The whole point of external reasons statements is that they can be true independently of the agent's motivations" ("Internal and External Reasons," p. 107). His example there is from a James story—Owen Wingrave's father insists that Owen has a reason to join the military even if Owen has no motivation to do so; his desires all lead in other directions and he hates everything about military life and what it means. Very few philosophers have tried to affirm that there are external reasons in *this* sense. (In fact, as Williams himself seems to acknowledge, this is a strange example since it is very unlikely that Wingrave really *has* any good reason to give his son, one that could stand up to any scrutiny. The reason *this* isn't an external reason is, very likely, not because there are no such reasons, but because this is a bad one.) The rationalist response is usually to try to show that various considerations can meet the internalist constraint without being "relativized" to some existing, contingent "motivational set." In the recent literature, this response is common to Nagel and Korsgaard despite their differences. It is also common to Kant and Hegel, I am claiming, and the point then is to see how they differ on what *could not* be unmotivating, a matter of indifference.

25. Hegel, *PhG*, p. 326; *PS*, p. 366.

26. Hegel, *PhG*, p. 334; *PS*, pp. 376–77.

27. Hegel, *PhG*, p. 358; *PS*, p. 404.

28. Hegel, *GPR*, p. 112; *PR*, p. 151. More poetically put: "The laurels of pure willing are dry leaves which have never been green." *GPR*2, p. 184; *PR*, p. 153.

29. Hegel, *GPR*, p. 117; *PR*, p. 159.

30. This means that the dispute between them does not concern a difference between Hegel's doctrine of "internal reasons" and Kant's commitment to a theory of psychological causation, as Wood claims in *Hegel's Ethical Thought*. I agree that Hegel believes in the possibility of motivational overdetermination for an action and does not think moral worth could require the isolation of some "pure motive." But I don't think the reasons he believes this, and why he objects to Kant's theory of moral worth, have to do with views about reasons and causes in Kant. I agree here with Henry Allison's statement of Kant's own commitment to internal reasons, *Kant's Theory of Freedom* (Cambridge: Cambridge University Press, 1990), p. 189.

31. Hegel, *GPR*, p. 142; *PR*, p. 189.

32. This acceptance is the import, I take it, of the passages from Hegel's *Philosophy of Right* quoted above, as well as § 132.

33. Cf. the concluding remarks of W. K. Frankena, "Obligation and Motivation in Recent Moral Philosophy," in *Essays in Moral Philosophy*, ed. A. Melden (Seattle: University of Washington Press, 1958), pp. 40–81.

34. Indeed, it is possible to be an objectivist of some sort and still accept it. One could hold that perceiving the world in a certain way *is* thereby already motivating, that discerning the morally salient features of a situation or possible goal thereby gives one an unavoidable motivation to act. One would accept the constraint suggested by P but argue that it is a mistake to separate such moral discernment from, as a separate question, "what does the motivating" when I proceed to act on such perception. There is no way I could come to see it that way and experience any motivational gap. If I did, that would be good evidence that I hadn't seen what was there to see. (Irrationality is in the perceiving, or what clouds the perceiving, not in the willing or strength of will.)

35. As we have also already noted in the case of Hegel, the preferability of one course of action over another, or all "value," is something conferred, not discovered. A principle or goal can function as a norm, governing my evaluation of possible actions, only if self-imposed, a claim which forces the issue back to the conditions for a genuine self-imposition, or a truly justifiable valuing. (On this conception, that is, finding something valuable is not justified by being able to point to an inherently valuable quality of the thing, in the world, but by having reasons for the estimating or esteeming that do not rely on some consideration that is beyond justification or merely "given.") Just as in Kant, this in turn raises for Hegel the question of the relation between what, prima facie, might seem like merely my own reasons for acting, reasons relevant just to me and my situation, or subjective reasons, and the general considerations I must appeal to in justifying those reasons to myself, or, ultimately, objective reasons.

That Hegel has this view of the problem in mind is signaled everywhere by the terms we have already quoted and in many other places. He objects to what he regards as a Kantian opposition between subjective, or heteronomously determined, ends and objective, or autonomously determined, ends, implying that such objectivity is ultimately a condition of the justifying power of any consideration. He speaks metaphorically of our having to "take up" what is subjectively and contingently compelling and "purify" it, "raising it up" to a level of "self-creating" "infinity" wherein our "subjective right of satisfaction" is completed in "rationality" itself, and so on.

These views, all of them shifting the question of the rationality of norms to questions of justifiability and the relation between subjective and objective reasons, raise their own problems. For one thing, such approaches tend to "over-solve" the problem and tend to treat all subjective reasons as reasons only if finally objective, thus grossly undervaluing the personal, or agent-centered, point of view. But at issue now is a final clarification of how Hegel's position on *Sittlichkeit* looks in the light of these considerations.

36. More generally, this is the problem with all "Humeanism" in ethics, or with any inclination to treat my "passions," desires, ground projects, or motivational set as a basic reason to act. Such a position must take account of the possibility, and ultimately the priority, of "motivated," or rationally induced, desires, not just "unmotivated desires." For useful discussions of this version of the isssues, see: R. Jay Wallace, "How to Argue about Practical Reason," *Mind* 99 (1990), pp. 355–85; Rachel Cohen, "Hume and Humeanism in Ethics," *Pacific Philosophical Quarterly* 69 (1988), pp. 99–116; Michael Smith, "The Humean Theory of Motivation," *Mind* 96 (1987), pp. 36–61; Philip Petit, "Humeans, Anti-Humeans, and Motivation," *Mind* 96 (1987), pp. 531–33; Michael Smith, "On Humeans, Anti–Humeans, and Motivation: A Reply to Pettit" *Mind* 98 (1988), pp. 589–95.

37. "The subject is in its home in that which is objective, it is in its element." Hegel, *VPRN*, p. 122.

38. Cf. Nagel, *The View from Nowhere*, pp. 14, 18.

39. Hegel, *VRPN*, p. 124. (I am indebted to Terry Pinkard for drawing my attention to these formulations.)

40. Ibid., p. 125.

41. This is Williams's language in "Internal and External Reasons." See also the notion of a "ground project" in "Persons, Character, and Morality," in *Moral Luck*, pp. 1–19.

42. The general issue of Hegel's disagreements with moral realism, and his own position of how values are conferred, and on the conditions for any such conferring, are obviously quite complex. But it might help to note that one of the models Hegel is probably thinking of here is Kant's for the justifiability of aesthetic judgments. There too the value, beauty, is conferred by subjects, not found; but there too not conferred contingently, as a result of dispositions and desires we happen to share. The expectation that others *ought* to find this beautiful rests on a general assessment of who they are and so what they could not be unaffected by, if, as in most cases, it were not for something distorting or blocking such a reaction and conferring.

43. See Korsgaard, "The Reasons We Can Share."

44. One of the ways Hegel tries to show this concerns the problems of moral judgment, in cases when moral or rights-based claims are understood to be the claims they are by being formulated in terms of an abstractly conceived moral

subject. Understanding the problem of moral justifiability in terms of avoiding treating myself as an exception, or avoiding a maxim that would deny others the standing of free agents, agents who can be motivated by reasons, etc., will certainly end up prohibiting broad classes of action. But all moral life requires fairly fine-grained moral judgment, and while there are not application rules for such judgment, if the general orientation is provided only by such a "thin" conception of persons, the results, he claims, will be worrisome. Such a reliance will ensure, he argues, that I will have no criterion of judgment to rely on in deciding what counts as treating another as means or end except my own "conscience," or the depth of my personal conviction. And this, he tries to show, will ultimately allow everyone to claim some form of moral purity, agreement in moral principle, but widespread self-indulgence in moral practice. Avoiding such a result will require some more complex view of our unavoidable, historically "thick" bonds with others and *thereby* the kinds of reasons to act, or norms, which could not but be motivating, given such conditions.

Kant of course denies this and has a doctrine of virtue. I have tried to argue elsewhere that that doctrine does not meet this objection. Cf. my "Hegel, Ethical Reasons, Kantian Rejoinders."

45. This sort of limitation of morality is discussed in a Hegelian spirit by Williams in *Ethics and the Limits of Philosophy*, chap. 10.

10

Is Subjectivity a Non-Thing, an Absurdity [*Unding*]? On Some Difficulties in Naturalistic Reductions of Self-Consciousness

Manfred Frank

Self-consciousness and subjectivity designate not one topic of interest among others but rather *the* basic interest that has gripped modern philosophy from Descartes to Husserl (and Sartre). The interest in this theme grew from the fact that modern thinkers again and again held self-consciousness to be an indubitable principle. It counted as the "*fundamentum inconcussum*" from whose intelligibility one hoped to be able to deduce all other insights, step by step. This audacious foundational claim was given up already by the skeptical German early romantics; today it is really not maintained any more. But self-consciousness still counts as important. It even plays a major role in contemporary philosophy of mind.

The intuitions that stand behind this revived interest in the subject can be made intelligible in three ways:

1. If we renounce understanding ourselves as subjects (in a sense essential for our self-description), we cannot practice philosophy at all any more. For then that which we have in mind when we consciously relate to ourselves cannot be distinguished from physical entities. If we accept this conclusion as valid, then to be consistent we must also recognize that physicalism provides the only fitting description of our actuality. After all, *physicalism* is the term for the conviction that there exists only that which falls under the scope of the procedures that the natural sciences (and, in the last instance, physics) have developed. Quine has named this standpoint "naturalized epistemology."[1] In its most radical form,[2] it is tantamount to denying outright the existence of conscious phenomena. Here the mental is not reduced to something else, e.g., a "causal role"—as "functional state identity theory"[3] supposes. Rather, it is maintained that what we mean by "mental phenomena" are in actuality physical appear-

ances—and nothing more. With the expression "and nothing more," the mental is "eliminated." But in the same stroke, the ground is taken away from philosophy as a form of theory distinct from natural science. Since philosophy is occupied with consciousness in a way that is essential for it, philosophy itself is eliminated with the elimination of consciousness.

2. A second intuition calls upon the form of expression specific to philosophy: argumentation. *This* is what distinguishes philosophy essentially from scientific and also everyday discourse. Arguments lead to convictions in a manner different from that of the compulsion of analytic evidence or causality exercised on those who find themselves exposed to them. In this I see an anticipation of freedom.[4]

Here I cannot and do not need to justify this thesis. It is only to provide a transition to the real thesis of my paper, which is that the discourse of philosophy presupposes irreducible subjectivity. Because argumentation essentially rests not on the compulsion of physical necessitation or analytic evidence, it demands a special description for those beings who can be called the subjects of argumentation. Only free subjects, conscious of themselves, can engage in argumentation games with one another.

3. The third intuition in favor of a revival of a philosophy of the subject connects with this point. It involves seeing in subjectivity an unrenouncible presupposition of ethics. From this, one can explain what is called our humanity. After all, how am I to take seriously something like Kant's categorical imperative, according to which I am to treat persons fundamentally as ends, not as objects, if persons just *are* objects[5] and nothing more? If *there is* nothing like nonobjective subjectivity, then this imperative loses its addressee. Thus argumentation and ethics need a "*fundamentum in re*." In my opinion, this is the irreducibility of subjects to objects or events.

For a while the thesis of the "death of the subject" became fashionable. Like all fashions, it is already awaiting its replacement by a change in contemporary interest. Nietzsche, Heidegger, and their French followers treated the subject as the final offshoot of the Western repression of being and as the source of the "will to power." Let us suppose there is something to this thesis. Then we must still say the following: whoever attacks the injurious effects of the basic tendency of Western philosophy that culminates in the "self-empowerment of subjectivity" can do so sensibly only in the interest of the preservation of subjects. Who else but a subject is to be assaulted and repressed by the regimentations of discourse or the "dispositions of power" expressed by Foucault's powerful incantations? A C-fiber in the brain cannot suffer a "crisis of meaning," for the simple reason that only subjects can recognize something like a meaning.

I

The problem that lies in this (admittedly somewhat rhetorical) formulation will also not be removed if one concedes: pains arise only when a C-fiber (or its functional equivalent) is stimulated. Even if, now that the microstructure of the brain is better known, due to refined histological techniques (in particular the electron microscope and silver-tracings), we can more easily imagine that in fact the brain indeed has a structure that enables it to be the material substrate of all conscious achievements and experiences, there remains a barrier in regard to the intelligibility of the psycho-physical connection. Colin McGinn has spoken of a "cognitive closure." It consists in the fact that in principle I cannot represent in my consciousness the middle term that connects the neural and the mental.[6] It remains for me an insoluble riddle[7] that electrochemical processes in neural paths are supposed to stand in an intrinsic relation to what we call subjective experiencing.[8] Emil Du Bois-Reymond, the founder of experimental physiology, already took this to be a fundamental riddle. In a famous lecture of 1872, "On the Limits of the Knowledge of Nature," he said:

> Now at some point in the development of life on earth, which we do not know and the determination of which does not matter here, there arises something new, something unheard of before, something . . . incomprehensible. The thread of understanding spun out in a negative infinite time tears, and our knowledge of nature comes to an abyss, over which no bridge, no wings carry: we stand at the . . . limit of our wit. This . . . incomprehensible thing is consciousness. Now I will show, in what I believe is a compelling fashion, that it is not only for the present state of our knowledge that consciousness is not explicable from its material conditions, which everyone no doubt concedes, but also that it is in the nature of things that it is not explicable from these observations.[9]

Du Bois-Reymond describes the riddle more closely this way:

> What conceivable connection is there between specific movements of specific atoms in my brain on the one hand, and, on the other, the original and for me undeniable, not further definable, facts, "I feel pain, feel pleasure; I taste sweetness, smell rose fragrance, hear the sound of an organ, see red." . . . After all, it is entirely and forever incomprehensible that it would matter for a heap of carbon, hydrogen, nitrogen, oxygen atoms, etc., how they are situated and how they move, how they were situated and how they moved, how they will be situated and how they will move.

> There is no way to comprehend how consciousness can arise from their being together.[10]

It just is the case that in every thinkable instance of their arising, conscious experiences are certain, whereas propositions of science (e.g., those of neurobiology, which presuppose psycho-physical identity) can be false.[11] To put it another way: I am in pain even if I take the neurophysiological proposition "This pain is a C-fiber stimulation" to be false (or if this and all other [such] propositions are supposed to be false or remain unverifiable). Thereby the old Cartesian evidence,[12] that the mental is better known to me than the bodily ("*quod [mens] sit notior quam corpus*"), is vindicated.

But with this observation we probably have not completely captured what made Emil Du Bois-Reymond believe that in principle there are reasons that ground the claim that the riddle of consciousness cannot be solved. How did he come to this conviction? We all know in some way what it means to "be there" in a conscious way: We have sensory experiencings (such as seeing blue or having pains or hearing an augmented fifth); we have feelings (such as being in love, grief, or anxiety) or moods (such as being well or badly disposed). From our own experience we know intentions (such as yearning for something, believing something, hoping for something) thoughts (such as that Fermat's hypothesis was said to be recently proven by an English mathematician), and much else. All these consciousnesses[13] have something in common (and this is what first allows us to subsume them under one concept): they exist only on the condition that we are also immediately familiar with their taking place. In this sense Fichte, for example, could say: every consciousness *of* something (objective) has some *nonobjective and immediate self-consciousness* as its presupposition.[14] For it just does not make sense (or only an arduously justified sense, as for example with psychoanalytic concepts) to say: I do have horrible anxiety, but I don't know anything of it. Or: I think that *p*, but *that* I think that is not known to me. Even more comical would be the following claim: right now it really does hurt me in the right knee, but I sense nothing there.[15] I can have knowledge regarding something that I am not experiencing. But there seems to be an analytic relation between experiencing and consciousness of experiencing.

This familiarity is immediate. I mean by this that it does not come about by way of a detour via a second consciousness, such as "by means of" an act of judgment. For I also have a toothache when I do not think of having it, or sorrow in love when I do not claim to be in love, or exam anxiety when I am not reflecting about it. "Toothache" is already a concept with which I describe something later that at first I was aware of nonconceptually.[16] Naturally, the choice of this concept can be false or inappropriate. Perhaps I have not properly named how it felt to be in this unpleasant condition. But the essential point is still this: one is "aware" of "what it is like" in oneself even when one does not know in the slightest way how one should classify the feeling.[17]

Only the existence of *contents of consciousness* has its measure in consciousness. We would not say (at least without qualification) of objects in the world that they exist only insofar as we are aware of them. Now the material processes in our brain (or more generally, in our central nervous system), which the neurobiologists assure us are the physical basis of our consciousness, are doubtless among the objects or events which we would *not* assume to have a consciousness of themselves (such as we have of our experiencings and acts). And thus arises the problem how something in which there is no trace of consciousness can be the cause of or even be identical with something whose being consists in being-familiar-with-itself.

Let us call M the material side of the event of consciousness and E the conscious experiencing. Then a contradiction appears to arise between the identity assertion "$M=E$" and the two propositions "I know [*kenne*] E immediately" and "I do *not* know [*kenne*] M immediately." But, one will object, this contradiction arises only because one mixes up realist and epistemological perspectives that are out of place. (Even if Jocasta *is* Oedipus' mother, Oedipus still need not know her as such.) Correct. But don't we have a right to demand that the assertion of a "subsisting" identity of matter and experiencing represents something that in principle can be *intelligible* to us (thus, made accessible to our own consciousness)?[18] But this is precisely where the "cognitive closure" comes in, the a priori nature of which Emil Du Bois-Reymond described so impressively.

Now the neurobiologist will say: I do not understand your amazement. For, in nature we constantly experience transitions between states that have nothing in common with what can be grasped by our senses: such as the burning of wood to ashes or the transformation of water into steam. And as for the identity of matter and consciousness, how is it more of a riddle than the identity of energy and matter or of waves and particles? And if it is not, then what justified Du Bois-Reymond's assertion that "consciousness is not explicable from its material conditions"?

Moreover, do we really *believe* in this riddle ourselves? We do not at all seriously dispute but are rather completely convinced that nothing transpires in our mind without electrochemical activity in our neural paths, specifically in our neurons. Quite often we exert an influence on our body in order to change our consciousness: we drink to meet thirst, we take antineuralgesics for our pains, we jog to get awake, we seek out the sun in order to heal our depression. We are familiar with all that; we don't doubt for a second the dependence of our consciousness on bodily processes, nor the dependence of our body on consciousness: we will something, and then our body carries it out; we decide to clench our teeth together, and pain recedes; we have anxiety, and our heart starts beating; we are scared and become pale. Nonetheless: we simply cannot understand how that which we experience with immediate familiarity and which we even believe would *not* be possible *without* something bodily, thereby comes into being already *through* bodily processes. We do not at all dispute that important areas of our world are physical. Our objection to physicalism is that the world cannot be exclusively physical.[19] Our obstinate intuition fools us with the following thought experiment: If there is nothing in an organism as we know it as an object of our observation that reveals *that* characteristic which we call consciousness, then everything could transpire in it exactly as it does, *without* our having to ascribe consciousness to it.

Let us call such an automaton (as Davidson does) "Art."[20] He appears to greet us like one of us and speaks like one of us; the convictions that he expresses are precisely those which we expect from him; he even has the typical weaknesses that we know of him, for example, that of not cleaning his shoes when he comes into our room after the rain or of lighting up a cigarette without first asking; he publishes the kind of books that we value him for; and when friends greet him, the same kind of smile shows in his features as if he were really enjoying himself. But we know: he does not enjoy himself; his greeting is a meaningless gesture; he has no convictions; he is never in any way minded. We can establish in him only the neural counterparts (or causal roles) of what with us would be accompanied by experiences. But how do we know that we ourselves are not Arts, just like the beautiful, only somewhat stiff, Olimpia in Hoffmann's tale "The Sandman"? The question is odd, because we just do *have* consciousness and because we *know* for sure that we have it.[21] We know this so surely that we could more easily doubt meaningfully that we inhabit a body than this: that we live in a conscious way. What the neurobiologist can explain to us about consciousness is thus precisely what we see when we have a soulless automaton before us that only seems to have experiences. The processes in its neural paths are like ours. Yet there is nothing but electricity and chemistry (or, as Valerio jokes in "Leonce and Lena," "cardboard and clocksprings");[22] and this being that resembles us in all observable characteristics like one egg to another is separated from us by an abyss: it does not have what we call mental states. It does not feel, does not see, does not think, does not wish. It produces merely mechanically those behavioral expressions that we accompany with our conscious states and accomplishments. It is absolutely unintelligible why such a being (one which the neurobiologist presents to us as the model of a person) should in our case also be a subject such as we know from our own intimate familiarity with consciousness. Du Bois-Reymond was thinking of this when he said it is not understandable how from the combination of carbon, hydrogen, and oxygen and other atoms something could be produced like a being-minded, a being-familiar, an experiencing. The more we reflect on this, the more decisively the feeling forces itself upon us that with the subjective perspective of experience, something radically new arises in the world of things and events, something that we cannot make understandable through the study of material accompanying circumstances (or, if you prefer, the causes) of our mental states and acts. It appears that for the neurobiologist, nothing at all would change if there were no subjective experiencing. All that interests him would still be present. For, that which we call "familiarity" is not needed by him. He carries through his psychological experiments on the basis of observable behavioral expressions (or on the basis of types of causal roles, which he identifies in the functioning totality of our organism). And so he commits himself confidently to the standpoint of eliminative materialism.

But *we*—what will *we* do? We cannot get out of the perspective of experience from which the world opens to us. And we are familiar with it in a way that a priori closes off the position of eliminative materialism. Whoever has been familiar once with consciousness can never return to a state of unfamiliarity like that to which Undine succumbs after she has to lose her soul again and mingle among the unconscious elementary spirits.

II

Now we want to see whether we can succeed in saying something more about this state of being-familiar-with-oneself than just this: that it necessarily escapes the view of the eliminative physicalists. Thereby we can take our lead from the question of precisely *why* the physicalist does not know anything of conscious experiencing.

A first approximation to an answer could be: because the physicalist has an attitude of observation, of sense perception or experimentation, with regard to his object. Whoever observes something does in fact relate himself to an object. But we said of the subject that it is not an object at all. Thus how should it be able to reveal itself to the objectifying view of observation?

Perhaps you will say: This answer is too cheap, it even rests on a trick. And above all, it operates with a presupposition that has yet to be corroborated. Perhaps one should turn the tables on the adepts of self-consciousness and contend the following: All knowing is related to an object, to that of which it is a knowing.[23] Now, either this mysterious familiarity (in consciousness) *consists* in a knowing (and then for it the same thing must hold) or it does *not* consist in a knowing, and then the fans of subjectivity would already be at the end of their argument.

Indeed, the whole Western tradition, and in its wake natural science as well, operates with a model of cognition (or knowing) that one could describe as the subject-object schema. There is someone who cognizes and, opposed to her or him, something cognized. The cognized is the *object* of the cognizing. One could also speak of a schema of re-presentation ("*Vor-stellung*" = "placing before"). This telling expression already gives away what it is made out of: to represent ("place before" [*vorstellen*]) something means: to present something before oneself (*vor sich stellen*). The represented is numerically distinct from the representing, it is the "ob-ject" (literally translated: "thrown against" ["*Gegenwurf*"]) to the "subject," which is "thrown under" ["*Unter(ge)worfenen*"] it.

The naturalistic eliminativist employs this schema when he reproaches us that either we can have only a knowing of our subjectivity (and then the subject would fall into the position of the re-presented)[24] or we must give up the claim of the epistemic relevance of our phenomenon—and that would be a declaration of bankruptcy for the philosophy of the subject. For what would a science [*Wissenschaft*] be that can't base itself on any knowing [*Wissen*] of its object?

This alternative sounds decisive—and yet it rests on thin ice. It collapses as soon as the naturalistic eliminativist takes one more step. Since he infers self-consciousness only from observed expressions and since these are found only on the side of the represented, the position of an object, he now falls into an explanatory circle.[25] For how is he to see an object (or, if you wish, an observable behavioral expression) *as* the expression of a *self*, if previously he was not acquainted with a self at all? Thus he can only presuppose the criterion according to which he identifies the object of his observation as a mental phenomenon. "He can only presuppose it" means: his explanation goes in a circle because he must already have known that which is to be explained in the explanation. And this prior acquaintance was precisely what we previously have called "immediate." It is to be called "immediate" because it does not come about by means of something other than itself, thus, e.g., not by an observation of behavior (or mirror images). We do not observe ourselves in order to get the idea that we have pains, as we do with others; we simply *have* this idea. (To be sure, with formulations like "I feel pain," ordinary language seduces us into the assumption that pain is itself the object of a sensation. That is of course nonsense: pains are themselves already sensations—without any further perceptual orientation.)[26]

III

Now what is the structure of this familiarity? So far we have heard about it negatively, namely that it cannot be explained as an objective (perceptually based) self-representation, e.g., not as an observation of behavior.[27] Fine, you may say. But we do also *have* a cognition of ourselves as observable bodies. And we can relate to other persons and their mental states at all only through observations. My reply is: Who is denying that? But *how* do we have consciousness of ourselves as observable bodies in space and time? The only important question in this context is: How can we recognize a body *as ours*? According to what has been said, the correct answer cannot be "Because I see it, e.g., in the mirror." For suppose we had a magical mirror: as in an idealized cubist artwork, it would synoptically offer us all observable views of us and even make visible all mental states and properties. Then we still would not know per se that this is *our* body and *our* soul. The use of the pronoun of the first person singular is never unproblematic in epistemic contexts. It is tied to actual familiarity-with-ourselves as its condition. We cannot introduce talk of the mineness of our body independently of expressions like "this knee, whose torn ligament I feel" or "this eye, which hurts me" or "this heart, whose beating I feel"—and thereby we have in each case used verbs of consciousness.[28] Yet, to ascribe familiarity to them was precisely unproblematic. Now if we are able to show that something bodily is familiar to me as something of mine only insofar as it is disclosed to me through something mental, then we have a new confirmation for the Cartesian intuition that our mind is "better known" to us than our body (or that our body is certain to us *as ours* only to the extent that it is familiar to us through something mental).

From this we learn that it would be circular to want to illuminate our epistemic familiarity with ourselves as consciousnesses in expressions that function only in the world of objects. And we can also (and more fundamentally) formulate these insights this way: self-consciousness is absolutely not analyzable in expressions that do not already presuppose it. Besides expressions of sensory observation, this also holds for expressions of demonstrative reference (through indexicals such as "this-there" or "here" or "now") or (Fregean) descriptions [*Kennzeichnungen*].[29] What does that mean in particular? First, that we are originally more familiar with self-consciousness than with that which, from an observer's perspective, we obtain from others (or ourselves in the mirror) in behavioral expressions.[30] Otherwise, how could we grasp as *ours* an observational datum that in itself carries no indication of its bearer? But second, our self-consciousness is also more original than everything that we can refer to with indexicals such as "here" and "this-there."[31] For, whoever was not previously familiar with the referent of 'I' cannot even situate himself in space and time in order to use demonstratives meaningfully. For example, how is a person who stands before a map, in which a red arrow indicates "you are here," to know who is being spoken of, if she hasn't previously learned how to identify his body through the I?[32] And how is she to understand "now it is night" when she has not previously read the indication of time from her own mental presence? Third, if we are successfully to refer a description (*Kennzeichnung*) (such as "being the largest man in the city") to *ourselves*, and not merely to any person who fulfills this description, we must be familiar with the bearer of this property in a way that cannot be explained *from* the description itself. This is what the talk of the unanalyzability of self-consciousness means.[33] Fourth and finally, self-consciousness also cannot be described as the object of a knowing. For all knowing is relative to a theory that could be false. But I am familiar with mental states even when I do not know a theory on the basis of which I hold them to be true (it can also happen that I am in love without a valid theory about love).[34] For this reason, animals and children can have self-consciousness prior to language acquisition. And for this reason it can happen that, without lacking self-consciousness, I literally "don't know" precisely how I am mentally.

Several specific points about familiarity have an exact parallel in a related phenomenon: so-called *de se* attributions. They differ from (phenomenal) "experiencings" (feelings with a knowledge of how one is mentally) because of their cognitive character. While it was always possible to deny the character of "knowing" to "knowledge of what it is like to be like a bat,"[35] this is precisely not disputable for the class of self-ascriptions to be characterized more precisely below. The basic underlying idea here actually stems from Johann Gottlieb Fichte, but in our time Hector-Neri Castañeda has taken it up again with great effect.[36] The issue concerns locutions with "he/she," an intentional verb, and "he himself/she herself" (e.g., "she believes that she herself is the Wine Queen of Schriesheim"). These locutions take their peculiar certainty from the logical irreplaceability of the I-perspective that is implicit in conscious self-references. This logical irreplaceability of the I-perspective has brought some[37] to dispute the propositional theory of self-consciousness that is widespread among analytic philosophers.[38] According to this theory, self-consciousness is a case of knowing that is expressed in assertions of the form "I know that I ø." But the normal function of expressions with "I" (or other deictic expressions) is not at all to express propositions.[39] From this it follows that some knowledge (*Kenntnis*) is not propositional but is still an instance of knowing (in the cognitively relevant sense of the term).[40] As noted, that can be illustrated by a peculiarity of belief sentences with "he/she" and "himself/herself." If I believe something about myself, I need in no way to ascribe to myself cognitions expressed in propositions (and resting on information), as third parties would do.[41] I can even mistrust my mirror image, take my biography to be a dream and deny my character. Even then I will be familiar with myself (and possibly with my doubts about my biography) with infallible certainty. Now what kind of thing is this I? It is by no means a person, if "person" means a spatiotemporal object with a causally traceable history whose elements can be arranged in propositions. If Descartes doubts that he himself is Descartes, he is by no means putting into question the certainty of the "Cartesian *cogito*"—on the contrary, he is showing that its certainty exceeds that of any information about one's body.[42] Or if Narcissus, looking dreamily at his reflection in the spring water, cries out in delight, "How beautiful you are," then he need not by any means be relating himself to himself thereby *as* to he himself. In his *self*-reference there definitely can be lacking a self-*consciousness* (thus the consciousness of himself as being *himself*; when Echo's own *words* call back to him, he does not know these are *his* words). It is precisely this explicit self-consciousness, which Narcissus lacks and which Artemis punishes him with only later, that the following formulation expresses: "Narcissus believes that *he himself* is beautiful." For, in this locution the believer has absolutely no logical possibility of going wrong in the referential object of his believing. That is, he has referred directly to the logical subject of self-ascription, no matter how this is to be specified further in an objectifying description. Thus, even when he does not know who or what it is to which he refers, or whether what he believes about himself is true, he is still aware with Cartesian certainty of this belief's being *about himself.*

Behind this somewhat tiresome linguistic exercise, a cardinal discovery with far-reaching consequences is concealed. Wittgenstein characterized it as the subjective use of 'I' (or 'he').[43] Examples are "I have a toothache" or "I feel tired." The essential thing in such thoughts is that they necessarily and directly reach their referential object (me myself) whoever I am. I may be a brain that is swimming desolately in the vat of the experimentation of a sadistic neurobiologist (and whose nerve endings are connected with a supercomputer). Even when I know nothing more at all about my bodily appearance (because I have never seen myself in that circumstance, nor will I ever get to see me or in any other way perceive me)—even then, I can always grasp the thought, "My God, I won't let this happen again."[44] And the 'I' in these thoughts refers with dead certainty to *me*, even when I have no perception and no description of myself. It is otherwise with the objective use of 'I'. This occurs in propositions such as "I have a bump on my forehead" or "I am standing next to the table." In both cases 'I' refers not to the logical subject of the thought but rather to my body (or a part of it or to its location, etc.)—but *that* this is so, I need not know. I need not feel the bump, and I may not have seen the table. I obtain this information only by perception. And in the case of direct epistemic self-reference there is nothing that I can fail to perceive or in whose identification I could go astray. 'I' is just not an object of perception that I could identify as the self that has the perception.[45] May we conclude from that that it is not an object at all but rather a subject?[46] Friedrich Schlegel once wittily remarked, "Very striking is the expression '[the free subject] is an absurdity [*Unding*]'; it is also the only non- and counter-thing [*Nicht- und Gegending*]."[47]

A story about poor Ernst Mach also shows us in an amusing way that self-identification through observational predicates (but not epistemic self-reference) is deceptive. When he stepped into a Viennese bus, he saw a man step in on the other side at the same moment, of whom he thought, "What a shabby pedagogue is the person who has just entered"[48]—not knowing that he was referring to himself because he had not seen the mirror.[49] (If Lacan were correct in his theory of the mirror stage,[50] we would all find ourselves in the unenviable situation of Ernst Mach for all our life.) Epistemic self-ascriptions are thus not captured in logical terms by attributions *de dicto* or *de re*; the perspective of the first person is irreplaceable for the self-situating of subjects in the world and in practical interactions. Closely connected with the theory-independence of self-consciousness is the fact that self-consciousness must be something prelinguistic—which generations of philosophers of language and analytic philosophers from Herder to Ryle had denied. If we understand by "language" the totality of that which can be made communicable and intelligible in propositions, then self-consciousness is not a linguistic phenomenon at all (which of course does not mean that it does not allow of being articulated in language). Some of our cognitions (*Kenntnisse*) thus do not articulate a knowing (*Wissen*) (expressible in propositions).[51] Attempts at reductionism, such as the private language argument or the semantic nominalism based on that are thereby rebuffed or proven to be subreptions.[52]

IV

In conclusion, you will ask: What result have we arrived at with these increasingly technical reflections? We have seen that the grounds that speak against the reducibility of self-consciousness are of an *in principle* nature. Self-consciousness is in principle not touched at all by our discussions about expressions or objects. That we nonetheless believe from rich evidence that consciousness is identical with certain types of physical events (or with a causal role) makes it necessary to have a theory that does justice to the peculiarity of this identity. That is not my topic in this paper. In any case, the continuing interdisciplinary debate that is conducted about this topic nowadays shows that we do not yet possess such a theory. While neurobiology makes breathtaking progress in the comprehension of functions of our brain, we are as before confronted by the question of the experimental physiologist Du Bois-Reymond: What contribution can even the best physical theory make to fathoming the peculiarity of familiarity? We can observe the physical (or infer it from physical effects or control it adequately through theoretical terms) but not the mental. "Cognitive closure" consists precisely in the fact that the connection of one with the other is not in turn disclosed to us. And as long as we cannot understand it, we have good grounds for meeting the optimism of the naturalists with the old epistemological reserves of idealism.[53]

This must have consequences for the form of philosophy as a theory—in its demarcation from the natural sciences. In philosophy, the concerns of subjectivity as such, unabbreviated, must come to expression.

One can naturally ask if there is not something more important than the execution of such guardian tasks, far from the ordinary world, at least when "important" means only what concerns the course of the world as a cosmological whole. After all, the course of the world does not bother itself, as far as we know, about the rationality of arguments or the inwardness of subjects. But it is precisely here that our interests differ: if it is indifferent to the course of the world what becomes of subjects (or whether some living beings take themselves to be subjects), then that cannot be something of no account to *us*. And it is, I believe, to remind us of that, that philosophy exists.[54]

Notes

1. Willard Van Orman Quine, "Epistemology Naturalized," in *Ontological Relativity and Other Essays*, 2nd ed. (New York and London: Columbia University Press, 1971).

2. Represented by, e.g., Richard Rorty, "Incorrigibility as the Mark of the Mental," *Journal of Philosophy* 68 (1970), pp. 399–424; and Daniel Dennett, *Consciousness Explained* (Boston, Toronto, and London: Little, Brown and Co., 1991).

3. In the words of Ned J. Block and Jerry Fodor, it says that, "for any organism that satisfies psychological predicates at all, there exists a unique best *description* such that each psychological state of the organism is identical with one of the

machine tables relative to that description" ("What Psychological States Are Not," *Philosophical Review* 81 [1972], p. 165; reprinted in *Readings in Philosophy of Psychology*, vol. 1, ed. N. Block [Cambridge, Mass.: Harvard University Press, 1980], p. 240; cf. Block, "Troubles with Functionalism," pp. 270 f.). Underlying this is the assumption that all systems that can be characterized by mental properties can be described as probabilistic automata. Here a probabilistic automaton is a generalized Turing machine whose machine table contains instructions that are connected with the positive probability of less than or equal to one. Cf. also Kim Sterelny, *The Representational Theory of Mind: An Introduction* (Oxford: Blackwell, 1990), esp. pp. 6 ff.

4. I am relying on Stephen Toulmin, *The Uses of Argument* (Cambridge: Cambridge University Press, 1958; 6th ed., 1983), above all on pp. 94–145. Habermas has taken up this thesis in the theory of argumentation in his essay "Truth Theories," in *Vorstudien und Ergänzungen zur Theorie des kommunikativen Handelns* (Frankfurt: Suhrkamp, 1984), pp. 127–83, esp. pp. 161 ff.

5. Kant speaks of "means," but means are also always objects. Cf. *Groundwork of the Metaphysic of Morals*, trans. H. J. Paton (New York: Harper & Row, 1964), Ak. vol. 4, pp. 428 f.; page references are to the following edition: *Kants gesammelte Schriften* (hereafter Ak.) (Berlin: Königliche Preussische Akademie der Wissenschaften, 1900 ff.).

6. Colin McGinn, "Can We Solve the Mind-Body Problem?" in *The Problem of Consciousness* (Oxford: Blackwell, 1991), p. 3: "A type of mind *M* is cognitively closed with respect to a property *P* (or a theory *T*) if and only if the concept-forming procedures at *M*'s disposal cannot extend to a grasp of *P* (or an understanding of *T*)." The reason is: "Conscious states are simply not, qua conscious states, potential objects of perception: they depend upon the brain but they cannot be observed by directing the senses onto the brain. You cannot see a brain state *as* a conscious state. In other words, consciousness is noumenal with respect to perception of the brain."

7. To quote the title of Peter Bieri's Marburg Inaugural Lecture: "What Makes Consciousness a Riddle?" in *Spektrum der Wissenschaft*, vol. 10 (1992), pp. 48–56. Both quotations from Emil Du Bois-Reymond are also found there.

8. No one has analyzed this aspect as penetratingly as Thomas Nagel. Cf. several essays in his collection *Mortal Questions* (New York: Cambridge University Press, 1979; 6th ed., 1985), esp. essays 12–14; and *The View From Nowhere* (New York: Oxford University Press, 1986), above all the first three chapters. Cf. also Frank Jackson's classic essay "Epiphenomenal Qualia," *Philosophical Quarterly* 32 (1982), pp. 127–36; reprinted in *Mind and Cognition: A Reader*, ed. W. G. Lycan (Oxford: Basil Blackwell, 1990), pp. 469–77.

9. In Du Bois-Reymond, *Vorträge über Philosophie und Gesellschaft* (Hamburg: F. Meiner, 1974), p. 65.

10. Ibid., p. 71. There is also an echo of Du Bois-Reymond's talk in a remark of Julian Huxley's, which Colin McGinn has placed as a motto before his essay "Can We Solve the Mind-Body Problem:" "How it is that anything so remarkable as a state of consciousness comes about as a result of initiating nerve tissue, is just as unaccountable as the appearance of the Djin, where Aladdin rubbed his lamp in the story" (p. 1).

11. Thus Saul Kripke in "Identity and Necessity," in *Identity and Individuation*, ed. M. K. Munitz (New York: New York University Press, 1971), pp. 162–64.

12. It is formulated in the heading of the second *Meditation*.

13. I intentionally express myself this way, for they are not all to be grasped *stricto sensu* as "states"; some of them are rather acts (like wishing the end of this lecture hour), others are rather happenings (like suffering suddenly now from a throbbing toothache), and others are rather dispositions (like violent temper or jealousy), etc.

14. E.g. in Fichte's 1797 *Versuch einer neuen Darstellung der Wissenschaftslehre*, in *Johann Gottlieb Fichtes sämmtliche Werke*, ed. I. H. Fichte (Berlin, 1845–6; reprint, Berlin: de Gruyter, 1971), vol. 1, pp. 519–34 (cf. esp. chap. 1: "all consciousness is determined by the immediate consciousness of our self," pp. 521 ff.).

15. What Bishop Berkeley wanted to say of being in general does hold for consciousness: *esse est percipi*. The subsistence, the being of conscious states or acts, has its necessary and also its sufficient criterion in the mental familiarity that we have of them.

16. The difference between the immediate (not conceptually self-ascribed) and infallible "having" of experiences, and the (linguistic) expressions in which I express this having (which, like all assertions, can be false) has been worked out by no one more clearly than A. J. Ayer, *The Problem of Knowledge* (New York: St. Martin's Press, 1965; original ed., 1956), chap. 2, "Scepticism and Certainty," pp. 36 ff., esp. pp. 61 ff.

17. One can quickly convince oneself of this by the following consideration: assertions and thoughts can be true or false, my toothache (or how it is felt) cannot. It can only take place or not, and *if* it takes place, then I know about it absolutely without further mediation. My consciousness is here (probably *only* here) the measure of the being of its content. In common terms, "what I don't know doesn't hurt me."

18. If we make the identity conditions dependent on the conditions of their epistemic accessibility (thus take up an antirealist standpoint), then we must be ready to allow that epistemic contexts are always "inexact." I can always precede every reference with a "transcendental prefix," an "I know (think, believe, see, feel) that so and so," so that all knowing of the world becomes a knowing *de dicto*. Now if we are not made aware of *M* in *E*-consciousness, then one can say with Kant that it is "nothing for me." A modern variant of this notion is presented by A. J. Ayer in *The Problem of Knowledge,* p. 96. There the transition between the proposition "It seems to me that I am seeing a cigarette case right now" into the other one, "I am now seeing a seeming-cigarette case" is justified: "These seeming-objects are sense-data; and the conclusion may be more simply expressed by saying that it is always sense-data that are directly perceived." A similar relativization of all reference to *de dicto* referrings of a subject was proposed by Hector-Neri Castañeda, "The Self and the I-Guises, Empirical and Transcendental," in *Theorie der Subjektivität* (Festschrift for Dieter Henrich), ed. K. Cramer et al. (Frankfurt: Suhrkamp, 1989), pp. 105–49.

19. Cf. Jackson, "What Mary Didn't Know," *Journal of Philosophy* 83 (1986), p. 392: "Physicalism is not the noncontroversial thesis that the actual world is largely physical, but the challenging thesis that it is entirely physical. This is why physicalism must hold that complete physical knowledge is complete knowledge simpliciter. For suppose it is not complete: then our world must differ from a world, W(P), for which it is complete, and the difference must be in nonphysical facts; for our world and W(P) agree in all matters physical. Hence physicalism would be false at our world (though contingently so, for it would be true at W(P))." Similarly Thomas Nagel, who in *The View from Nowhere* (cf. pp. 25 ff., 90 ff.) presents the thesis of the incompleteness of objective (physical) reality quite strongly and says "the brain has nonphysical properties" (p. 30).

20. Donald Davidson, "The Material Mind," in *Essays on Actions and Events* (Oxford: Clarendon Press, 1980), pp. 245–59. Cf. also the example of "swampman" in "Knowing One's Mind," *Proceedings of the American Philosophical Association* 60 (1987), pp. 441–58, here pp. 443 f.

21. There is a longstanding debate in analytic philosophy (since Wittgenstein) over whether (so-called "phenomenal") experiencings, which on logical grounds do not stand at all under the alternative true/false, may be appropriately designated as "knowings" (*Wissen*). Connected with this is the question whether familiarity with experiencing is in general propositionally structured (if one identifies a proposition with the set of possible worlds in which it is true, as in David Lewis, "Causation," in *Philosophical Papers*, vol. 2 [New York: Oxford University Press, 1986], p. 160, n. 3). But epistemically it does make a difference if I know of an experiencing only in general or if I know how it is to me when in that state. Cf. Jackson, "Epiphenomenal Qualia," and "What Mary Didn't Know," pp. 291–95; also *The Nature of Mind,* ed. D. Rosenthal (New York: Oxford University Press, 1991), pp. 392–94. Later I will

show that a second case of "familiarity," namely the self-ascription of a property, in which I make an intentional reference to the world ("attitude *de se*"), is definitely excluded from doubts about cognitive relevance.

22. Georg Büchner, *Dichtungen*, ed. H. Poschmann with the collaboration of R. Poschmann (Frankfurt, 1992), pp. 126 f.

23. It doesn't matter if this object is concrete or abstract, simple or composite.

24. This would contradict the assertion of the immediacy of familiarity.

25. Thus, e.g., David Armstrong, who has presented a "defense of inner sense" and attempted to understand self-consciousness according to a model of "inner perception," in *Consciousness and Causality*, with Norman Malcolm (Oxford: Basil Blackwell, 1984), pp. 108 ff. But Thomas Metzinger, for example, also understands self-consciousness as metapresentation (thus as the representation of a prior representation). He believes circular complications would be avoided if representation and metapresentation are "thought as distinct processes." (*Subjekt und Selbstmodell: Die Perspektivität phänomenalen Bewusstseins vor dem Hintergrund einer naturalistischen Theorie mentaler Repräsentation* [Paderborn: Schöningh, 1993], p. 100). But if the two are distinct, then talk of *self*-consciousness loses its meaning and becomes indistinguishable from believing *de re*. Self-reflexive relations presuppose identity.

26. Cf. Sydney Shoemaker's 1968 essay "Self-Reference and Self-Identity," reprinted in *Identity, Cause, and Mind: Philosophical Essays* (New York: Cambridge University Press, 1984), pp. 6–18, here p. 15: "Our language may suggest that pains are perceived, but it does not suggest—and it seems to me clearly not to be true—that one perceives feeling or the 'having' of one's pains." Likewise, cf. Ayer, *The Problem of Knowledge*, p. 107.

27. "The latter point is especially important; it shows that the knowledge in question is radically different from perceptual knowledge. The reason one is not presented to oneself 'as an object' in self-awareness is that self-awareness is not perceptual awareness, i.e., is not the sort of awareness in which objects are presented. It is an awareness of facts unmediated by awareness of objects. But it is worth noting that if one were aware of oneself as an object in such cases (as one is in fact aware of oneself as an object when one sees oneself in a mirror), this would not be held to explain one's self-knowledge. For awareness that the presented object was ø would not tell one that one was oneself ø, unless one had identified the object as oneself; and one could not do this unless one already had some self-knowledge, namely the knowledge that one is the unique possessor of whatever set of properties of the presented object one took to show it to be oneself. Perceptual self-knowledge presupposes non-perceptual self-knowledge, so not all self-knowl-

edge can be perceptual" (in Sydney Shoemaker and Richard Swinburne, *Personal Identity* (Oxford: Basil Blackwell, 1984), pp. 104 f.).

28. This is also an insight that Sydney Shoemaker has presented, especially clearly in his famous essay "Self-Reference and Self-Awareness," pp. 17 f.

29. This is translated by Russell as "definite descriptions."

30. For this reason self-ascription or attribution *de se* is precisely not to be reduced to other-ascription or attribution *de re*. Cf. Lewis, "Attitudes *De Dicto* and *De Se*," *Philosophical Review* 88 (1979), pp. 513–43; reprinted in *Philosophical Papers*, vol. 1, (New York: Oxford University Press, 1983), pp. 133–59, esp. pp. 151 f., 156 f.). Lewis also speaks of a relation of acquaintance: "Here is my proposal. A subject ascribes property *X* to individual *Y* if and only if the subject ascribes *X* to *Y* under some description *Z* such that either (1) *Z* captures the essence of *Y*, or (2) is a relation of acquaintance that the subject bears to *Y*" (p. 155).

31. This was a basic thesis of Hector-Neri Castañeda, "Indicators and Quasi-Indicators," in *Sprache und Erfahrung. Texte zu einer neuen Ontologie* (Frankfurt: Suhrkamp, 1982), pp. 116 f. John Perry also holds this thesis (in reliance on Castañeda) in "The Problem of the Essential Indexical," *Nous* 13 (1979), pp. 3–21, here p. 16.

32. Cf. Perry, "Frege on Demonstratives," *Philosophical Review* 86 (1977), pp. 474–97, esp. p. 492; also "The Problem of the Essential Indexical," pp. 4 f., 10 f.; as well as Lewis, "Attitudes *De Dicto* and *De Se*," pp. 138 f. For this reason there is a circularity in Thomas Metzinger's explanation of self-consciousness by "a little red arrow in the complete flight-simulator" that is to indicate to the pilot exactly where he is (*Subjekt und Selbstmodell*, pp. 241 ff.).

33. Thus Castañeda, "'He'. A Study in the Logic of Self-Consciousness," *Ratio* 8 (1966), pp. 130–57, here p. 131.

34. In recent work Donald Davidson has offered a compromise proposal according to which self-consciousness is in fact a nontheoretical "presumption" but still constitutes a genuine knowing (*Wissen*). (The presumption consists in this, "that if he knows that he holds a sentence true, he knows what he believes.") But Davidson purchases this concession (with reference to Rorty) with the assumption that self-consciousness is still, like all knowing, subject to error (cf. "First Person Authority," *Dialectica* 38 (1984), pp. 101–11, esp. pp. 110 f.).

35. For this reason, I have spoken of "self-*consciousness*" or "familiarity" (also of "acquaintance" ["*Bekanntschaft*" or "*Kenntnis*"]), in contrast to cognition ("*Erkenntnis*").

36. Castañeda has repeatedly referred to Kant but also to Fichte and Sartre, e.g., in "The Self and Its Guises" and in "The Role of Apperception in Kant's Deduction of the Categories," *Nous* 24 (1990), pp. 147–57; Castañeda refers explicitly to Fichte and Sartre in "Persons, Egos, and I's: Their Sameness Relations," in *Psychopathology and Philosophy*, ed. M. Spitzer et al. (New York: Springer, 1988), pp. 210–24, and in "Self-Consciousness, I-Structures, and Physiology," in *Philosophy and Psychopathology*, ed. M. Spitzer and B. Maher (New York: Springer, 1991), pp. 118–45. Reference to Fichte is found most expressly in Robert Nozick, who likewise allies himself with Castañeda in "The Identity of the Self," in *Philosophical Explanations* (Cambridge, Mass.: Harvard University Press, 1981), pp. 27–114, esp. p. 76 n. 89 and p. 108. The expression "attribution *de se*" comes from David Lewis, who in any case also refers to Castañeda and Perry.

37. E.g., John Perry; David Lewis; and Roderick Chisholm, *The First Person* (Brighton: The Harvestor Press, 1981), p. 15.

38. I should say more generally: of attitude ascriptions, where "attitudes" ("*Einstellungen*") stand for intentions and translates "propositional attitudes."

39. Chisholm, *The First Person*, pp. 5, 17.

40. Lewis, "Attitudes *De Dicto* and *De Se*," p. 139: "But if it is possible to lack knowledge and not lack any propositional knowledge, then the lacked knowledge must not be propositional."

41. Of course, the question then is how I can transform pre-propositional experiencings into true assertions. Chisholm has attempted to understand this according to a model of supervenience (*The First Person*, p. 82). I cannot pursue this question here.

42. Cf. Elizabeth Anscombe, "The First Person," in *Collected Papers*, vol. 2 (Minneapolis: University of Minnesota Press, 1981), p. 22.

43. Ludwig Wittgenstein, *Preliminary Studies for the 'Philosophical Investigations' Generally known as The Blue and Brown Books*, 2nd ed. (Oxford: Basil Blackwell, 1969), p. 66. Also, Shoemaker, "Self-Reference and Self-Awareness," pp. 7 ff.

44. Cf. Anscombe, "The First Person," pp. 31–32.

45. "[T]here is no object of experience that one could perceive as the self that is doing the perceiving. However it is that one identifies an object of experience as oneself, whenever one does, one identifies an object in experience with a thing which is not a part of experience, and this thing is the one to which the person in question will refer to by 'I' (or its translation in other languages), and another person will refer to by 'he*' or 'he himself' in the special S[elf-ascription] use"

(Castañeda, "He," pp. 142 f.). In other words, one cannot make understandable by perception why a perceptual object should be identical with something essentially nonperceivable. Subjective states—as Davidson has also emphasized lately—are not objects at all, because they are not situated on the object side of a re-presentation. "The source of the trouble is the dogma that to have a thought is to have an object before the mind" ("Knowing One's Own Mind," pp. 454 f.) Cf. "What Is Present to the Mind," *Grazer Philosophische Studien* 36 (1989), p. 15; and "The Myth of the Subjective," in *Relativism, Interpretation and Confirmation,* ed. M. Krausz (Notre Dame, Ind.: Notre Dame University Press, 1989), p. 171.

46. Above, I have indicated one possibility for justifying this transition from *de dicto* to *de re* (thus from the epistemic/semantic to the ontological standpoint). But how am I to recognize that what is ascribed *de se* is the nonobjective *mode* of givenness of certain spatiotemporal objects? The problem of making plausible any kind of identity theory (such as I seek) will always consist in the fact that it also must overcome "cognitive closure." In other words, I must be able to *recognize* that I *myself am* the *de re* (thus independently of my subjective perspective) identified body (or a functionally identified causal role or whatever).

47. Friedrich Schlegel, *Kritische Ausgabe,* ed. E. Behler et al. (Munich, Paderborn, and Vienna, 1959 ff.), vol. 19, p. 115.

48. Ernst Mach, *Beiträge zur Analyse der Empfindungen* (Jena, 1886), p. 34.

49. Perry gives a similar example in "The Problem of the Essential Indexical," p. 3.

50. Jacques Lacan, "Le stade du miroir . . ." in *Écrits* (Paris: Editions du Seuil, 1966), pp. 93–100.

51. David Lewis has spoken of nonpropositional knowledge: ". . . if it is possible to lack knowledge and not lack any propositional knowledge, then the lacked knowledge must not be propositional" ("Attitudes *De Dicto* and *De Se,*" p. 139). Casteñeda has gone into this position (whose main representatives he takes to be Lewis and Chisholm and which he calls the "Direct Attribute View") in "Self-Consciousness, Demonstrative Reference, and the Self-Ascription of Believing," in *Metaphysics: Philosophical Perspectives, vol. 1,* ed. J. E. Tomberlin (Atascadero, Calif.: Ridgeview, 1987), pp. 404–54, esp. p. 409. Castañeda bases the "self-transparency" of episodes of consciousness on their "immediate intelligibility (which is independent from the understanding of others, intersubjectivity, and truth values)," pp. 412 f., 414 f., 418.

52. This also holds analogously for pragmatic attempts to reduce self-consciousness to intersubjectivity. It can be shown against these that sooner or later they get caught in the same circles that we know already from theoretical reduc-

tions of phenomena (cf. my "Wider den apriorischen Intersubjektivismus," in *Gemeinschaft und Gerechtigkeit*, ed. M. Brumlik and H. Brunkhorst (Frankfurt: Fischer, 1993), pp. 273–89; see also other literature there). In these attempts, an acquaintance with the phenomena to be explained is regularly already presupposed in a hidden way; indeed, without such pre-acquaintance, the attempt at explanation could not see its goal. This situation also does not improve if I interpret the reflex, which supposedly teaches me about the being of my self, as a role which is projected on me by interactions with other persons. That I am I myself, and that my experiencings are mine, cannot be a teaching that is made familiar to me by the intersubjective validity of a proposition. It is similarly impossible that it could be myself to me by my mirror image. And other persons as well, whom I encounter in contexts of action, in which the role of an inter-subject falls to me, could teach me about my selfhood only at the price of a manifest explanatory circle.

53. This is not in fact the line of Lewis's argumentation. But he agrees with the consequences: "Some say, condescendingly, that scientific knowledge of our world is all very well in its place; but it ignores something of the utmost importance. They say there is a kind of personal, subjective knowledge that we have or we seek, and it is altogether different from the impersonal, objective knowledge that science and scholarship can provide. Alas, I must agree with these taunts, in letter if not in spirit. Lingens has studied the encyclopedia long and hard. He knows full well that he needs a kind of knowledge they do not contain. Science and scholarship, being addressed to the world, provide knowledge of the world; and that is knowledge *de dicto*, which is not knowledge *de se*" ("Attitudes *De Dicto* and *De Se*," p. 144).

54. The English version of this essay is based on a translation by Karl Ameriks.

11

Self and Reason: A Nonreductionist Approach to the Reflective and Practical Transitions of Self-Consciousness

Dieter Sturma

Any attempt to defend a nonreductionist view of subjectivity and morality must pay attention to idealist theories, but one has to be aware that even these theories are not free from reductionist tendencies. In the case of philosophical Idealism especially, the question of where to draw the borderline between reductionism and nonreductionism can be answered only with great difficulty. Idealist theories can claim a nonreductionist status only if they allow for some kind of independence of states of consciousness from merely physical states, and that means they have to allow for some kind of dualism. By their advocates as well as their critics, dualist models of consciousness and morality are generally associated with Cartesian and transcendental philosophy. I shall be defending a modified version of such models against reductionist approaches. A reconsideration of such models is justified in particular by the fact that Descartes's theoretical philosophy and Kant's practical philosophy continue to be accused of dogmatism, and defenders see themselves almost entirely in the role of deflating such accusations. But both sides overlook that Cartesian and Kantian nonreductionism contain considerable systematic potential for a philosophical analysis of subjectivity and morality. Accordingly, I intend to develop a dualist approach in characterizing a connection between self and reason that includes perspectives on the philosophy of mind and moral philosophy inaugurated by Descartes and Kant. Furthermore, this analysis of the relation between self and reason should provide an account of the systematic core of a philosophy of person in which conceptions of the subject in theoretical and practical philosophy converge.

In the following outline of the step from self to reason, i.e. the transition from the self-evidence of the Cartesian *cogito* and the identity of self-consciousness over time to the realm of practical attitudes, there will be eight stages: (1) the subject of mental activity, (2) the elusiveness of the self, (3) traces of the self in consciousness, (4) the activity of the self, (5) autonomy and reason, (6) the examined life, (7) the rational life-plan, and (8) the other person as a fact of reason.

The Subject of Mental Activity

For most recent philosophers of mind, Descartes represents the prime case of the original theoretical sin. In particular, for philosophy of mind that has been influenced by the linguistic turn, Cartesianism is viewed as the greatest obstacle to an adequate understanding of the nature of human consciousness.[1] This criticism is directed primarily against the reifications that accompany the concept of the *res cogitans*, against metaphysical dualism, and against a theory of introspection and epistemic privacy attributed to Descartes.

Methodologically, the criticism of Cartesianism is for the most part reductionist. Consciousness is to be explained by recourse to materialist, behaviorist, and functionalist models—to mention only the best-known ones here. The assumption made at the outset of the reduction is that self-consciousness is not a unique state of consciousness. These anti-Cartesian approaches hope to make the appearance of uniqueness disappear by showing that self-consciousness does not contain any mysterious properties and is composed of structures that are to be found in other simpler cases of consciousness as well.

From the perspective of more recent criticisms of Cartesianism, Descartes's *cogito* argument, which originally functions only as an epistemological propaedeutic to his metaphysics, takes on almost monstrous features. In the caricatures that accompany this criticism, the epistemological function of the *cogito* argument is totally misunderstood, just as is its actual systematic content. Contrary to widespread assumptions, the *cogito* argument contains neither a model of introspection nor a concept of a private object, as Wittgenstein's criticism assumes.

In fact, the *cogito* argument develops a model that has had and still has a paradigmatic meaning for theories of subjectivity—a meaning that is independent of its original metaphysical context. Underlying this model is the insight that self-referential states of consciousness are structurally unlike the cognitive consciousness of spatiotemporal objects[2]—a thesis that, ironically, happens to be confirmed in an impressive way by Wittgenstein.

Descartes never completely understood the reasons for the structural peculiarity of self-referential states, although he was certainly able to use them for his own theoretical purposes. This is especially true for his formulae of self-certainty: the sentences *I exist* and *I think*. One cannot deny that Descartes moves from these formulae to a reification of a *substantia cogitans*, but there is no objective reason to identify the reification of the 'I think' with the systematic potential of the formula *I think*.

The formula of self-certainty implicitly contains a concept of self-consciousness that is composed of four structural properties:

1. The structure of self-consciousness is unlike all other states of consciousness.
2. Self-consciousness is a state of self-familiarity that must not be derived from other mental states.
3. Self-consciousness is infallible.
4. Self-consciousness is a state of epistemic privacy.

However, one cannot immediately derive properties of the *subject* of self-consciousness from these structural properties. Rather, one must make a strict distinction between the properties of self-consciousness and the properties of the self. Descartes was certainly aware of this distinction. When he characterizes the referential structure that underlies self-consciousness, he is initially very cautious. His first answer to the question "What is the self?" is that it is the subject of mental activity.[3] And this answer has its own philosophical significance that is independent of Descartes's further intentions.

Descartes's *cogito* argument has exclusively negative consequences for characterizing the referential structure of his concept of the self. No inferences about the content of the self can be made from the formal function of being a subject of mental activity, because within the framework of radical doubt, all properties of spatiotemporally identifiable objects have been excluded from the realm of indubitable evidence. Only the irreducibility of self-consciousness and the formal assumption of a subject of states of consciousness are beyond any doubt. This *minimal* Cartesianism that is indispensable for recent theories of subjectivity can thus be summarized in the claim that the self is the irreducible subject of mental activity.

The Elusiveness of the Self

Attempts at adding further properties to the concept of the self are confronted with the problem of the elusiveness of the self. Critics of Cartesianism have taken this problem as an occasion for calling into doubt the assumption of an irreducible concept of the self. The classical and most influential example of this kind of reductionism is Gilbert Ryle's thesis of the elusiveness of the 'I'.

According to Ryle, reflective states of consciousness are performances of higher order acts: "To concern oneself about oneself in any way, theoretical or practical, is to perform a higher order act, just as it is to concern oneself about anybody else."[4] These higher order acts are nonreflective, and that is why they must be silent about themselves: "Self-commentary, self-ridicule and self-admonition are logically condemned to eternal penultimacy."[5] Although Ryle at least allows for a partial nonparallelism between the notion of 'I' and other indexicals, he does not find anything mysterious about the phenomenon of self-consciousness:

> there is nothing mysterious or occult about the range of higher order acts and attitudes, which are apt to be inadequately covered by the umbrella-title 'self-consciousness'. They are the same in kind as the higher order acts and attitudes exhibited in the dealing of people with one other. . . . The only anomaly of the 'I' consists in its systematic elusiveness: 'I' is like my own shadow; I can never get away from it, as I can get away from your shadow. There is no mystery about this constancy, but I mention it because it seems to endow 'I' with a mystifying uniqueness and adhesiveness.[6]

If one takes into account the demanding techniques of argumentation that are attached to Ryle's approach in particular, his criticism of Cartesianism must appear astonishingly inconsistent and ambivalent. Although initially he claims that self-consciousness is not a mysterious phenomenon and can be explained by recourse to other states of consciousness, later he gives (perhaps unintentionally) an argument for the anomaly of self-consciousness—an anomaly that has already been discovered by Kant. In this case, indifference towards the history of philosophy, which early analytic philosophy has made part of its approach, turns out to be methodological incompetence.

Despite what Ryle, Kenny, and many others assume, self-consciousness *has* a "mystifying uniqueness and adhesiveness," a phenomenon that is analyzed by Kant and Wittgenstein. Therefore, any adequate criticism of Cartesianism should direct itself if not towards Kant, then at least towards Wittgenstein and not towards any of his apparent followers. Wittgenstein explicitly portrayed the linguistic illusion that is responsible for the Cartesian paralogism:

> We feel then that in the cases in which 'I' is used as subject, we don't use it because we recognize a particular person by his bodily characteristics;

> and this creates the illusion that we use this word to refer to something bodiless, which, however, has its seat in our body. In fact *this* seems to be the real ego, the one of which it was said, '*Cogito, ergo sum*'.[7]

It is striking that Wittgenstein does not deny "the peculiar grammar of the word 'I'" but rather explicitly emphasizes it.

> The word 'I' does not mean the same as 'L. W.' even if I am L. W., nor does it mean the same as the expression 'the person who is now speaking'. But that doesn't mean: that 'L. W.' and 'I' mean different things. All it means is that these words are different instruments in our language.[8]

The referential structure of self-consciousness thus does not lose any of its mysterious character in Wittgenstein's linguistic analysis. Wittgenstein does attempt to counteract the special role of self-consciousness by explaining it in terms of a complex structure of self-referential linguistic use, but he speaks explicitly of a differentiated linguistic use and does not adopt the further reductionist position that "mental concepts cannot be understood apart from their function in explaining and rendering intelligible the behavior of human agents."[9] To this extent, Wittgenstein's analysis of the I's peculiar grammar is a linguistic confirmation of the special referential role of self-consciousness and is in no way a refutation of the Cartesian argument for the irreducibility of self-referential states.

Traces of the Self in Consciousness

In an often misunderstood passage from the *Critique of Pure Reason*, Kant presents a systematically ambitious analysis of the anomalous referential structure of self-consciousness.[10] When Kant emphasizes that in our attempt to judge anything at all about the I, we are turning around our selves in a perpetual circle, he does not mean to be pointing out, as is often assumed, a difficulty in his own arguments but rather a constructive displacement [*konstruktive Verstellung*] of the I. It follows from Kant's critical epistemology as well as from his ensuing critique of the self—condensed in the famous passage at B404[11]—that self-referential mental acts cannot be identified with knowledge of a "self." The self-reference of consciousness initially contains only the idea of a subject of consciousness that is known only indirectly through the contents of consciousness "as its predicates," and as a form of consciousness it is not identifiable *through* consciousness. This constructive displacement of the I results from Kant's model of consciousness, according to which consciousness of spatiotemporal objects is structured by a categorial synthesis according to the conditions of possible self-consciousness. However, this model contains only the presupposition of a concept of the subject that designates nothing more than an instance of self-reference and does not contain any characterization of the content of this subject.

The special feature of Kant's theory consists in the fact that the constructive displacement of the I does not depend on any vicious circularity but is rather a consequence of irreflexive relations. The doctrine of the transcendental unity of self-consciousness is composed of transcendental characterizations that are due entirely to the analysis of the conditions of the possibility of experience. Kant explains further that the meaning of reflective attitudes is internally dependent on the position of the subject in space and time. This characterization is of particular importance for contemporary theories of self-consciousness, because in this way, the demand stated especially by analytic philosophers that a theory of self-ascription must take into account the spatiotemporal position of a person can be met without any commitment to a reductionist approach. Kant believes in the irreducibility of the givenness of the empirical context of the life of persons, just as he is convinced that experience and self-consciousness along with its subject are not determined exclusively empirically.

Neither the elusiveness of the self nor the constructive displacement of the 'I think' entails the irreducibility of self-consciousness. The elusiveness of the self only bars its direct identification. Revealing the constructive displacement of the 'I think' excludes only the possibility of identifying the self, but, on the other hand, it is already an important indication of the presence of a subject of mental activity. The limits of our knowledge and language must not be confused with the limits of our consciousness. Although there is a limitation to our application of concepts expressing states of self-consciousness, we have rich external evidence of reflective states of consciousness.[12] This is true particularly for the experiential perspective of a person's consciousness.

Personal existence implies an irreducible subjective perspective with respect to cognitive, reflective, and practical attitudes. This perspective constitutes an ontological property of persons. The description of the life of a person would be incomplete if it did not contain an experiential perspective with existential properties. In contrast to mere particularity in space and time, a dimension of existential consciousness is opened up with this experiential perspective. Therefore, the experiential perspective stands for a specific ontological quality, namely that of existing subjectively as a person.

Contrary to a number of anti-Cartesian interpretations of Wittgenstein's private language argument, the experiential perspective is an exclusive realm for which there is in each case only one individual and a privileged mode of access. And that is the epistemological reason for the epistemic and linguistic elusiveness of the self. For the concept of the self refers to the experiential perspective of a person, and to this extent it stands not for an object but rather for the complex connection between the subjectively formed dispositions and experiences of a person.

The Activity of the Self

According to Kant's epistemological analysis, the experiential perspective of persons is a positional self-awareness, that is, it is interpretable in terms of spatiotemporal indexicals and not from a monolithic standpoint. For Kant, the 'I think' always includes the 'I am.' For this reason he says that the sentence "I think or I exist as thinking" is an empirical sentence,[13] especially since the consciousness of my own existence is the immediate consciousness of other things outside of the standpoint of reflection, and consciousness of other things outside of me also includes states of consciousness that refer to my physical properties. In this respect, self-consciousness contains *difference*. In classical German philosophy, this difference is alluded to in much broader theoretical and argumentative contexts by concepts such as reflection, *Entzweiung* (self-division) or *Entäusserung* (self-externalization). The characteristics of the difference within self-consciousness reveal that the self can remove itself from the given immediacy of its life by means of its self-referential consciousness.

Indexicality and quasi-indexicality[14] are thus the formal linguistic means by which people primarily orient themselves in a reflective way towards their ontological and social contexts. In the medium of language, indexicality, and quasi-indexicality are the immediate expressions of human subjectivity. In a general sense, indexicality and quasi-indexicality are linguistic manifestations of the ontological position of a person that can be expressed in basic philosophical concepts such as space, time, consciousness, and self-referentiality.

The epistemic meaning of self-consciousness and self-knowledge is justified by the difference within self-consciousness, for an epistemic relation towards one's own existence that cannot be separated from the specific perspective of the subject is always contained in forms of self-ascriptions. Even if self-consciousness as such is not yet self-knowledge, the 'I that thinks' experiences "the position of itself (*dabile*) as determinable in space and in time (*cogitabile*),"[15] and one should add: to be determined in space and time. Therefore, a self-conscious person is already related to his existence in space and time—regardless of the absence of empirical content in self-consciousness.

Self-consciousness is not transcendence but rather the perspective of an existing consciousness that always includes itself. In this respect, the difference within self-consciousness, i.e., the "twofold I in the consciousness of myself,"[16] is already practical. One can speak of the alteration of self-consciousness that is necessitated by this twofold structure as an *action*, for in its reflected positionality, the subject of self-consciousness—the self—is immediately related to itself in an altered form. On the basis of this requirement, which is contained in every form of reflective existence and which excludes *not* being able to act, the immediate self-relation of self-consciousness is an alteration, and its subject, the self, is both a principle of change and its object.[17]

Although the physical appearance of a person does not seem to undergo any changes from the perspective of an external observer, an activity can nonetheless be present, namely whenever the mental situation has changed—even if this happens only by means of a transition to an intensified state of reflective attention. For this reason, the Wittgensteinian criterion for the presence of mental processes does not apply. A person can do literally nothing but attend to this inactivity itself in a reflective state, without altering her behavior, and this would still qualify as action. This fact is revealed in the case of a denial of first aid in which this denial is covered up by pretending not to notice the emergency.

Because self-consciousness as an implicit instance of alteration has epistemic consequences, consciousness of one's own existence immediately gains the status of a practical relation to the world. The unity of positionality and reflection produces an unavoidable connection between epistemic and practical attitudes, because awareness of one's position in space and time changes a person's attitude towards the external contexts of existence, towards other persons, and therefore towards oneself. The process that lets a person refer to what that person is *not* is already initiated with self-consciousness—this is the meaning of the 'difference' within self-consciousness. The activity of self-consciousness has in this respect an eccentric form: it binds the self to what it is not and forces it to relate to it explicitly.

This self-referential difference within self-consciousness has a structural analog in a person's practical attitudes. Insofar as a person achieves self-consciousness, that person is always related to her existence in the spatiotemporal world. As a positional consciousness, the experiential perspective of self-consciousness has the status of an instance of alteration, for within self-consciousness a person experiences that she is affected in a certain manner by a conscious state or event to which she must relate herself in the world. This self-referential and intrinsically differentiated relation takes the form of a practical dualism: a person does not live in two worlds, but a person leads an intellectually differentiated existence in one world.

One of the possible consequences of these self-referring attitudes is the attempt to oppose dependence on external things with reasons for actions. In individual cases, one will only rarely have to decide whether such attempts have really been successful—the epistemic privacy of self-consciousness and the influence of the unconscious prohibit this—but even a person's attempt to establish reason in the course of action clearly breaks through the world of mere events and opens up the perspective of practical reason.

Autonomy and Reason

The self as the subject of self-consciousness is the center of the experiential perspective of an individual who exists in space and time and whose essential properties include acting from reason. And it is this constellation of self and reason that determines the meaning of the concept of a person in a narrow sense. It is a necessary condition of the life of persons as subjects of reflective and practical attitudes to be able to alter the world of events. On the basis of this property one must grant persons a special status in the world of events,[18] for persons are not necessarily objects of change but are capable of altering the world of events in a reasonable way. To this extent the complete ontology of a person already involves a transition from self to reason. And this fact is the ontological cornerstone of the dual aspect theory that is defended here.

Self and reason represent an ontological difference in the world of events. Unlike the dualism generally attributed to Cartesianism, in dual aspect theory the irreducible concepts of self and reason do not signify metaphysical enclaves but rather integrated components of the lives of persons in the world of events. Otherwise personal life could not have self-determined elements. Accordingly, reason is the perspective of a person's specific potential for action, not a relationless noumenal realm. If reason were to be banned to a noumenal realm, then at best, features of negative freedom could be assumed in the world of events. However, autonomy would be impossible with negative freedom alone, because self-determination can come about only as an event within the world.

On the other hand, the ontological conditions of autonomy should not be confused with autonomy itself. Even though the existence of persons qua rational individuals reveals an ontological difference in the world of events, autonomy still needs to be brought about practically in an additional act; that is, autonomy as a natural property does not attach from the start to the activities of persons. If autonomy is not a natural property of the agency of persons, then it can be instantiated only with the help of nonnatural features of personal life. And the nonnatural perspective of agency that allows for autonomy is the standpoint of reason.

The widespread conviction of classical German philosophy has been that the standpoint of autonomy can be conceived only as a standpoint determined by reason. This conviction has found its best-known expression in Kant's theory of practical reason. It presupposes a concept of the moral self that is defined by a relation between the first- and third-person perspectives. And it was Kant's ambitious task to resolve the moral and psychological tensions that result from the conflict between the first- and third-person perspectives.

The concept of the moral self is given a powerful formula in Kant's famous expression of the "moral law within."[19] This formula says that the self gives itself a law and in this way constitutes the formal structure of autonomy. The internal differentiation of the concept of the self does not proceed according to the standards of a merely formal relation to one's self, for the moral law qua autonomy of reason must be construed from an impersonal standpoint. From this situation the tensions arise that are peculiar to Kant's moral philosophy, namely that autonomy can be properly understood only from a subjective perspective, whereas justifiable self-determination can be construed only from an impersonal standpoint.

In Kant's moral philosophy, however, subjective and impersonal standpoints are not simply placed next to each other without any relations, contrary to what several critics assume. In the categorical imperative, no *immediate* impersonal determination of the will is intended.[20] The impersonal perspective is meant to refer rather to maxims, and maxims are subjective principles of volition[21] in the form of rules of acting that do not yet imply any immediate moral obligation. A person's maxims manifest values that select and structure courses and situations of action in a practical way and place them in relation to future actions. To this extent maxims refer to the contexts of the life of persons and depend to a large degree on their character and dispositions.

Persons accompany their actions at least implicitly with moral evaluations that can be resisted only with great difficulty. This can be seen clearly in the case of awareness of injustice or egoistic actions. As long as repressive or self-deceptive processes have not yet become routine, a person knows quite well that she has acted immorally, or at least in a way subject to criticism, even if that is very seldom admitted in public.

Moral insights that go against one's own will provide the empirical basis of Kant's theory of practical reason,[22] and it is this basis that makes clear the methodological profile of Kant's dual aspect theory. Surprisingly enough, Kant's arguments are supported by a view that is generally taken by intuitionist approaches. However, a Kantian moral philosophy can be successful only if its deontological ambitions can connect up with moral facts in a way appropriate to the phenomena. Even if several formulations seem to point in a different direction, there are decisive passages in Kant's writings on moral philosophy that point towards what he calls the "fact of reason." The fact of reason does not lead, as many critics want to suggest, to a one-sided rationalistic interpretation of actions but rather to a systematic interpretation of "moral sense." Whether a person in fact acts morally is not crucial in judging a person's reason. The point that is important for the nonreductionist dual aspect theory is that the person is capable of acting morally and examining his life in terms of reason.

The Examined Life

The examined life is the explicit transition from a referentially indeterminate concept of the self to the standpoint of the person as a subject of self-determination through practical reason. Obviously, the standpoint of reason is not the only source of motivation in people's lives. Rather, in practical attitudes and in processes of decision-making there is a plurality of different motivational levels. Generally the motivational counterpart to reason is the realm of emotions. Without going into the details of the complicated meaning involved in the concept of emotions, it must be pointed out that the emotional constitution of human beings is not simply a passive foundation for an otherwise rationally determined consciousness; this constitution already forms the dispositions and acts of persons. That is why attempts at developing a strict separation between the realms of reason and emotions must fail. The emotional nature of personal existence can be approached by psychological analysis only to a limited extent. Schelling and Hegel in particular have shown that the mental dimension of rational individuals is much broader than the realm of phenomena that occur in explicit states of consciousness. In human modes of behavior, the transitions between the realms of reasons and emotions cannot be identified; one must, therefore, speak of indeterminate relations. For both Schelling and Hegel this fact is characteristic of human existence.[23] And long before Freud, they had shown repeatedly that the grounds of behavior that are attributed to a person either by herself or by others need not necessarily have been the cause by which this mode of behavior was generated.

Despite these indeterminate relations, reason can function as a corrective for emotional dispositions. The most important level in this context is that of the norms and ideals that are effective in a person's actions. Normative corrections of conduct are dispersed over various time periods and contexts of personal life and can even disappear throughout the course of time. However, it is normally possible for a person to increase the effect of practical reason in her life, even if this effect is difficult to discern in individual cases. From the standpoint of reason, the meaning of the life of a person lies in how the person emphasizes the direction of an examined and self-determined life and not in critical evaluations of the moral worth of individual actions.

The examined life obviously provides reasons for action. In contrast to a self that only proceeds from one alternative to the other, actions in an examined life are performed by a "strong evaluator."[24] The differentiations of a "strong evaluator" contain a plurality of possible courses of action that are not present at an unreflective level of personal existence. Charles Taylor summarizes this point as follows:

> A person is a being who has a sense of self, has a notion of the future and the past, can hold values, make choices; in short, can adopt life-plans. At least, a person must be the kind of being who is in principle capable of all this, however damaged these capacities may be in practice. Running through all this we can identify a necessary (but not sufficient) condition. A person must be a being with his own point of view on things. The life-plan, the choices, the sense of self must be attributable to him as in some sense their point of origin.[25]

Accordingly, in the practical perspective of an examined life this sense of self always takes on a temporally extended form. And the focal point of practical reason over time is the rational life-plan.

The Rational Life-Plan

The examined life must be carried out in light of values and the setting of goals that are highly context-dependent. Thus the life of a person cannot be lived "according to plan" in a literal sense. A life-plan is not a rigid outline towards which life's individual events can be directed. Even a life-plan's ultimate goals are mutable and must be changed in light of unforeseen circumstances. For this reason a life-plan can be understood neither as a unified or unifying concept under which all particular goals and actions are to be subsumed, nor as an abstract framework from which a person's life can take its starting point. Rather, a person finds that the normative models to which she will orient herself are already present in social life, and the contingent conditions under which a person has to lead her life contribute to this orientation.

A life-plan is a normative perspective that can be brought about only partially. But the quality of self-determination depends on this partial fulfillment. The goals of a rational life-plan can be achieved only bit by bit, but within the framework of reason, persons can design and follow a life-plan and thus establish the continuity of their lives.[26] A rational life-plan in no way excludes diversity, especially since reasonable grounds of motivation undergo changes through time. Accordingly, the execution of a rational life-plan must proceed in light of the fact of reasonable diversity.[27] Attempts at eliminating this fact run contrary to the claims of autonomy and will always take the form of massive oppression in the political arena.

A rational life-plan presupposes a specific conception of the practical unity of a person over time. According to this conception, personal narratives are to be conceived such that in the future, no need for revision will arise: ideally a person at one time will not in a certain sense blame the actions of that same person at another time.[28] Because the course of every action is subject to contingent conditions, it is neither possible nor desirable to pursue a completely rational life-plan. Nevertheless, a person should still adopt maxims of acting according to what appear to be the best reasons at each point in time, for there is a close connection between a rational life-plan and the continuity of a person over time. Whoever does not understand himself as a person extended in time who can and should lead his life according to the perspective of reason must necessarily lack respect for his own future needs and those of other persons, and will thus, morally speaking, act irresponsibly.[29]

The Other Person as a Fact of Reason

The fact of reason is revealed in the reciprocal relations that result from the presence of other persons in social life. Due to this presence of others, the standpoint of reason is always a step of the self to the Other. This step is a fact of practical reason and belongs to the unquestioned phenomena of everyday experience. Persons refer to each other *as* persons and attribute self-consciousness to each other reciprocally. The basis for this step is the recognition of the other self. Persons do not first perceive each other as mere objects in space and time and then clarify in a further step the status of the reality of other minds. Rather, they already assume that others have a moral self that presupposes moral states such as love, hate, respect, contempt, pride, shame, guilt, gratitude, resentment, remorse, and so on.[30] The recognition of the other self occurs immediately and without the express knowledge of each of the persons. And the social life with which we are all familiar depends on this recognition of the other self; where such recognition is lacking, one cannot speak of personal life: the recognition of the other self distinguishes a society of persons from a colony of ants.

Both the reality of reason and the reality of the self are manifest in the practical recognition of the other self. In this way, the issue of the elusiveness of the self that could be encountered so far only in indirect arguments can find an impressive practical solution. The solution finds its linguistic analog in the semantic fact that the concept of the self can be applied in the same way to different persons. The linguistic objectivity of the concept of the self is thus revealed in its invariant meaning and its varying reference.

Irreducible reciprocal relations are the core of the practical reason of persons; amongst them the self functions as a subject and as an object at the same time; that is, persons perceive each other as subjects with equal or at least similar interests, properties and possibilities. In this way, practical reason transcends the narrow borders of selfish and egoistic affects and sets up justifiable grounds for recognition and the reciprocal relations of persons. This complex state of affairs can be summarized by saying that the self's faculty of reason is *a*—proponents of classical German philosophy would say the *only*—justifiable perspective of self-determined externalization in reflection and practice.[31]

Notes

1. See Anthony Kenny, *The Metaphysics of Mind* (New York: Oxford University Press, 1989).

2. See René Descartes, *Meditations on First Philosophy*, trans. J. Cottingham (New York: Cambridge University Press, 1986), pp. 27–28 (pagination of *Œuvres de Descartes*, vol. 7, ed. C. Adam and P. Tannery [Paris: J. Vrin, 1964]): "I know that I exist; the question is, what is this 'I' that I know? If the 'I' is understood strictly as we have been taking it, then it is quite certain that knowledge of it does not depend on things of whose existence I am as yet unaware; so it cannot depend on any of the things which I invent in my imagination."

3. See Descartes, *Meditations*, p. 28: "But what then am I? A thing that thinks. What is that? A thing that doubts, understands, affirms, denies, is willing, is unwilling, and also imagines and has sensory perceptions."

4. Gilbert Ryle, *The Concept of Mind* (New York: Hutchinson's University Library, 1949), p. 195.

5. Ibid.

6. Ibid., p. 198.

7. Ludwig Wittgenstein, *Preliminary Studies for the 'Philosophical Investigations' Generally known as The Blue and Brown Books*, 2nd ed. (Oxford: Basil Blackwell, 1969), p. 69.

8. Wittgenstein, *Blue and Brown Books*, p. 67. Cf. Ryle, *The Concept of Mind*, p. 197: "An 'I' sentence indicates whom in particular it is about by being itself uttered or written by someone in particular. 'I' indicates the person who utters it." Wittgenstein has shown that this not the meaning of 'I'.

9. Kenny, *Metaphysics of Mind*, pp. 5–6.

10. For discussion and criticism of recent misinterpretations of Kant's theory of self-consciousness, see Karl Ameriks, "Kant and the Self: A Retrospective," in *Figuring the Self* (Albany: SUNY Press, forthcoming); "Understanding Apperception Today," in *Kant and Contemporary Epistemology*, ed. P. Parrini (Boston: Kluwer Academic Publishers, 1994), pp. 331–47.

11. See Immanuel Kant, *Critique of Pure Reason*, trans. N. K. Smith (New York: St. Martin's Press, 1929), A346/B404 (pagination of the first/second German editions): "Through this I or he or it (the thing) which thinks, nothing further is represented than a transcendental subject of the thoughts = *X*. It is known only through the thoughts which are its predicates, and of it, apart from them, we cannot have any concept whatsoever, but can only revolve in a perpetual circle, since any judgment upon it has always already made use of its representation. And the reason why this inconvenience is inseparably bound up with it, is that consciousness in itself is not a representation distinguishing a particular object, but a form of representation in general, that is, of representation in so far as it is to be entitled knowledge; for it is only of knowledge that I can say that I am thereby thinking something."

12. Cf. Thomas Nagel, *The View from Nowhere* (New York: Oxford University Press, 1986), p. 23.

13. See Kant, *Critique of Pure Reason*, B428. Cf. my *Kant über Selbstbewusstsein. Zum Zusammenhang von Erkenntniskritik und Theorie des Selbstbewusstseins* (Hildesheim and New York: Olms, 1985), pp. 93–106.

14. See Hector-Neri Castañeda, "Indicators and Quasi-Indicators," *American*

Philosophical Quarterly 2 (1967). Cf. Manfred Frank, "Hat Selbstbewusstsein einen Gegenstand?" in *Selbstbewusstsein und Selbsterkenntnis: Essays zur analytischen Philosophie der Subjektivität* (Stuttgart: Reclam, 1991).

15. See Kant, *Kants gesammelte Schriften* (hereafter Ak.) (Berlin: Königliche Preussische Akademie der Wissenschaften, 1900 ff.), vol. 22, p. 47.

16. See Kant, Ak. vol. 20, p. 268–69. Cf. my "Das doppelte Ich im Bewusstsein meiner selbst. Zur Struktur von Kants Begriff des Selbstbewusstseins," in *Proceedings of the Sixth International Kant Congress*, vol. 2/1, ed. G. Funke and T. Seebohm (Washington, DC: Center for Advanced Research in Phenomenology & University Press of America, 1989), pp. 367–81.

17. See my "Perspektiven der Person. Der Zusammenhang von Reduktionismuskritik und Epistemologie der Freiheit," in *Perspektiven des Perspektivismus*, ed. V. Gerhardt and N. Herold (Würzburg: Königshausen & Neumann, 1992), pp. 126–29.

18. Cf. Susan Wolf, *Freedom within Reason* (New York: Oxford University Press, 1990), p. 10.

19. See Kant, *Critique of Practical Reason*, 3rd ed., trans. L. W. Beck (New York: Macmillan, 1993), Ak. vol. 5, pp. 161–63.

20. See Kant, *Groundwork of the Metaphysic of Morals*, trans. H. J. Paton (New York: Harper & Row, 1964), Ak. vol. 4, p. 421: "There is therefore only a single categorical imperative and it is this: '*Act only on that maxim through which you can at the same time will that it should become a universal law*'." Cf. Henry Allison, *Kant's Theory of Freedom* (New York: Cambridge University Press, 1990), p. 189: "the centerpiece of Kant's conception of rational agency is the Incorporation Thesis, that is, the claim that an incentive . . . can determine the will only insofar as it has been incorporated into a maxim."

21. See Kant, *Groundwork*, Ak. vol. 4, p. 400 n.: "A *maxim* is the subjective principle of a volition."

22. Cf. my "Autonomie und Kontingenz. Kants nicht-reduktionistische Theorie des moralischen Selbst," in *Akten des Siebenten Internationalen Kant-Kongresses*, ed. G. Funke (Bonn: Bouvier, 1991), pp. 573–87.

23. See Friedrich Wilhelm Joseph Schelling, *On the History of Modern Philosophy*, trans. A. Bowie (New York: Cambridge University Press, 1994), pp. 108–13 (pp. 92–98 of *Sämmtliche Werke*, vol. 10); Georg Wilhelm Hegel, *Enzyklopädie der philosophischen Wissenschaften im Grundrisse (1830)* (Hamburg: Felix Meiner, 1969), §§ 387–482. Cf. my "Hegels Theorie des Unbewussten. Zum Zusammenhang

von Naturphilosophie und philosophischer Psychologie," *Hegel-Jahrbuch* 1990; "Odyssee des Geistes. Schellings Projekt einer naturphilosophischen Geschichte des Selbstbewusstseins," in *Philosophie der Subjektivität? Zur Bestimmung des neuzeitlichen Philosophierens*, ed. H. M. Baumgartner and W. Jacobs (Stuttgart-Bad Cannstatt: Frommann-Holzboog, 1993).

24. See Charles Taylor, "What is Human Agency?" in *Human Agency and Language: Philosophical Papers 1* (New York: Cambridge University Press, 1985), p. 23.

25. Taylor, "The Concept of a Person," in *Human Agency and Language*, p. 97.

26. Cf. John Rawls, *A Theory of Justice* (Cambridge, Mass.: Harvard University Press, 1971), pp. 407–24.

27. Cf. Rawls, *Political Liberalism* (New York: Columbia University Press, 1993), pp. 54–58.

28. See Rawls, *A Theory of Justice*, p. 423.

29. See ibid.: "One who rejects equally the claims of his future self and the interests of others is not only irresponsible with respect to them but in regard to his own person as well. He does not see himself as one enduring individual." Cf. my "Person und Zeit," in *Zeiterfahrung und Personalität*, ed. Forum für Philosophie Bad Homburg (Frankfurt: Suhrkamp, 1992).

30. See Peter F. Strawson, "Freedom and Resentment," in *Freedom and Resentment and Other Essays* (London: Methuen, 1974). Cf. Strawson, *Analysis and Metaphysics* (New York: Oxford University Press, 1992), p. 138: "In a variety of ways, inextricably bound up with the facts of mutual human involvement and interaction, we feel towards each other as to other selves; and this variety is just the variety of moral and personal reactive attitudes and emotions which we experience towards each others and which have their correlates in attitudes and emotions directed towards ourselves." Cf. Thomas Nagel, "Moral Luck," in *Mortal Questions* (New York: Cambridge University Press, 1979), p. 37.

31. The English version of this essay is based on an original translation by Eric Watkins.

12

From Kant to Frank: The Ineliminable Subject

Karl Ameriks

I

The defenders of subjectivity today have to fight a multifront battle. In this struggle, it is useful to distinguish strategic plans from tactical decisions and to remember that alliances built on fundamentals can thrive on differences that are incidental. Because of its strategic position alone, Manfred Frank's philosophy of the subject is surely one of the most important and promising of our time. His goal, as I see it, is to rescue the role of the subject "across the board," i.e., for ethical, methodological, epistemological, and possibly even ontological purposes. This goal can be seen as a continuation of the Heidelberg school's call for a "theory of self-consciousness" that is grounded both systematically and historically in the classical tradition of German philosophy.

In a seminal article in the Gadamer Festschrift, Dieter Henrich outlined the crucial preconditions for such a theory, most notably that it overcome the dilemmas of what he called the "Reflection Theory" of self-consciousness.[1] At about the same time, he also argued that the first approximation to an adequate critique of the Reflection Theory was to be found in an "original insight" of Fichte's,[2] and in later work Henrich has often contended that this insight was a crucial advance on Kant. (Elsewhere I have critically examined some current attempts to employ this insight in regard to Kant's notion of apperception.)[3] More recently, Frank has joined forces with Henrich, and argued that from Descartes on, through Kant and even contemporary non-German theory of mind, the Reflection Theory is the cardinal enemy for the camp of those who take subjectivity seriously.[4] Now Frank has also moved on to show in more detail how there is an advance beyond the Reflection Theory that actually predates Fichte's work, since it can already be found in the sketches of the early romantics, as opposed to the mainline German idealist systems.[5]

Even more impressively, Frank has used insights from this early romantic notion of the self to construct a contemporary position that, roughly speaking, is meant to save an existentialist account of consciousness, presented most clearly by Sartre, from the extreme antisubjectivist positions found in its Heideggerian predecessors and its post-Heideggerian, "postmodern" variants.[6] The Achilles' heel of these extreme positions is that their famous assault on the fundamental position of subjectivity rests on an inappropriately restricted notion of the subject, a notion that still presumes that a subject is something that must be understood originally from the standpoint of reflection. Since such an understanding of the subject leads to demonstrable absurdities, it is then inferred, all too quickly, that the subject as such must be given up.

To the considerable extent that modern philosophy does rest on the unhappy notion of the subject that Heidegger meant to deconstruct, Frank can join in its burial. However, insofar as there is also an ineliminable prereflective notion of the subject that can be vindicated, Frank can and does argue that the *cogito* can be resurrected without fear—and also without having to take the literally self-defeating but ever-popular measures of replacing the subject's fundamental position by an historicist principle of intersubjectivity (as in Habermas)[7] or a naturalistic principle of universal objectivity (as in much analytic philosophy).

More specifically, Frank follows Tugendhat in arguing that Heidegger is best understood as having saved the study of being from "objectivism" by showing first that being needs to be approached via our understanding of, or access to, being, and second that this shows in turn that in addition to all the beings that there are, which simply exist or do not exist, there is a capacity for judgment (grounded for Heidegger in what he calls the "disclosure" that makes judgment possible) that generates statements that can be either true or false.[8] The crucial point here is that as long as the "access" to beings is understood simply in terms of the old model of something being present to mind (*"vor-gestellt,"* re-presented), there is no real difference between seeing nothing and not seeing anything, and this leaves only two options, presence and nonpresence. However, once the importance of the domain of judgment is appreciated, we can see the need to distinguish at least three fundamental situations, namely, (1) not saying something, (2) saying something that is not (i.e., something that is false), and (3) saying something that is the case. In this way, it turns out that a particular kind of subjectivism, i.e., a model of the subject as a mere "mirror" of the presence of things (here one can see the roots of Rorty's attack on the "mirror of nature" view), is what underlies the unfortunate rise of a kind of "objectivism," i.e., the impoverished view that there are only things and not frameworks of understanding, which are what first genuinely disclose things and require the three fundamental possibilities noted above. (Heidegger's basic idea here is an obvious radicalization of Husserl's challenges to objectivism; in our own time, the point has been stressed most vigorously in the works of Gerold Prauss.[9])

One can now see Frank's response to the Heideggerian challenge to subjectivism as itself a natural radicalization of the argument begun by Heidegger. Just as Heidegger attempted to wrest the study of being from the limitations of objectivism by disclosing its roots in an improper (presence-modeled) underlying notion of the subject, Frank has proposed to save the study of the subject itself by arguing that we do not need to move away from self-consciousness as the basis of philosophy; rather, we need only move away from the Reflection Theory's account of self-consciousness, for this account turns out to be but another variety of objectivism. This is because the Reflection Theory rests on the notion that the self exists only when it is reflected upon, thus made an object of itself. The theory seems both obviously absurd and yet inevitably appealing, for, one might ask, how else does one "catch" the self except by turning back upon it? The appeal of such a theory comes out in many ways, and recently (in an apparently quite independent manner) it has even caught the momentary fancy of a leading analytic philosopher of mind: in Daniel Dennett's "cognitive theory of consciousness," conscious states are defined as precisely those to which the being has "access."[10] In this way, the mystery of consciousness can be dissipated; where there are such "self-monitoring" systems, there consciousness exists; where not, there is nothing. The operationalism explicit in this procedure is disturbing for more than phenomenological reasons, and this should make one want to do precisely what Frank attempts: namely, to construct a model of the subject that does not eliminate its most basic (not reflected on) states and absurdly replace them with what are surely higher and more objective capacities.

II

Frank's whole strategy is so appealing in its fundamentals that my response here can amount only to advancing for consideration a few friendly amendments and to indicating that some steps toward an alternative to the Reflection Theory can be found not only in Fichte or the early romantics, but also in the original "pre-Fichtean," namely Kant. (I also believe that not only in Kant's thought, but in Heidegger's as well, one can find underlying agreements with Frank's basic program—but in this article there will be space only to begin the reexamination of Kant).[11] My general hypothesis is that, even if it is undeniable that the philosophies of Kant and

Heidegger have been the major influences (at the beginning and end of the late modern period, respectively) on the development of extreme and unpalatable views of subjectivity, it may still turn out that the return of the subject to its proper place is also inspired in large part by some deeper aspects of precisely these philosophies.

Before entering into the exegesis of Kant, it would help to know what the doctrines are that we would like to be able to find. Let us take one of Frank's own most recent summaries of the privileges of subjectivity (in this volume). Here are four basic claims:

1. "we are originally more familiar with self-consciousness than with that which . . . we obtain from others . . . in behavioral expressions. . . . Otherwise, how could we grasp as *ours* an observational datum that in itself carries no indication of its bearer?"[12]

2. "our self-consciousness is also more original than everything that we can refer to with indexicals such as 'here' and 'this-there'"—for how else is a person to understand a map that says "you" are here?[13]

3. "if we are successfully to refer a description . . . to *ourselves*, . . . we must be familiar with the bearer of this property in a way that cannot be explained *from* the description itself."[14]

4. "self-consciousness also cannot be described as the object of a knowing. For all knowing is relative to a theory that could be false."[15]

These points can be brought together by speaking of self-consciousness, in its immediate sense, as having a priority over *observation, orientation, description*, and *objective knowledge*. Such claims obviously rest on presumptions about the terms with which self-consciousness is contrasted, and these presumptions are quite controversial. Nonetheless, I think most of the claims can be understood easily enough in common sense terms and as expressing views that are persuasive for many today largely because of an indirect effect (e.g. via Wittgenstein) of Kantian considerations. The "observation" claim, for example, corresponds fairly closely to what one would expect a Kantian to say after noting that the 'I think' of transcendental apperception is not equivalent to (but is rather what must be able to accompany) any particular observation that one makes of objects, let alone outer objects. Similarly—the second point, the point about orientation—especially as spelled out in terms of the example of reading a map, corresponds precisely to what one would expect given Kant's distinction between mere intuition and apperception and his early discussion of how we locate ourselves in regions of space, namely not merely by the sensible data before us. It would be somewhat anachronistic to presume that the third point, the linguistic issue of description, was a direct Kantian concern, and yet it too is certainly suggested by the notorious claim (B409) that the "being itself" of self-consciousness is given, "although nothing in myself is thereby given for thought." This could be taken easily enough to mean that one is acquainted with oneself independently of any determining proposition (something "given for thought") that one has at hand.[16] Finally, the fourth and ultimately most controversial claim, the claim about knowledge, appears to correspond nicely to the Kantian idea that the paradigm of knowing is empirical theoretical determination and that we are aware of something in us that is not captured by any such determination.

These points of correspondence are, of course, very general, and there is also a significant aspect of Frank's argument that does not *seem* directly to match the thrust of most of Kant's discussions. Put most simply, the difference is that here Frank is most concerned with aspects of the ineliminability of an *individual* concretely identifying itself, whereas usually Kant can *appear* concerned rather with structures of consciousness *in general*. For example, in the Kantian contrast between empirical and transcendental apperception, and in the critical thrust of the Paralogisms, it would seem that Kant is trying to remind us precisely that the empirical knowledge that a particular person is, say, so and so old, tall, etc., is at a different level than the transcendental representation of the I, which is simply a necessarily possible component of any such knowledge, and not, as it was for dogmatic philosophers, a determining intuition of particular features of an individual.

There is a crucial ambiguity here which I believe is not always made clear in Kantian discussions. One hears of a "view from nowhere" that takes one beyond the spatiotemporal limits of one's actual position as a finite person. Presumably, this view is to contrast with a view "from somewhere," a view that has the limitations of such an actual position. This is a nice image, and it has an obvious Kantian tone and heuristic value in ethical as well as theoretical discussions. Note, however, that at least two very different kinds of surpassings of the "somewhere" could be meant.[17] On the one hand, there is a view that is distinguished by *taking into account all* the particular somewheres and privileging none of them. Thus we might get an ideal scientific description of the world as a whole, which would contrast with the limited perceptions of an actual person, seeing things just from here and now. Similarly, we can imagine an ideal utilitarian calculation of what needs to be done to make the sum of pleasures highest for all, which can contrast with the particular narrow thoughts and pleasures of any actual person. In these thought experiments, we see things from "nowhere" in the sense of no particular somewhere (and so from what is sometimes called the Standpoint of the Universe), and yet what we see then could be captured by some idealization of the totality of the typical *empirical* knowledge of particular persons. Note that on this contrast, one can make a distinction between the "subjective" (= the particular) and the "objective" (=the total, or ideal) that is *still within* a framework of what is wholly *objective* or empirical in a broad sense. The latter aspect of this framework, which one could label the "nowhere because centerless" perspective, has an obvious similarity to the Kantian notions of apperception and morality ("*Wille*," or pure practical reason) thought of as general and impartial structures that nonetheless apply to us. Thus, as Kant himself stresses, there can be a close fit between empirical (e.g., particular facts) and transcendental (e.g., fundamental laws) perspectives with respect to the objective domain.

It is a different and more radical kind of perspective that emerges when one attends to the phenomena that fascinate Frank. Self-consciousness in the primordial sense of a self-familiarity of a sort that apparently escapes (because it precedes) all observation, orientation, description, and knowledge is "from nowhere" now in the new sense that, rather than being in principle "from everywhere," it is instead from an extraordinarily concrete "somewhere," a somewhere so concrete that any description of it would be too general to guarantee unique applicability.[18]

As was noted, this view may seem very different from what concerned Kant, but in fact he does seem to have been aware of it as well. Consider his mysterious note that the "I think expresses an indeterminate empirical intuition . . . an indeterminate perception . . . something real that is given . . . not as appearance nor as thing in itself (noumenon), but as something which actually exists."[19] It has often been remarked that here we seem to have the true "*Unding*" (non-thing, or absurdity) of Kant's system[20]—something outside both appearances and things in themselves. And yet there need be nothing absurd here, for the crucial term "indeterminate" is stressed by Kant, and the point can be simply that *if* by "determinate" one means an aspect of the individual that is fully captured by standard descriptions or observations, *and* if one understands (as Kant often does) the domain of appearances as defined by such determinations, then, with any *given particular* 'I think,' there is still something "real" here[21] and yet something that also does not by itself allow us to say anything specific about things in themselves. This "something real" is not an extra or transcendent self; it is simply that aspect of the self that each one of us is familiar with immediately. Note that within this framework, there is what can be called a view from the "most concrete somewhere," and *also*—in contrast to the previous "nowhere because centerless" perspective—something that could equally well be labeled a "nowhere *because* centered" perspective. Thus there arises a contrast between the subjective ("what it is 'like' from here") and the objective (how, on the basis of this familiarity and all that I know, I can then observe, orient, describe what I know to be *myself* as such) that now falls *within subjectivity* in a broad sense. For example, even though the fact that I see myself as indicated by "here" on a map is a known fact, and not simply an immediate aspect of self-consciousness, it is not something that could be known from the "nowhere because centerless" view alone. Yet, although it involves that view, it is also understood as something that is known by the very self that has an immediately centered awareness of "how it is" for it (compare Heidegger's notion of *Stimmung* and Thomas Nagel's notion of "what it is like to be a bat").

The philosophy of the subject thus discloses a self that is "pure" in two related but also very different ways. There is, on the one hand, the pureness of the whole subjective framework. This includes both the simplest states of mind, i.e., states that involve a particular self-awareness that can occur prior to observation, and prior to objective orientation, and perhaps even, as Frank says, prior to language and concepts; and also those more complex states of explicit self-identification that involve a coordination of immediate self-familiarity and what we understand from description, observation, etc. On the other hand, there is the pureness of objectivity as such, of what we ascend to once we see that in a sense we are an empirical thing and yet also more than just one particular thing in the world, that we are part of a general structure that can hold no matter what particular things come and go. (The language of a "view from nowhere" is but one version of this traditional philosophical perspective; perhaps the most developed version of this pure self is the objective correlate of Husserl's depiction of the "life" of the transcendental ego.)

In addition to the general question of how to understand the connection between the two extreme pure selves, i.e., the most primitive subjective states and the most general objective view, there is the more specific question that concerns us now of how to understand the relation between the two sorts of subjectivity described above. To begin to understand this relation, i.e., the relation between the states within which one "recognizes" oneself as such and the primitive subjective states themselves (which are immediately recognized), it helps to return to a related duality: the duality of the intentional and pre-intentional, as expressed in the major accounts of the self that immediately preceded Frank—namely those of Heidegger and of Henrich.

Recall that Frank followed both Heidegger's argument that the understanding of being that allows our grasp of truth and statements is something prior to and more than sheer presence (or absence) to consciousness and also Henrich's argument that the subject is fundamentally prereflective. There is a tension between these two arguments, one that also mirrors the contrast that has been drawn between the "general" and the "indeterminate" Kantian notions of the 'I think'. Henrich's argument appears to hinge more on the basic and indeterminate aspects of the self than on the "projective," intentional capacities of the subject stressed by Heidegger (in the latter part of the analytic of *Dasein* in *Being and Time)* and the hermeneutical tradition. One way of stating Henrich's argument is to say that the Reflection Theory is subject to a vicious circle: if self-consciousness is to be a consciousness that re-cognizes itself, then it would seem that some familiarity with the self must precede that recognition, for otherwise how would one know that it is *one's own self* that one is finding? The point here is that this familiarity cannot (on pain of circularity) itself be explained in terms of reflection, since it is precisely what is needed to make the reflection (involved in recognition) intelligible to begin with. (Similar considerations can be shown to underlie the four irreducible aspects of subjectivity stressed in Frank's four claims summarized earlier.) Henrich and Frank express this point by saying that this basic self-consciousness *cannot* originally be an intentional activity, and this in a double sense: it itself is not something which one "tries" to accomplish, and it is not something that has an "object" in the sense of having a content whose referent is separate and may or may not be there.[22] But then it may seem that on this account, self-consciousness itself has ended up as a kind of simple object after all; it is just either present or not. And one might then ask why it is even called "self-consciousness" and why "consciousness" or something even simpler would not be enough.

The triple structure of judgment (noted above), which Husserl and Heidegger (and Kant as well, I would add) used to overcome objectivism, can seem to be lost at this basic level. On this prereflective model, self-consciousness seems mute; if it cannot go wrong, isn't this just because it does not have, as such, a structure that can be said possibly to misapply (or, in good cases, to apply)? It is revealing that sometimes Frank defends the irreducibility of the subject by appealing not to such sheerly prereflective states but rather to its clearly intentional capacities (especially when he stresses the moral self and the importance of "style"). Meanings, he stresses, are not given things but are matters that subjects always construe or interpret.[23] Without disputing this point (although it can be overdone, if one always speaks of literally "creating" meanings), it should be emphasized that if one were to try to defend the subject in only this way, one would be departing from (though still possibly supplementing in a consistent way) the notion that the self has a wholly primordial, *pre*reflective primacy. Yet it is not accidental that there is a tendency to shift from "lower" to "higher" order aspects of subjectivity, for as soon as one tries to specify what the allegedly primordial self-consciousness is like, the dilemma arises of either being able to say nothing or of having to say something that after all involves intentional and descriptive features that can threaten a return of the Reflection Theory, that is, threaten to turn the subject back into an object after all.

III

To avoid this dilemma I propose the following revisionist Kantian tactic within the broadly subjectivist strategy. As I have argued in more detail elsewhere,[24] the crucial first step is to distinguish between mere representation, consciousness, and self-consciousness, and then between various levels within self-consciousness.

Representation, for Kant, is a capacity that is nonmaterial and can be assumed to exist in prehuman beings and in certain lower levels of our own mental life. It involves "feeling" and the primordiality of the sense of "what it is like," which corresponds to one aspect of the irreducibility of subjectivity as analyzed by Frank. However, representation in this general sense does not necessarily involve intentionality, and it is not what Kant understands as consciousness proper, which is more than sensation and involves representation of a specific type, which is not "nothing to me."[25]

I have proposed that this "not nothing to me" level of fully "conscious" representation be understood precisely not in terms of a model of presence or reflection but rather as simply an indication of Kant's doctrine of apperception; representations are "something to me" just when they can be understood as involving at least an implicit 'I think', an 'I think' that functions as a prefix to a that-clause and marks the fact that here we have some intentional and propositional content.

Since an 'I think' is involved, should we say that at this level there is already actual *self*-consciousness or at least the necessity of possible self-consciousness? Kant's doctrine of transcendental apperception appears to be making precisely this claim; it says that all of these "conscious" representations already prefixed by a particular 'I think', must also be capable of being prefixed by a further, collective 'I think'. The further unifying 'I think' is obviously a form of self-consciousness, but what of the initial particular 'I thinks'? What I propose is that each of the first-level, "pretranscendental" 'I thinks' *can also* be called a kind of *self*-consciousness and that this is so even if one does not insist on a strong (orthodox) Kantian thesis that an accompanying transcendental 'I think' is *really* possible for *each* of them. (Note that to say that the first-level consciousness *exists only via* the "further" 'I think' would be to fall prey again to the

Reflection Theory.) It might seem unnecessary to speak of "self"-consciousness here, but I believe it is fair to say that there is a kind of "selfness" here that comes simply from the fact that there really has to be a *subject* involved *as such* in the event,[26] i.e., a subject using its mind in a structured way, even though that subject need not be reflecting upon itself (e.g., it is simply *in* the state "I think that it is hot here," not "I think that I think that it is hot here").

In this way there arises a position similar to that which Frank has been calling for, namely, a modification of Kant's theory in the direction of diminishing the role of reflection. However, note again that it is only once one gets beyond this primordial "self-consciousness" in conscious representations as such that one gets into most of the aspects of self-awareness that are discussed by Frank—i.e., both those particular "view-from-nowhere-because-centered" states that involve the *recognition* of one's position and identity as such and then all the even higher intentional acts that reflect one's freedom and interpretive style. With respect to both of these particular kinds of irreducible states, I would propose that, *without* falling back into a Reflection Theory, it can be said that in all these cases, there is a kind of intentional "(self)-consciousness" (as I will refer to it). We do see and grasp and describe and know who we are and where we are as such (and how we want to interpret), even if this is not to be explained *simply* by typical propositional knowledge. To use Dieter Sturma's terms, we might say we have the self as a "quasi-object" at this level.[27] Confusions can arise, because there is always also present a first prereflexive level of awareness, the "animal" awareness of being a certain way, which need not be conceived as intentional. This level coexists with our actual simple intentional awarenesses and may seem to give a level of total immediacy to them that they do not have in all their concrete totality. But the paradigm instance of consciousness is what I have called the basic (self)-consciousness that exists "between" the lowest levels of mere animal representation and the various higher kinds of recognitive, reflective, or interpretive intentionality.

It is this middle kind of (self)-consciousness, consciousness of the form "I think that so and so," which on my interpretation is also the key premise of Kant's transcendental deduction.[28] In contrast, the Henrich school has seen the deduction as being meant by Kant to be based on a reflective certainty of the I's identity.[29] Such a reading does force one to regard Kant as a prime obstacle to a sustainable ("prereflective") theory of subjectivity. However, without recapitulating the challenges that have been offered to this (Henrich school) reading, one can note that it would surely be more appealing and charitable to have the welcome consequence of allowing for a strand in Kant that is free from the absurdities of the Reflection Theory. One can also note that the bare Kantian notion of apperception as such does not seem to have any absurd reflective component immediately built into it, if it is taken simply to stand for the capacity to combine representations in a judgmental fashion, i.e., to give them cognitive significance. There can be higher and more complex states of mind than this basic level of apperception, but if such a level is acknowledged as central, then we have finally succeeded in isolating a kind of (self)-consciousness that is free from becoming either an absurdly complex reflective object or merely a mute and all too simple entity. In this way, without denying that there are formulations in Kant that may also lead to the misconceptions of subjectivity that Frank and others have been trying to correct, one could still regard Kant as an ally in the rescue of the subject today. As long as the possibility of such an alliance is not foreclosed, the development of philosophy from Kant to Frank can also be, in part, a productive move back to (and with) Kant.

Notes

1. Dieter Henrich, "Self-Consciousness, A Critical Introduction to a Theory," *Man and World* 4 (1971), p. 3–28. German version, "Selbstbewusstsein: Kritische Einleitung in einer Theorie," *Hermeneutik und Dialektik* (Tübingen: Mohr, 1970), pp. 257–84.

2. Henrich, *Fichtes ursprüngliche Einsicht* (Frankfurt: Klostermann, 1967); translated as "Fichte's Original Insight," in *Contemporary German Philosophy*, vol. 1 (University Park, Pa.: Pennsylvania State University Press, 1982), pp. 15–53.

3. In "Understanding Apperception Today," *Kant and Contemporary Epistemology*, ed. P. Parrini (Dordrecht: Kluwer, 1994), pp. 333–49, I argue against certain ways in which some American neo-Kantian discussions of the self miss the truly *subjective* potential of Kant's theory; in "Kant and the Self: A Retrospective" (delivered at the University of Iowa conference on "Figuring the Self," April 1992), I argue against certain ways in which some neo-Fichtean discussions of the self appear to miss the truly *antireflective* potential of Kant's theory.

4. See esp. Manfred Frank, *Selbstbewusstsein und Selbsterkenntnis* (Stuttgart: Reclam, 1991), chap. 2.

5. See esp. Frank, "Philosophical Foundations of Early Romanticism," in this volume.

6. Frank, "Is Self-Consciousness a Case of *présence à soi*? Towards a Meta-Critique of the Recent French Critique of Metaphysics," in *Derrida: A Critical*

Reader, ed. D. Wood (Oxford: Blackwell, 1992), pp. 218–34. The last half of this paper is focused on Derrida, but many of the ideas are also meant to apply against other "neo-structuralists."

7. See esp. Frank, *Selbstbewusstsein und Selbsterkenntnis*, chap. 3.

8. Frank, "Présence," p. 221. Cf. Ernst Tugendhat, *Vorlesungen zur Einführung in die sprachanalytische Philosophie* (Frankfurt: Suhrkamp, 1976).

9. See Gerold Prauss, *Erscheinung bei Kant* (Berlin: de Gruyter, 1971); *Einführung in die Erkenntnistheorie* (Darmstadt: Wissenschaftliche Buchgesellschaft, 1980); and my "Contemporary German Epistemology," *Inquiry* 25 (1982), pp. 125–38.

10. Daniel Dennett, *Brainstorms* (Montgomery, Vt.: Bradford Books, 1978), pp. 150, 159, 169. This theory, like much of Dennett's work, may owe some of its inspiration to Ryle. For a similar criticism of a theory like this, cf. Colin McGinn, *Problems in Philosophy: The Limits of Inquiry* (Oxford: Blackwell, 1993), pp. 29–30.

11. One step in the strategy of defending Heidegger would be to contend that a Heideggerian critique of objectivism and the metaphysics of presence need not fall prey immediately to a tendency to understand the disclosing subject itself *only* in reflective and thus "objective" terms. Frank notes some damning, but not clearly typical, uses of the notion of reflection in Heidegger ("Présence," pp. 223–24), but the main point of his attack seems to be that any theory that, like Heidegger's, seems to give primacy to our focus on the "outside" must distort the self's immediate grasp of itself. Yet it may be that, as in Kant's theory and especially his "Refutation of Idealism," one can combine an account of how the subject knows itself *determinately* only *via* an "outside" (i.e., judgments of external objects; cf. Prauss, *Erscheinung*) with a claim that there is *also* a form of nonobjective, prereflective existence of the self.

12. Frank, "Is Subjectivity a Non-Thing, an Absurdity [*Unding*]?" in this volume, p. 185.

13. Ibid.

14. Ibid., p. 186.

15. Ibid.

16. Cf. my *Kant's Theory of Mind* (Oxford: 1982), p. 176, n. 103.

17. Cf. Thomas Nagel, *The View from Nowhere* (New York: Oxford University

Press, 1986), pp. 54 f. I believe his seminal account does not fully clarify this ambiguity, but parts of his discussion involve an almost parallel distinction, in reverse order, of the two views "from nowhere" that I distinguish. See his opening remarks on the problem of "particular subjectivity," i.e., the fact that descriptions always seem too incomplete to have to reach *me*; and then, secondly, the problem of "how can I be merely a particular person," which presumes a "centerless" or "perspectiveless" conception of a contrasting and ideal "objective self."

18. Cf. Frank's discussion of the phenomenon of "*de se*" properties, in "Subjectivity," this volume, pp. 186–88.

19. Immanuel Kant, *Critique of Pure Reason*, trans. N. K. Smith (New York: St. Martin's Press, 1929), B422–23 n. (pagination of the first/second German editions).

20. Cf. Frank, "Fragmente einer Geschichte der Selbstbewusstseinstheorie von Kant bis Sartre," in *Selbstbewusstseinstheorien von Fichte bis Sartre* (Frankfurt: Suhrkamp, 1991), p. 421 f. On my proposal, Kant is saved from having to imply a "fully determinate" "intellectual intuition" here (cf. Frank, "Fragmente," p. 425). See also my "Kant and Mind: Mere Immaterialism," in *Proceedings of the Eighth International Kant Congress* (Milwaukee: Marquette University Press, 1995).

21. Hence Kant says "empirical"—but in a special, *non*determined sense. I would argue that he does and can in principle also allow the entertainment of nonempirical implications of this "real" given, e.g., its ultimate freedom and nonmateriality. Cf. Colin McGinn's remarks about consciousness as "noumenal" in "Can We Solve the Mind-Body Problem?" in *The Problem of Consciousness* (Oxford: Blackwell, 1991), p. 3; cited above by Frank, "Subjectivity," this volume, p. 190, n. 6.

22. See, e.g., Frank, *Selbstbewusstsein und Selbsterkenntnis*, p. 71.

23. "*Deuten*"—this term seems unavoidable (it has also played a central role in Prauss's account of the subject). See Frank, "Towards a Philosophy of Style," *Common Knowledge* 1 (1992), pp. 54–77; cf. Prauss, *Einführung*.

24. Cf. my "Understanding Apperception Today."

25. Kant, *Critique of Pure Reason*, B131–32.

26. Here I am trying to develop an "in between" position that avoids the difficulties that Frank *(Selbstbewusstsein und Selbsterkenntnis*, pp. 309 f., 328 f.) finds in H. N. Castañeda's notion of "internal reflexivity" and in R. Chisholm's notion of "subjectless" consciousness (*The First Person* [Minneapolis: University of Minneapolis Press, 1981], chap. 7).

27. Dieter Sturma, *Kant über Selbstbewusstsein* (New York: Olms, 1985). Sturma has spoken of this level as involving "self-reference" without "self-consciousness" (p. 59); I believe this is consistent with what I am saying, since the "(self)-consciousness" I am speaking of is so only in an extended sense, and what Sturma means to exclude is a higher-order state of mind, e.g., an explicit reflection or grasp of a self as a typical object.

28. See, e.g., my "Kant's Transcendental Deduction as a Regressive Argument," *Kant-Studien* 69 (1978), pp. 273–85; my "Recent Work on Kant's Theoretical Philosophy," *American Philosophical Quarterly* 19 (1982), pp. 1–24; and my "Kant and Guyer on Apperception," *Archiv für Geschichte der Philosophie* 65 (1983), pp. 295–302. Cf. also Sturma, *Kant über Selbstbewusstsein*, chap. 2.

29. Henrich, *Identität und Objektivität* (Heidelberg: Winter, 1976). Cf. Frank, "Fragmente," pp. 416 ff.

Selected Bibliography

Books

*Allison, Henry E., *Kant's Theory of Freedom* (Cambridge: Cambridge University Press, 1990).

*Ameriks, Karl, *Kant's Theory of Mind* (Oxford: Clarendon Press, 1982).

*Aschenberg, Reinhold, *Sprachanalyse und Transzendentalphilosophie* (Stuttgart: Klett-Cotta, 1982).

*Beiser, Frederick, *The Fate of Reason* (Cambridge, Mass.: Harvard University Press, 1987).

*Beiser, Frederick, ed., *The Cambridge Companion to Hegel* (Cambridge: Cambridge University Press, 1993).

Bowie, Andrew, *Schelling and Modern European Philosophy: An Introduction* (New York and London: Routledge, 1993).

Brands, Hartmut, *"Cogito ergo sum," Interpretationen von Kant bis Fichte* (Freiburg: Alber, 1982).

*Breazeale, Daniel, and Rockmore, Thomas, eds., *Fichte: Historical Contexts/Contemporary Controversies* (Atlantic Highlands: Humanities, 1994).

Brook, Andrew, *Kant and the Mind* (Cambridge: Cambridge University Press, 1994).

Carl, Wolfgang, *Der schweigende Kant: Die Entwürfe zu einer Deduktion der Kategorien vor 1781* (Göttingen: Vandenhoeck & Ruprecht, 1989).

Chisholm, Roderick, *The First Person* (Minneapolis: University of Minnesota Press, 1981).

This limited bibliography is meant only as a starting point for readers who wish to explore further recent work in English or German directly concerning the authors and topics central to this volume. Some works with additional extensive bibliographical material are indicated above by an asterisk.

*de Vries, Willem, *Hegel's Theory of Mental Activity* (Ithaca: Cornell University Press, 1988).

Förster, Eckart, ed., *Kant's Transcendental Deductions: The Three 'Critiques' and the 'Opus postumum'* (Stanford: Stanford University Press, 1989).

Frank, Manfred, *Die Unhintergehbarkeit von Individualität* (Frankfurt: Suhrkamp, 1986).

Frank, Manfred, *Selbstbewusstsein und Selbsterkenntnis* (Stuttgart: Reclam, 1991).

Frank, Manfred, ed., *Selbstbewusstseinstheorien von Fichte bis Sartre* (Frankfurt: Suhrkamp, 1991).

*Frank, Manfred, ed., *Analytische Theorien des Selbstbewusstseins* (Frankfurt: Suhrkamp, 1994).

*Guyer, Paul, ed., *The Cambridge Companion to Kant* (Cambridge: Cambridge University Press, 1992).

Henrich, Dieter, *Fichtes ursprüngliche Einsicht* (Frankfurt: Klostermann, 1967), translated as "Fichte's Original Insight," in *Contemporary German Philosophy*, vol. 1 (University Park, Pa.: Pennsylvania State University Press, 1982), pp. 15–53.

Henrich, Dieter, *Selbstverhältnisse. Gedanken und Auslegungen zu den Grundlagen der klassischen deutschen Philosophie* (Stuttgart: Reclam, 1982).

Henrich, Dieter, *Konstellationen: Probleme und Debatten am Ursprung der idealistischen Philosophie (1789–1795)* (Stuttgart: Klett-Cotta, 1991).

Henrich, Dieter, *Der Grund im Bewusstsein: Untersuchungen zu Hölderlins Denken (1794–1795)* (Stuttgart: Klett-Cotta, 1992).

*Henrich, Dieter, *The Unity of Reason: Essays on Kant's Philosophy*, ed. Richard Velkley (Cambridge, Mass.: Harvard University Press, 1994). [This book includes a full bibliography of Henrich's writings.]

Hespe, Franz, and Tuschling, Burkhard, eds., *Psychologie und Anthropologie oder Philosophie des Geistes* (Bad Cannstatt: Frommann-Holzboog, 1991).

Kienzle, Bertram, and Pape, Helmut, eds., *Dimensionen des Selbst. Selbstbewusstsein, Reflexivität und die Bedingungen von Kommunikation* (Frankfurt: Suhrkamp, 1991).

*Kitcher, Patricia, *Kant's Transcendental Psychology* (New York: Oxford University Press, 1990).

McDowell, John, *Mind and World* (Cambridge: Harvard University Press, 1994).

McGinn, Colin, *The Problem of Consciousness* (Oxford: Blackwell, 1991).

*Mohr, Georg, *Das sinnliche Ich. Innerer Sinn und Bewusstsein bei Kant* (Würzburg: Königshausen & Neumann, 1991).

Nagel, Thomas, *The View from Nowhere* (Oxford: Oxford University Press, 1986).

Neuhouser, Frederick, *Fichte's Theory of Subjectivity* (Cambridge: Cambridge University Press, 1990).

Nozick, Robert, *Philosophical Explanations* (Cambridge, Mass.: Harvard University Press, 1981).

*Pippin, Robert, *Hegel's Idealism: The Satisfactions of Self-Consciousness* (Cambridge: Cambridge University Press, 1989).

Powell, C. Thomas, *Kant's Theory of Self-Consciousness* (Oxford: Oxford University Press, 1990).

Prauss, Gerold, *Kant über Freiheit als Autonomie* (Frankfurt: Klostermann, 1983).

Rosenberg, Jay F., *The Thinking Self* (Philadelphia: Temple University Press, 1986).

Ross, George MacDonald, and McWalter, Tony, eds., *Kant and his Influence* (Bristol: Thoemmes, 1990).

Schulz, Walter, *Ich und Welt. Philosophie der Subjektivität* (Tübingen: Neske, 1979).

*Siep, Ludwig, *Praktische Philosophie im Deutschen Idealismus* (Frankfurt: Suhrkamp, 1992).

*Stolzenberg, Jürgen, *Fichtes Begriff der intellektuellen Anschauung. Die Entwicklung in den Wissenschaftslehren von 1794–95 bis 1801–02* (Stuttgart: Klett-Cotta, 1986).

*Sturma, Dieter, *Kant über Selbstbewusstsein. Zum Zusammenhang von Erkenntniskritik und Theorie des Selbstbewusstseins* (New York: Olms, 1985).

Taylor, Charles, *Sources of the Self: The Making of the Modern Identity* (Cambridge, Mass.: Harvard University Press, 1989).

Tugendhat, Ernst, *Selbstbewusstsein und Selbstbestimmung. Sprachanalytische Interpretationen* (Frankfurt: Suhrkamp, 1979); translated as *Self-Consciousness and Self-Determination* (Cambridge, Mass.: MIT Press, 1986).

*Wildt, Andreas, *Autonomie und Anerkennung. Hegels Moralitätskritik im Lichte seiner Fichte-Rezeption* (Stuttgart: Klett-Cotta, 1982).

Wood, Allen, ed., *Self and Nature in Kant's Philosophy* (Ithaca and London: Cornell University Press, 1984).

Wolff, Michael, *Das Körper-Seele-Problem. Kommentar zu Hegel, Enzyklopädie (1830) § 389* (Frankfurt: Klostermann, 1992).

Articles

Allison, Henry, E., "The Concept of Freedom in Kant's 'Semi-Critical' Ethics," *Archiv für Geschichte der Philosophie* 68 (1986), 96–115.

Allison, Henry, E., "Morality and Freedom: Kant's Reciprocity Thesis," *Philosophical Review* 95 (1986), 393–425.

Allison, Henry, E., "Kant's Refutation of Materialism," *Monist* 72 (1989), 190–208.

*Ameriks, Karl, "Recent Work on Kant's Theoretical Philosophy," *American Philosophical Quarterly* 19 (1982), 1–24.

Ameriks, Karl, "Contemporary German Epistemology," *Inquiry* 25 (1982), 125–38.

Ameriks, Karl, "Kant and Guyer on Apperception," *Archiv für Geschichte der Philosophie* 65 (1983), 295–302.

Ameriks, Karl, "Hegel's Critique of Kant's Theoretical Philosophy," *Philosophy and Phenomenological Research* 48 (1985), 1–35.

Ameriks, Karl, "The Hegelian Critique of Kantian Morality," in *New Essays on Kant*, ed. B. den Ouden (New York: Peter Lang, 1987), 179–212.

Ameriks, Karl, "Kant on the Good Will," in *Grundlegung zur Metaphysik der Sitten: Ein kooperativer Kommentar*, ed. O. Höffe (Frankfurt: Klostermann, 1989), 45–65.

Ameriks, Karl, "Reinhold and the Short Argument to Idealism," in *Proceedings: Sixth International Kant Congress 1985*, ed. G. Funke and T. Seebohm (Washington, D.C.: The Center for Advanced Research in Phenomenology and the University Press of America: 1989), vol. 2, part 2, 441–53.

Ameriks, Karl, "Kant, Fichte, and Short Arguments to Idealism," *Archiv für Geschichte der Philosophie* 72 (1990), 63–85.

Ameriks, Karl, "Kant on Spontaneity: Some New Data," in *Akten des Siebenten Internationalen Kant-Kongresses*, vol. 2/1, ed. G. Funke (Bonn: Bouvier Verlag, 1991), 573–87.

Ameriks, Karl, "Hegel and Idealism," *Monist* 74 (1991), 386–402.

Ameriks, Karl, "Recent Work on Hegel: The Rehabilitation of an Epistemologist?" *Philosophy and Phenomenological Research* 52 (1992), 177–202.

Ameriks, Karl, "Kantian Idealism Today," *History of Philosophy Quarterly* 9 (1992), 329–42.

Ameriks, Karl, "Kant and Hegel on Freedom: Two New Interpretations," *Inquiry* 35 (1992), 219–32.

Ameriks, Karl, "Understanding Apperception Today," in *Kant and Contemporary Epistemology*, ed. P. Parrini (Dordrecht: Kluwer, 1994), 331–47.

Ameriks, Karl, "Kant and the Self: A Retrospective," in *Figuring the Self: Individual, Spirit and the Absolute in Classical German Philosophy*, ed. D. Klemm and G. Zöller (Albany: SUNY Press, forthcoming).

Ameriks, Karl, "Kant and Mind: Mere Immaterialism," in *Proceedings of the Eighth International Kant Congress*, ed. H. Robinson (Milwaukee: Marquette University Press, 1995).

Aquila, Robert, "Self-Consciousness, Self-Determination and Imagination in Kant," *Topoi* 6 (1987), 63–77.

Breazeale, Daniel, "Fichte's 'Aenesidemus' Review and the Transformation of German Idealism," *Review of Metaphysics* 34 (1981), 545–68.

Breazeale, Daniel, "Between Kant and Fichte: Karl Leonhard Reinhold's 'Elementary Philosophy'," *Review of Metaphysics* 35 (1982), 785–821.

Breazeale, Daniel, "The 'Standpoint of Life' and 'The Standpoint of Philosophy' in the Jena *Wissenschaftslehre*," in *Transzendentalphilosophie als System: Die Auseinandersetzung zwischen 1794 und 1806*, ed. Albert Mues (Hamburg: Felix Meiner, 1989), 81–104.

Breazeale, Daniel, "Why Fichte Now?" *Journal of Philosophy* 87 (1991), 424–31.

Breazeale, Daniel, "Fichte on Skepticism," *Journal of the History of Philosophy* 29 (1991), 427–53.

*Breazeale, Daniel, "Fichte and Schelling: The Jena Period," in *The Age of German Idealism*, ed. Robert C. Solomon and Kathleen Wright, *The Routledge History of Philosophy*, vol. 6 (London: Routledge, Chapman, and Hall, 1993), 138–80.

Breazeale, Daniel, "Philosophy and the Divided Self: On the Existential and Scientific Tasks of the Jena *Wissenschaftslehre*," *Fichte-Studien* 6 (1994), 1–29.

Cassam, Quassim, "Kant and Reductionism," *Review of Metaphysics* 43 (1989), 72–106.

Castañeda, Hector-Neri, "The Self and the I-Guises, Empirical and Transcendental," in *Theorie der Subjektivität* (Festschrift for Dieter Henrich), ed. K. Cramer, H. Fulda, R.-P. Horstmann, and U. Pothast (Frankfurt: Suhrkamp, 1987), 105–40.

Cramer, Konrad, "Über Kants Satz: Das: Ich denke, muss alle meine Vorstellungen begleiten können," in *Theorie der Subjektivität*, ed. K. Cramer, H. Fulda, R.-P. Horstmann, and U. Pothast (Frankfurt: Suhrkamp, 1987), 167–202.

di Giovanni, George, "The Facts of Consciousness," in *Between Kant and Hegel: Texts in the Development of Post-Kantian Idealism*, ed. G. di Giovanni and H. S. Harris (Albany: SUNY Press, 1985), 3–53.

Düsing, Edith, "Sittliche Aufforderung. Fichtes Theorie der Interpersonalität in der *Wissenschaftslehre nova methodo* und in der *Bestimmung des Menschen*," in *Transzendentalphilosophie als System. Die Auseinandersetzung zwischen 1794 und 1806*, ed. Albert Mues (Hamburg: Felix Meiner, 1989), 174–97.

Düsing, Edith, "Das Problem der Individualität in Fichtes früher Ethik und Rechtslehre," *Fichte-Studien* 3 (1991), 29–50.

Düsing, Klaus, "The Constitution and Structure of the Self-Consciousness: Kant's Theory of Apperception and Hegel's Criticism," in *Midwest Studies in Philosophy*, vol. 8, 409–31.

Frank, Manfred, "The Text and its Style. Schleiermacher's Hermeneutic Theory of Language," *boundary 2* 11 (1983), 11–28.

Frank, Manfred, "'Intellektuale Anschauung.' Drei Stellungnahmen zu einem Deutungsversuch von Selbstbewusstsein: Kant, Fichte, Hölderlin/Novalis," in *Die Aktualität der Frühromantik*, ed E. Behler and J. Hörisch (Paderborn: Schöningh, 1987) 98–126.

Frank, Manfred, "Schelling's Critique of Hegel and the Beginnings of Marxian Dialectics," trans. Joseph P. Lawrence, *Idealistic Studies* 19 (1989), 251–68.

Frank, Manfred, "Fragmente zu einer Geschichte der Selbstbewusstseinstheorien von Kant bis Sartre," in *Selbstbewusstseinstheorien von Fichte bis Sartre*, ed. M. Frank (Frankfurt: Suhrkamp, 1991), 415–599.

Frank, Manfred, "Two Centuries of Philosophical Critique of Reason and Its 'Postmodern' Radicalization," trans. Dieter Freundlieb and Wayne Hudson, in *Reason and Its Other: Rationality in Modern German Philosophy and Culture*, ed. Freundlieb and Hudson (Providence and Oxford: Berg Publishers, Inc., 1993), 67–85.

Frank, Manfred, "Is Self-Consciousness a Case of *présence à soi*? Towards a Meta-Critique of the Recent French Critique of Metaphysics," in *Derrida: A Critical Reader*, ed. David Wood (Oxford: Blackwell, 1992), 218–34.

Frank, Manfred, "Die Wiederkehr des Subjekts in der heutigen deutschen Philosophie," in *Conditio Moderna. Essays, Reden, Programm* (Leipzig: Reclam, 1993), 103–17.

Frank, Manfred, "Philosophische Grundlagen der Frühromantik," *Athenäum* 4 (1994), 37–130.

Frank, Manfred, "The Subject v. Language," trans. Laurence K. Schmidt and Barry Allen, *Common Knowledge* 4 (1995).

Fulda, Hans F., "Spekulatives Denken und Selbstbewusstsein," in *Theorie der Subjektivität*, ed. K. Cramer, H. Fulda, R.-P. Horstmann, and U. Pothast (Frankfurt: Suhrkamp, 1987), 444–79.

Gerhart, Volker, "Selbstbestimmung. Über Ursprung und Ziel moralischen Handelns," in *Metaphysik nach Kant? Stuttgarter Hegel Kongress 1987*, ed. D. Henrich and R.-P. Horstmann (Stuttgart: Klett-Cotta, 1988), 671–88.

Gerhart, Volker, "Selbständigkeit und Selbstbestimmung. Zur Konzeption der Freiheit bei Kant und Schelling," in *Die praktische Philosophie Schellings und die gegenwärtige Rechtsphilosophie*, ed. H.-M. Pawlowski, S. Smid, and R. Specht (Stuttgart-Bad Cannstatt: Frommann-Holzboog, 1989), 59–105.

Guyer, Paul, "Kant on Apperception and a priori Synthesis," *American Philosophical Quarterly* 17 (1980), 205–12.

Henrich, Dieter, "Self-Consciousness, A Critical Introduction to a Theory," *Man and World* 4 (1971), 3–28.

Henrich, Dieter, "Selbstbewusstsein und spekulatives Denken," in *Fluchtlinien. Philosophische Essays* (Frankfurt: Suhrkamp, 1982), 125–81.

Henrich, Dieter, "The Identity of the Subject in the Transcendental Deduction," in *Reading Kant: New Perspectives on Transcendental Arguments and Critical Philosophy*, ed. Eva Schaper and Wilhelm Vossenkuhl (New York: Blackwell, 1989), 250–80.

Henrich, Dieter, "Die Anfänge der Theorie des Subjekts," in *Zwischenbetrachtungen. Im Prozess der Aufklärung*, ed. Axel Honneth et al. (Frankfurt: Suhrkamp, 1989), 106–70.

Horstmann, Rolf-Peter, "Ontologischer Monismus und Selbstbewusstsein" in *All-Einheit, Wege eines Gedankens in Ost und West*, ed. D. Henrich (Stuttgart: Klett-Cotta, 1985), 230–46.

Horstmann, Rolf-Peter, "Gibt es ein philosophisches Problem des Selbstbewusstseins?" in *Theorie der Subjektivität*, ed. K. Cramer, H.-F. Fulda, R.-P. Horstmann, and U. Pothast (Frankfurt: Suhrkamp, 1987), 220–50.

Horstmann, Rolf-Peter, "Kants Paralogismen," *Kant-Studien* 84 (1993), 408–25.

Meerbote, Ralf, "Kant's Functionalism," in *Historical Foundations of Cognitive Science*, ed. J. C. Smith (Dordrecht: Reidel, 1989), 161–87.

Mohr, Georg, "Vom Ich zur Person. Die Identität des Subjekts bei Peter F. Strawson," in *Die Frage nach dem Subjekt*, ed. M. Frank, G. Raulet, and W. van Reijen (Frankfurt: Suhrkamp, 1988), 29–84.

Piper, Adrian, "Xenophobia and Kantian Rationalism," *The Philosophical Forum* 24 (1993), 188–232.

Pippin, Robert, "Kant on the Spontaneity of Mind," *Canadian Journal of Philosophy* 17 (1987), 449–75.

Pippin, Robert, "Hegel, Ethical Reasons, Kantian Rejoinders," *Philosophical Topics* 19 (1991), 99–132.

Pippin, Robert, "Hegel, Modernity, and Habermas," *Monist* 74 (1991), 329–57.

Pippin, Robert, "Idealism and Agency in Kant and Hegel," *Journal of Philosophy* 87 (1991), 532–41.

Pippin, Robert, "Horstmann, Siep, and German Idealism," *European Journal of Philosophy* 2 (1994), 85–96.

Pöggeler, Otto, "Selbstbewusstsein und Identität," *Hegel-Studien* 16 (1981), 189–217.

Rohs, Peter, "Über Sinn und Sinnlosigkeit von Kants Theorie der Subjektivität," in *Neue Hefte für Philosophie* 27–28 (1988), 56–80.

Stolzenberg, Jürgen, "Fichtes Satz 'Ich Bin'," *Fichte-Studien* 6 (1994), 1–34.

Sturma, Dieter, "Das doppelte Ich im Bewusstsein meiner selbst. Zur Struktur von Kants Begriff des Selbstbewusstseins," in *Proceedings of the Sixth International Kant Congress*, vol. 2/1, ed. G. Funke and T. Seebohm (Washington, D.C.: Center for Advanced Research in Phenomenology & University Press of America, 1989), 367–81.

Sturma, Dieter, "Hegels Theorie des Unbewussten. Zum Zusammenhang von Naturphilosophie und philosophischer Psychologie," *Hegel-Jahrbuch* (1990), 193–201.

Sturma, Dieter, "Autonomie und Kontingenz. Kants nicht-reduktionistische Theorie des moralischen Selbst," in *Akten des Siebenten Internationalen Kant-Kongresses*, vol. 2/1, ed. G. Funke (Bonn: Bouvier Verlag, 1991), 573–87.

Sturma, Dieter, "Logik der Subjektivität und Natur der Vernunft. Die Seelenkonzeptionen der klassischen deutschen Philosophie," in *Die Seele. Ihre Geschichte im Abendland*, ed. G. Jüttemann, M. Sonntag, and C. Wulf (Weinheim: Psychologie Verlags Union, 1991), 236–57.

Sturma, Dieter, "Person und Zeit," in *Zeiterfahrung und Personalität*, ed. Forum für Philosophie Bad Homburg (Frankfurt: Suhrkamp, 1992), 123–57.

Sturma, Dieter, "Perspektiven der Person," in *Perspektiven des Perspektivismus*, ed. Volker Gerhardt and Norbert Herold (Würzburg: Königshausen & Neumann, 1992), 113–29.

Sturma, Dieter, "Odyssee des Geistes. Schellings Projekt einer naturphilosophischen Geschichte des Selbstbewusstseins," in *Philosophie der Subjektivität? Zur Bestimmung des neuzeitlichen Philosophierens*, ed. H. M. Baumgartner and W. Jacobs (Stuttgart-Bad Cannstatt: Frommann-Holzboog, 1993), 580–90.

Sturma, Dieter, "Präreflexive Freiheit und menschliche Selbstbestimmung," in *F.W.J. Schelling. Über das Wesen der menschlichen Freiheit*, ed. Otfried Höffe and Annemarie Pieper (Berlin: Akademie Verlag, 1995), 146–69.

Sturma, Dieter, "Self-Consciousness and the Philosophy of Mind," in *Proceedings of the Eighth International Kant Congress*, ed. H. Robinson (Milwaukee: Marquette University Press, 1995).

Wiehl, Reiner, "Die Komplementarität von Selbstsein und Bewusstsein" in *Theorie der Subjektivität*, ed. K. Cramer, H. Fulda, R.-P. Horstmann, and U. Pothast (Frankfurt: Suhrkamp, 1987), 44–75.

Wood, Allen, "Fichte's Philosophical Revolution," *Philosophical Topics* 19 (1991), 1–28.

Zanetti, Véronique, "Kann man ohne Körper denken? Über das Verhältnis von Leib und Bewusstsein bei Luhmann und Kant," in *Materialität der Kommunikation*, ed. H. Gumbrecht and K. L. Pfeiffer (Frankfurt: Suhrkamp, 1988), 280–94.

Zöller, Günter, "Making Sense out of Inner Sense: The Kantian Doctrine as Illuminated by the Leningrad *Reflexion*," *International Philosophical Quarterly* 29 (1989), 263–70.

Zöller, Günter, "Lichtenberg and Kant on the Subject of Thinking," *Journal of the History of Philosophy* 30 (1992), 417–41.

*Zöller, Günter, "Main Developments in Recent Scholarship on the *Critique of Pure Reason*," *Philosophy and Phenomenological Research* 53 (1993), 445–66.

Zöller, Günter, "An Eye for an I: Fichte's Philosophical Contribution," in *Figuring the Self: Individual, Spirit and the Absolute in Classical German Philosophy*, ed. D. Klemm and G. Zöller (Albany: SUNY Press, forthcoming).

Zöller, Günter, "Thinking and Willing in Fichte's Theory of Subjectivity," in *New Essays on Fichte*, ed. Daniel Breazeale and Tom Rockmore (Lanham: Humanities Press, forthcoming).

Contributors

Henry E. Allison (California-San Diego), has written books on Lessing, on Spinoza, and on Kant's theoretical and practical philosophy. A collection of his recent essays on Kant is forthcoming.

Karl Ameriks (Notre Dame) has written a book on Kant and numerous essays on Kant, Fichte, Hegel, and contemporary philosophy. He is editing a translation of Kant's lectures on metaphysics.

Daniel Breazeale (Kentucky) has translated many works of Fichte, and has also edited and commented on several works of Fichte and Nietzsche.

Manfred Frank (Tübingen) has written and edited numerous books and essays on aesthetics, German romanticism, German idealism, modernity, self-consciousness, and neo-structuralism. He is presently completing a major study of the philosophical foundations of early romanticism.

Georg Mohr (Münster) has written a book on Kant and several articles on contemporary epistemology and philosophy of mind. He has edited a new edition of Kant's first *Critique*.

Robert Pippin (Chicago) has written books on Kant, Hegel, and modernity. He has also written numerous essays on themes such as aesthetics and politics in continental philosophy.

Ludwig Siep (Münster) has written several books on Fichte, Hegel, and practical philosophy, and numerous essays on metaphysics and ethics in contemporary American and German discussions.

Dieter Sturma (Lüneburg) has written a book on Kant, and numerous articles on classical German and contemporary philosophy of mind and ethics. He is completing a book on the philosophy of the person.

Véronique Zanetti (Fribourg) has co-edited a new edition of Kant's third *Critique*, and has written essays on Kant and topics in philosophical psychology and teleology and a book on Kant's third *Critique*.

Günter Zöller (Iowa) has written a book on Kant and several essays on Kant and Fichte. He is editing and translating a number of works by Kant, Fichte, and Schopenhauer.

Index